A LONG JOURNEY TO LOVE

Autobiography *of* Valerie Bartley

by

Valerie Bartley

Grosvenor House
Publishing Limited

The right of Valerie Bartley to be identified as the author of this
work has been asserted in accordance with Section 78
of the Copyright, Designs and Patents Act 1988

The book cover is copyright to Valerie Bartley

This book is published by
Grosvenor House Publishing Ltd
Link House
140 The Broadway, Tolworth, Surrey, Kt6 7Ht.
www.grosvenorhousepublishing.co.uk

A CIP record for this book
is available from the British Library

ISBN 978-1-83975-593-4

VAL'S BOOK

INTRODUCTION

Within these pages is a full record of my life, from the moment I was born until the present day.

I have not had an easy life. As the eldest of eight children I had to work hard in the home helping my mother, as well as in the fields, helping my father. Because I was needed at home and money was short, I had very little education. All I knew about was hard work and the beating I would get from Mamma if I dared to be a child and stepped out of line. That's how it was when I was growing up.

I came to England to make a better life for myself when I was eighteen. I married Eric, the man I had met in Bois Content in Jamaica, and who had then emigrated here. We wrote to each other and eventually he asked me to come and join him. We married and had three children.

Racism was widespread in the sixties and we suffered our fair share of abuse in the early years. It was also very difficult to find decent living accommodation but we worked hard and eventually managed to get a mortgage on a property of our own.

We suffered a serious setback when Eric fractured his head, broke both legs, and dislocated his shoulder in an accident and was unable to work. Our love for each other and sheer determination helped us through that bleak period and has sustained us through many equally harrowing episodes since.

As the family grew up, we decided to return to Jamaica and build a little house where we could relax and enjoy again the warm climate that we both missed. The move was very traumatic and when we arrived, the house was not finished. Then we were threatened at gunpoint by armed robbers and robbed of most of our possessions. They were murdering innocent people for their possessions. It was a terrifying experience, but when we went to the police we quickly realised that many of them were corrupt and we would get nowhere.

Our dream of a little house in the sun had turned to ashes and we returned to England, homeless and penniless, until we could sell our Jamaican property.

We were offered filthy, disgusting bedsits as emergency accommodation and life was not worth living, but we soldiered on together. We still had each other and that was what mattered.

Then Eric was diagnosed with Parkinson's Disease and I became his carer. That was a very challenging time for both of us and there were many tears, mostly of frustration and anger.

Out of the blue, and with no hint that anything was wrong, our lovely daughter, Yvonne, took her own life and I went into deep depression, at one stage trying to take my own life by overdosing on the tranquilizers that were supposed to make me feel calm. I began to understand why some people took that way out.

As I have said, my whole life has been hard; at times, almost intolerable. But I am not complaining and I am a cheerful person. I accept my lot and I am at peace with it. God is with me and helps me. When I am lost, he points me in the right direction and I follow His lead and get on with life. There is no room for bitterness.

Life could always be worse and there are many people out there who are worse off than I am. I understand how they feel... the temptation to give in or give up is always very strong, but I believe we have to battle on. Stay positive. Persevere. Have faith, and good will always win. And never forget how to laugh... it is like the sunshine, warm and healing.

There are five parts to my book which I have set out chronologically. You will notice that the first part, about my childhood, is written in the present tense. This happened quite naturally as my memories of those days were still so vivid that, as I wrote, I relived every moment as if it were all happening *now.*

For the future? Who knows what waits around the corner? But whatever comes, I will do what I believe I have to do. Life is for living... and do you know what? Oh boy, I have lived!

ACKNOWLEDGEMENTS

I would like to thank my loving daughter-in-law, Maria, for trying so hard over the years to get my book published. My wonderful grandson, Miles, and my good friend, Pamela, for all their help in proofreading and soft editing the book.

I would also like to thank the people at Commonword for all their support and encouragement in improving my writing.

PART ONE
OF CHILDHOOD

~ 1 ~

I am four years old and walking with my parents down a dirt track road which is slippery. I suddenly fall on my bottom, and now my best white dress is filthy.

"Valerie," my mother fumes. "Look what you've done."

Papa picks me up, brushes me down and I begin to skip with him holding my hand. We arrive at a thatched roof house with snow-white walls, and cracks running through the side. We can't get inside the house, as it is crammed with people dressed in hats and fancy shoes. But what puzzles me is that some of the people are humming songs that I've never heard before. Some are weeping and wailing. I think it is hilarious when big people cry.

Others are digging for their handkerchiefs and I begin to think that something must be wrong. But I carry on whizzing around without a care in the world as to why these strange people are bawling. I stand and gawp, surprised at those that scream so loud. I have to poke my fingers in my ears, to stop my eardrums from bursting. After all the crying stops we have something to eat and drink and we go home.

As time goes by, Mamma drags my memory back to what must have been a sad day. It seems as if her chest is going to burst, as she gulps air before she has the courage to tell me this old story. She tells me that it was my grandmother's funeral that we went to, my father's mother.

I shrug my shoulders and give her a puzzled look. I don't understand what death is. Mamma says that people who die go to heaven and they are with the angels in their gardens picking flowers forever.

She is telling me this as I'm about to climb the mango tree that has stood in our front garden before I was born. I want to pick some mangoes which I had been eyeing up for a few days. Mamma says not to throw stones at the mangoes, because I will knock the green ones off as well.

Which would be a waste, wouldn't it?

I think she should be more worried about me climbing up the mango tree, but all she wants to talk about are these old stories from a long time ago. I'm desperate to calm down the worms that are rumbling in my stomach because I only had one slice of roast breadfruit and a can of black tea that morning. So I'm not interested in her long-ago history, especially when I'm feeling so hungry.

She tells me how my grandmother adored me, and how beautiful she was with light skin and long silky, dark brown hair much like an Arawak Indian.

When I hear that, I wonder what kind of woman she was. She must have come from some foreign country. My mother is sitting comfortably below the tree, after working all the morning picking cocoa, with her dress wrapped between her long, ebony legs. She's fanning herself with a big cocoa leaf that she picked earlier from the bottom of the hillside.

But I'm getting annoyed, even though the stories fascinate me. Shouldn't she have the sense to make me come down off the tree first? Then, while I'm sitting eating the mangoes, she can tell me all the stories that are packed in her head.

Anyway, God must have been watching me, because I come down the tree faster than a mongoose. The hens sitting nearby patiently brooding on their eggs cluck with alarm at my sudden descent.

Mamma said "Thank God," for bringing me down safely. Now I can stuff myself, and I'm happy for her to continue her stories. Though intrigued, I will store them in my head.

She tells me that my grandmother always called out "Hold the dogs!" whenever she visited us. She would sweep me up into her arms and soak me with kisses, then gently put me down.

I listen intently to this unfolding tale.

Mamma tells me that one day, not so long after my grandmother died, her ghost came to visit us just like she is alive.

She saw her coming and she rushes towards the gate. Then she called out her name: "Mother Mary, Mother Mary! Don't you know that the living and the dead don't mix together?"

The juicy mango dropped from my hand and I can feel goose bumps all over my body.

"How could you meet her when she is dead?" I ask.

"It was her ghost," Mamma says.

"What did you do?" I ask.

"I tell her she must go back under the breadfruit tree, and rest until the Day of Judgment."

"What is 'judgment'?"

"It is when the world ends and we go to heaven".

I feel afraid and my heart begins to beat fast like a race horse running.

"Mamma, what did she say when you told her off?"

"She never said a word, she just vanished. Not long after, you get sick and I know it's her who blows bad air on you."

"What is bad air?"

"Oh, I don't want to talk about that now. You are a young bird, you never experience hurricane, but you will one day when you are older. Then you will have to learn how to ride in the wind by yourself and figure out how to stay up there, when the north wind starts to blow."

She nods her head wisely. "As you get older, you will see that the world is just like a big onion, beautiful, and full of adventures… and clouds of misery."

"I hope I never see her, or any other dead person."

Mamma flashes a huge frown that resembles a thunderstorm and says, "Not a pretty sight."

~ 2 ~

Mamma took me to a nursery school that is governed by my grand aunt.

Everyone calls her Aunt Rosy; she is my mother's auntie. She is a small lady with brown eyes and white curly hair, but the fairies stole two of her front teeth. She teaches the village children ABC and prepares them for Elementary school. The school is in her yard, where she keeps rabbits and guinea pigs.

Aunt Rosy teaches us the Blackbird's Game. We sit on the floor in a circle and she sticks bits of paper on our first two fingers. Then she recites:

"Two little blackbirds sat on a wall, one named Peter, one named Paul, fly away Peter, fly away Paul, come back Peter, come back Paul." The trick is we must have the two pieces of paper on our fingers when they come back, or else we will be out of the game. We have so much fun playing this game, especially when someone new joins in, and we want to show off our skills. Yes, Aunt Rosy has fun with us and we love her. Sometimes she speaks in a strange language to people and I don't know what she's saying.

Mamma speaks in a strange language too. She wakes up in the middle of the night chanting, as if she is rebuking something out of the house. I feel very frightened when she starts, especially in the dark bedroom. I button my head to the pillow and drag the skimpy sheet over my head and pretend I am asleep. I am frightened that I will see a ghost.

I have two sisters. Icis, whom I call Tootsie Pie, and Marjorie, whom I call Magic. My parents have three growing girls that they call their princesses. They don't have much, so sometimes when we are hungry we knock a few fruits off the trees, or suck the juice from some sugar canes. Mamma gives us green banana or cornmeal porridge that she cooks in goat's milk. I love to feel the warm, creamy milk washing my fingers when she lets me have a go at milking the goats, but I have to watch myself when they kick and bellow.

The normal starting age for Elementary School is seven years, but I go when I am six. Our neighbour, Teacher Thompson, is the headmaster at Ludford Mount Elementary School. My parents are friendly with him and his wife Miss Rose, so he allows me to start a year earlier.

He is a short man with big eyes and strong, stubby hands. My mother is a past pupil of Teacher Thompson, and she tells me some horrible stories, about how he beats naughty children. I'm not looking forward to that and now I'm frightened to go. But the day Mamma took me, I tried not to show that I was scared. I managed to make friends with Lories Berry who sat beside me. I love school and enjoy the days when I go. I'm not a brilliant pupil and my poor attendance doesn't help. A lot of time I'm sick with a sore throat and we have to go to Crawl Pass where Papa grows sugar canes.

Sometimes when I'm lying in bed, I can picture Teacher Thompson standing there like a statue, with his eyes pulping out of his sweaty face. His brown suit only leaves his back when he comes home after school and sits in their garden drinking red-stripe beer and smoking.

However, his wife Miss Rose is very kind to us. When she sees us hanging around their gate under the huge Kidney mango tree, she often invites us in, and offers us something to eat. They don't have their own children to play in their garden and I don't think she knows the real reason why we hang out near their gate. It's because the smell of her cooking is driving us wild when we come home from school hungry.

Her ackee and salt fish is delicious. As soon as she turns her back to get us some home-made lemonade, I start to lick the plate with my tongue that I didn't know was so long. She comes rushing back into the dining room and nearly dies from shock, when she sees what I am doing.

"Have you got a snake in your head, child?" She sounds quite annoyed.

"No, Miss Rose, it's my tongue."

"Don't let me see you do that again, OK?"

But I'm not going to let her annoyance upset me too much. My tongue mops up the delicious gravy quicker than my scabby fingers which are sore from grating coconut and cassava. I have a huge scar on my left thumb that I inherited one night while splitting an enormous cassava. I carried on after Mamma had bandaged it as if nothing has happened. The blood turns the slushy mixture into a beautiful shade of pink. Then I have to wring out the juice so that the air can blow through it, and Mamma will be able to bake cassava bread for our char and lunch in the morning.

I love English, Geography, and turning the globe, looking for countries in far away places. I dream about the day when I might visit those places. But the demands on me are very intense, and I'm off school for weeks, helping in the fields in the blistering heat, dropping corn and gungo peas, as Papa digs holes in the ground. I use my feet to rake the warm soil over the grains, and the end of my ragged dress to wipe the sweat from my face. The clothes I wear for these jobs have seen better days. Nevertheless, crisp Chambray clothes would only get stained and torn long before the sun sizzles out into the horizon.

~ 3 ~

I have a small bench that Papa made for me. He is a carpenter, a Jack of all trades. When I am eight years old, I use it as an ironing board to iron Mamma's bib for the first time. I try to push my hands down the deep pockets, but my fingers can't reach the bottom. The iron is heavy and hot, as it is filled with charcoal, but I'm very pleased that I manage it so well.

I didn't realise then that this is the beginning of duties that will haunt me throughout my childhood. But still there is some free time, with some nights spent pillow fighting with my sisters, and other nights spent roasting cashew nuts on the log fire, while we sit telling each other Anancy stories that we make up as we go along. At the same time we watch the kerosene pan that squats over the huge fire turning blacker and blacker, boiling the peelings for the pigs.

I have a list of jobs to do. Carrying water from the spring, feeding the pigs and goats and fetching wood…I must save some breath to tell you more. Icis and Marjorie soon follow, doing the same things. Most Fridays we don't attend school, because it is wash day, and we have to go to the river. We walk through Mass Sonny's pasture that has long Guinea grass and wade through with our hands. When the mango season comes, we pick up the mangoes that have fallen to the ground, even though there's a sign saying trespassers will be prosecuted. We love the Season and the Number Eleven mangoes as they are more delicious than the common ones.

However, we are taking liberties as Mass Sonny would be very cross if he knew that we were nicking his fruits. But if we don't nick them they would just stay there and rot away. He has so many mango trees that he sells truck loads to the market traders. Mamma tells us not to steal his fruits, and that we must never tell lies because if we do and she finds out we will be eaten by her wrath.

"Speak the truth and speak it well, cost it what it will; he who hides the wrong he does, does the wrong thing still," she says.

One day as we were going to the river we stopped and nicked some mangoes, but I was on the look out just in case Mamma was standing at the top of the hill watching us. As I put some mangoes in my bag, Mamma shouted, "Put them back!"

The bag dropped out of my hand.

"Come back up here the three of you!"

I started to cry because I know that she is going to beat us. She gave us a roasting with some brambles, and told us that when we get back we will get some more.

Anyway we had to admit that we were nicking some mangoes, even though her words were ringing in my ears as I stole the fruits. It is impossible for us to scrub the washpans of clothes all day, without something to eat. Times are hard, so we have to hunt for ourselves; and sometimes we do what she tells us not to do. Out of her sight we pick up some more. When we reach the river, we lay them into the slow running stream to keep cool for our lunch, and to build up our strength to scrub the clothes on the river stones. When we have a break, we sit and eat them and watch the grimy suds floats away.

Mamma's clothes are always washed first, and then neatly hung on the ferns and stones that cascade along the riverbank. She needs them to wear to the market in Kingston in the evening, but things don't always work out as planned. One day the clouds burst, and the raindrops are like bullets. I have to yank some banana leaves near the riverbank to cover her clothes. The juice stains like dye, and I'm half paralysed with fear that they will be ruined. We return home in the afternoon, just as the sun came out and dark shades hug the hill side.

All day, Mamma has been fetching fruits from the farmers with Hanna, the donkey. By the time the truck arrives at the end of our lane, the sun is sinking in the distance and the sky explodes into a shade of orange. I shield my eyes from the glare until it is out of sight. As dusk turns to night, we walk back down the lane with Papa carrying the youngest like a handbag. We misjudge the quickness of dusk and stumble in the dark without the bottle torch as Mamma drives out of sight.

Then we wash and get ready for bed, and the shade lamps glow a dim light in the rooms. The frogs and crickets are making a racket, and I wish I could record the exotic sounds and play them back when morning comes. Sometimes I'm so tired that as my head hits the pillow I'm in dreamland. But I will be interrupted, and will have to get up when my greedy little siblings start to scream in the middle of the night.

Papa is always in a deep sleep, and never seems to hear when they cry. It is amazing how I wake up as soon as they start, and even though I'm half asleep I'm ready to look after them. I soak a piece of cloth with kerosene oil, then light it on the floorboard and warm the lemon grass tea that has been brewing in the black pan since dusk. Then I pour it into the bottle and pull on the nipple. Sometimes it flies out of my hands and darts across the room. I feed the baby and his eyes start to close, then I put him down and try to sleep again.

But I wake up when the rats start nibbling and running around the room. Papa sets traps with delicious pieces of roast coconut to tempt them. I shudder when I hear the trap bang and the room suddenly becomes silent again. Papa wakes up sometimes and takes over, but he never gives me the pleasure of saying I have done well. He just takes it for granted, and that makes me feel angry and deflated. I wonder where I must run and hide to find a little peace.

I can't go to the cellar, as I'm afraid of the dark and the Duppy that people talk about every time someone dies. These ghost stories makes me feel afraid, and if the wind blows I panic, especially when I'm on my own with a screaming child. So, since I haven't got eyes like owls, and I can't fly up in a tree in the dark, I can't go to the cellar in case the scorpions start to crawl out of the junk that Papa hoards there.

I have visions of them stabbing me with their deadly tails and making a meal of me. So I decide to stay where I am and cradle my baby brother and sister. It is hard getting back to sleep when Papa is snoring those loud saxophone notes. I promise myself that, one day, when I'm older, I will share my experiences with the world.

~ 4 ~

Saturday is always a busy day for us. We have to sweep the huge yard that is divided into three sections; we sweep our section until it is free from dust, chicken droppings, and Cedar leaves that dance from the trees that Papa has planted all over the place. He has even given me a Cedar and says I can watch it grow into a mature tree.

We shine the wooden floor with beeswax and the coconut brushes that Papa makes from the dry coconuts until sweat runs down our faces. By the time I finish, I can see my face gleaming back at me, and my knees are bruised from the pressure of pushing and shoving.

Still we have to do it every week. My sisters and I take turns to watch the younger ones, while I fetch water from the spring and fill the barrels and drums.

Papa pads Hanna with two hampers, and goes off to the field to fetch food and wood. He doesn't return until late afternoon. He carries a bundle of Guinea grass on his head for Hanna's supper. It sweeps the ground behind him as he walks along the road while Hanna clip-clops in front of him, carrying the harvest home.

One Saturday when he went, I decided that we will have some fun time riding on my bench down the slopes behind the kitchen, and see who can race the fastest. I had to squeeze into the bench because I'm getting too big for it. I fell out and cut my elbow but I didn't cry. The scent of the tropical plants exploded as we brushed and rushed past, anaesthetising it and keeping the tears away. Then we stopped and had some oranges, star apples or anything that in season.

We usually make our own toys: kites, slingshots, gigs which some people call tops, and we entertain ourselves, because we never get any toys, either for birthdays or Christmas. Except for one Christmas when we were lucky and got a star light each. We were so delighted that we jumped up and down as they fizzed out fountains of light and we couldn't believe our luck. We just went hag wild, putting pieces of papers on combs and moving them along our mouths like mouth organs and making music!

The next day I manage to blast a few hummingbirds with my slingshot that I make myself and that gives me a thrill. I roast the birds on the fire and they taste divine. The colourful birds are delighted when there is a blaze of flowers to zip around. They flit around like busy bees sucking the nectar from the flowers of the young banana fingers, putting on an exotic dance, as they poke their beaks into the Hibiscus flowers at racing speed.

We do some daring things to brighten up our lives and as soon as Mamma and Papa are out of sight we say:

"Cat gone, rat take over." And we tear down the hillside, climb up the fruit trees, scrum for fruits and have a wonderful time. But one time I noticed that Papa had left his file that he needed to sharpen his machete, but I carried on having fun.

But we got a surprise when Papa returned home early, because we haven't done any of our duties yet. He was very angry with us; I can't remember ever seeing him so cross with us, he totally lost his cool. He quickly took off his belt and gave us a good hiding that I will always remember.

"I never like to spank any of you, because I know that it hurt. All of you could grow up until you leave home, without me laying a finger on any one of you, as long as you all do as you are told. Valerie, you are the oldest one and you should set a good example for the rest to follow. I am not going to spare the rod and spoil you all – who can't hear must feel."

Threading his belt back around his waist, he laid down his law, while we scatter in every direction, hollering and rubbing our stinging legs. He never hits us again, but we always have to watch out for Mamma. She hardly ever misses her target.

Still, there are good times. We play in the moonshine. I lie on the ground as my sisters put marbles, small lemons and oranges around me, then carefully lift me out of the creation without undoing the shapes that they have made. Mamma and Papa sit on the verandah and laugh. We take it in turns to let everyone have a go and we all have a whale of a time. Then we catch night beetles. Some people call them fireflies because they flash a dotting light as they fly around. We put them in jars, and gawp at them as they flop around inside. Some nights we play with them for a long, long time until Mamma says we must get to bed. By that time we are so hungry that we could scoff a cow and her calf.

When Papa brings home sugar canes he leans them up in a corner on the verandah, and then gives us a joint each. We feel like we are in Heaven before we go to bed. Other times we sit while Papa eats his dinner when he comes home late and wait for him to give us our rat baits. He cuts one dumpling into small pieces and hand them to us like they are pieces of gold. Even though the pieces are small we are delighted. Then we go to bed and sleep like logs, until the night sky says hello to the young sun as it bursts out into the sky. The day starts like no other before as we swing into action.

Sometimes when my sisters and I go to fetch water from the spring, we walk along the banks where the water spreads out. Other times we walk through the thick woods where the trees hug the banks, looking for birds' nests. There is joy when I find a nest with some baby chicks. I gape at them when I see how wide they open their beaks. I get such a buzz, but I always worry just in case Mamma decides to time me with her spit on the ground method, and watches it frizzle away before I return. Then I know that I will be in trouble.

Anyway, sometimes she is too busy making cassava bread for breakfast, or coconut milk to cook rundown for our dinner in the evening. The youngest child screams his head off and clings to the end of her dress as she tries to move around the kitchen. The smoke bellows out from all directions and her eyes are blood red and streaming tears. No wonder the younger ones always scream; the smoke is blinding them as well, but there is not a lot that she can do.

I'm always glad when she doesn't seem to notice how long I have been, but I don't try that scam very often because I know that if I get caught she will beat me. It is first things first and I don't mix my duties with pleasure when she is around. But still I manage to have adventures.

By the time I return to the nests, the chicks are fully fledged and ready to fly away. It's such fun to do things like that, but I have to look after my brothers and sisters. I hate the responsibility. However, I have no choice as our mother often goes to Kingston to sell fruits, and pretty much anything she can get her hands on.

Papa sharpens his machete and sneaks off to the field, or he is building houses for people that he never seems to get paid for, or sawing planks of wood with Uncle Man. It depends very much on what is available, but he never turns anything down. He needs every penny he can get.

I use coconut boughs to slide on down the hill side. It's a scary stunt as they're quite long, but we steer them around the trees, knocking off some of the blossoms and fruit, leaving a mixture of scents in the air. When we are having fun, the time goes quickly. Of course, we have no clock so I stand still in the blazing sun for a moment, and study the shape of my shadow. I can tell if it is twelve o'clock by the reflection and the position of my shadow. It depends where the sun is. We stand there with our ripped clothes hanging over our shoulders, and our feet covered in dust or mud, but the laughter is infectious. We laugh until our bellies hurt.

We pick oranges and lemons from the trees (and sometimes from other people's trees), and use them as a ball to play cricket. Just imagine if we are caught, as the fruits are not for playing ball games but for selling, to buy essentials such as oil for the lamps that enable us to see before we lay down our tired bodies when night comes. Still, we are luckier than some children who have to scrape up lumps of tar to make balls.

One day Mamma sent me to the shop to buy salted cod fish, coconut oil, and a pound of mixed flour (that is flour mixed with cornmeal). I pick at the salt fish and eat it but I'm careful not to let it show.

"I'm sure that the scales they're using in that shop have had its day," my mother says. "What am I going to do with this little scrap of fish to make it stretch to all these plates? I will have to make some flour sauce and colour it with curry to eke it out."

Then I feel pangs of guilt in my heart, and rush to get a drink of water because the salt fish is cutting my palate. I breathe a sigh of relief when I get away with my prank but promise myself not to do it again, because I know that I will be in trouble if Mamma finds out what I have been doing.

Sometimes Mamma buys a tin of condensed milk, which is thick, sweet and sticky, to put into the carrot or sour sap juice. It is like having a glass of wine with our dinner, but we don't have it often because it's a special treat! She sends one of us to buy some ice as we don't have a fridge. The ice melts quickly in the sun, so we have to run fast. Then I can drain my last drop of the juice and lick the glass.

I often pinch some of the milk and suck it from the tin when Mamma isn't looking. It is divine and I have to make myself stop before I empty it. I'm sure the rest of the children do the same. The trouble is one day when she goes to get the milk, the tin floats into her hand like a feather. She goes ballistic and tells us that if we don't own up she's going to beat every one of us until she finds out who did it.

"The good will have to suffer for the bad, because the cat cannot open the wagon door." When she starts to shout we know that trouble is brewing. Everybody starts to scatter and we keep our distance, because we know that her fiery sparks might catch us.

When we hear her voice ringing like a bell to let us know that dinner is ready, we walk slowly towards the kitchen door. We quickly take our plates and find a seat on the planks of wood that are lying under the shade out of the sun. But she calms down in the end like a ship that has lost its sail and is just bobbing up and down lazily on the waves.

~ 5 ~

I'm a tough little cookie, who loves a challenge because it gives me such a buzz. I also encourage my sisters and brother to break the rules as well. I do it many times, but only when our parents aren't around. I figure that we are only going to pass this stage in our lives once, and I don't want to miss out on the fun.

I'm an obedient child most of the time, not like my sister Icis. All she does is complain about some part of her anatomy hurting her. She is fragile like a piece of china when it suits her. We set off down the hill at the crack of dawn, to fetch water from the spring. The ground is damp and the dew bathes my legs. I pray not to slip as my feet grips the hill, with the pan of water balanced on my head. The pan leaks, and I bung the holes with clay, but it falls off when the water seeps into it. I'm soaked to the skin, trying to catch the water that drips from the pan with a cocoa leaf. By the time I reach home, a good amount of the water has gone. I pour it in the barrel and rush back down the hill with a spring in my matchstick legs. Icis is still crawling up the hill like a snail on eggshells. She never does as many trips as me and I hate her for being so mean.

Our Aunt Bertha says that she is impressed with my enthusiasm. It is good for those who benefit the most, but for me it is sheer hell. I'm worried that this trend will follow me into my adult life, and ravage my body with old age before I can wade out into the world. One day I hope to explore it from the huge continent of Africa to the South American jungle, where parrots fly around from trees. I always say a prayer to God and ask him to let me live long enough to fulfil my dreams of exploring the world.

Mamma sends Icis to one of her relatives who live up in Ginger Ridge, so that she can go to school up there, as she seems more interested in books and the finer things in life. She didn't have to fetch water because they have a water tank. They live several thousand feet up the mountain, and the bus has to wind its way around the hairpin bends to get there. I only visit a few times and I'm astonished how many houses nest on the hillside. I'm stunned when I see how low the clouds come down, touching the hillside.

It is chilly at night when the north wind is blowing in November and December, and the sugar canes are in flower, waving their huge pampas heads in the wind. When they appear, we are reminded that Christmas isn't far away. I have to work much harder while Icis is away, and I'm fed up.

Icis passes her exams, but returns home afterwards as my parents were having difficulty paying for her keep. On her return she slips back to her old ways with ease. She is more bookish than ever and I feel trapped and extremely angry.

I feel like a slave and I know that I'm being used, but there is nothing I can do about it because Mamma will beat me if I don't do all the jobs she gives me. I dream of running away... maybe to Kingston, but it's a big city and I don't know anybody there. I could end up on the streets, or even worse, working as a domestic, scrubbing clothes and floors. I don't want to be a slave for somebody else so I have to bear it, and blow the half-dead fire every morning with my mouth.

When the rainy season starts, the wood is so wet that I have to feed the fire with bits of paper, or some dry grass to get it going. All I get for a while is a plume of smoke that blinds my eyes and makes me cry. I wish we could have a nice gas cylinder stove like some of the town people.

Anyway, I got the fire going and roast some sweet potatoes and yams and hope that better times will come one day. Everyone knows when food is cooking, when they see the spiral of smoke splurge up into the sky. It's funny how people always turn up when the smoke dies down. They have noses like the John crows that glide around in the sky whenever Papa hacks off one of the goat's head and sells the meat to the neighbourhood. A flock of them always circles overhead.

One Sunday as we are having dinner, Mamma tells us that Miss Hilda is getting married, and she wants Icis, Marjorie, and me to be her bridesmaids. We can't wait to finish our dinner; but it doesn't take long because it's not much. Our bellies don't seem to have any bottoms and they never seem to fill. I'm sure that if we were given a whole roasted pig we would demolish it in no time.

Well, we can't wait to start practising how we are going to walk down the aisle on Miss Hilda's special day. I thought she was already married, as she and Batwing have lived in a two-bedroom house for as long as I can remember, with... make me count me fingers now... one, two, three, four or is it six children! Now they are planning to stop the herds of cows that stroll happily down the road cropping grass, with the excitement of their wedding. Anyway we start to walk up and down the yard, holding our heads up like penguins walking on sand, trying to practise fancy steps. That makes Mamma laugh out loud.

"No! That's too slow" She said.

But we carry on walking, and doing it our own way, which is fun. But at the back of my mind I know that tomorrow is not far away, when I will be carrying heavy loads again on my head. I just cringe as it pains me in my heart. My head is sore, even though I put a cottar on it before I put the load on. I make the cottar from wisps to take some of the pressure away; but my head still feels mashed up.

One day I'm standing in the sugar cane field, surrounded by a mountain of dead canes. I panic when I see the amount that has to be taken to the main road. The bees were buzzing and sucking the juice from the ends of the canes.

I watch my father, to see how he packs the sugar canes in the crocks that hangs over Hanna's back. It isn't long before I'm in charge of my own donkey, packing sugar canes and walking in the blistering sun for the two miles or so to the main road, where the men load them onto the trucks and take them to the estate to make all shades of sugar and rum. Sometimes when it is raining heavily, Hanna gets stuck in the clay mud. I struggle to free her and then I'm covered with mud to my knees.

It is very frightening, when the sugar canes start to slide out of the crocks, especially when we are going down a hill. The bees and wasps zip around sucking the juice as Hanna walks along and I worry about getting stung. When I arrive at the main road I stack the canes from the ground and tiptoe as far as I can reach to build the pile. But many time the flaming lot comes tumbling down, and I have to fix it… all over again. I'm shattered then, and cry silently in my heart. Icis and Marjorie start to do the same as me. It is a sight to watch: Sister Sade's three princesses loading up the three donkeys. Icis has Mercy, and Marjorie races around with Poppy.

Mamma and Papa don't know how we lick up the donkeys with the whip to see who can race back first. Daring to do some adventures like that really makes me feel special the work is a challenge, but it also makes us feels proud about ourselves, especially when we see the tons of sugar canes that we shift to the main road. Even though we get tired by the end of the day, after a good night's sleep we'll start again.

We sing songs like *Hill and Gully Rider*, or *Carry Me Ackee*, or *Daylight Come and Me Wanna Go Home*, just to cheer ourselves up and pass the time. It helps to make life worth living as we walk backwards and forwards in the blistering heat. The donkeys are our best friends as we spend so much time with them. We know their little tricks and they know how far they can push us. Many times they just stop and crop some grass by the side of the road. They never hurt us, except when they are flashing their tails and that stings a bit, but we constantly man- handle them and plague them with hard work. Every morning when they see us coming they start to bray as if to say, 'Here we go again,' flashing their tails in slow motion. The birds sing sweet songs overhead; the trees dangle their branches in the gentle breeze.

Some mornings the dew is still dripping from the leaves as we lead Hanna, Mercy, and Poppy from their night pen. We pad their backs with the soft wadding that Mamma has made, and they shrink their bellies as we plonk our feet against their sides and pull the girths tight. I feel sorry for them when I see how they suck up their bellies to their backs when the rope slices into their skin, but there is no other way to do it. In a way the poor donkeys are like us; they can't answer back, but they do have to jump and kick-up every now and then. We can't jump up, we are just like our African ancestors; slaves that tilled the land all day long until their dying days.

Being the oldest child is a huge burden on me. There isn't much I can do to get out of the situation. All I hear is, "Valerie, you are the oldest and you must set good example for the rest to follow." I hear it from the sun peeping up into the sky until it sinks into the Caribbean Sea.

Papa grins and his face looks like the sun when I gain confidence with the task he throws at me. Being a girl doesn't make much difference, as I do my jobs just like any boy would… even better because I take care to get it right. I show them that I'm able to do it like a boy, with a slingshot in his back pocket, a gig in his hand and a cheeky grin on his face.

When night comes we are too tired to do anything else but crawl into the huge bed that Papa made. It is for ten people and fills the room from one end to the other. It has planks of board neatly laid on top, supported by the posts that he has expertly planted into the ground. Mamma has made an enormous mattress and stuffed it with grass. I love the rustling sound that it makes and snuggle up to whoever is next to me as I drift off to sleep, until the first fingers of dawn creep across the sky.

However, morning comes before we know it, and we are woken by the constant crowing of the cocks or Mamma urging us to, "Wake up, wake up, wake up! It's time to get up! It's time to get up," As she nudges us gently.

I roll over for a moment and wish she would go away, but she tells us the same again, this time with more command in her voice. She is like an alarm clock ringing in my ear every morning. So I stretch my limbs and yawn, then slither out of bed like a snake, with half closed eyes.

The donkeys are braying, the cows mooing, the cocks crowing as they fly off their roosts and the world comes alive as the young sun glitters in the horizon, embracing us with its glow. Another long day of toiling lies ahead in the sun, rain and mud. Some days my feet are covered in animal muck. The smell lingers all day, like a century-old barrel of beer that has gone off.

I eat some sugar cane as I walk along, peeling it with my teeth. It exercises my mouth, invigorates my body and tantalise my taste buds, as we seldom get sweets. My teeth are strong and white because I clean them by chewing a special stick. So I never end up with rotten teeth I smile when there is nothing to smile about and the world smiles back at me.

Our father is very proud of us, and he draws other people's attention to whatever we are doing. We share many masculine tasks with him that most boys would love to do, but we are girls who wear ribbons in our hair when we dress up on Sundays to go to church.

People who know us often refer to us as 'Brother Lattie's boys' when they see the kind of work that we tackle. Being a girl doesn't make any difference. I'm like a boy, rough and tough, with scabby knees, and my father treats me like one because of what I have to do. The only thing missing is a middle leg… and that would confuse everyone now, wouldn't it?!

We are well behaved most of the time. We have to be, because we know we'll get a beating if we do something wrong. I never hear the word smack; only 'I'm going to spank your backside until it burn you'. That's the way it is. Rough, and tough, but we don't know any different and neither do our parents.

Maybe Mamma is not well but she just has to get on with it and work it off at home or in the field. When she is in a bad mood she beats hell out of the clothes with the clapper stick. I watch the suds flow down the river, swirling around the Swiss cheese plants and ferns that sway lazily, when I go to the river with her.

Mamma knows that there will be many days when she will not have such pleasure; to feel the water splashing around her long legs, or listen to it trickling on its way. So then she has a break and drinks up the sweet wine of the moment, observing the butterflies flopping and flitting amongst the flowers, and the ground doves twitching about their business. She only goes to the river once in a blue moon – I guess when she wants a break from the house, and to stop herself from knocking our brains out when we are just too much to cope with. I feel that she finds it very difficult to cope with so many children. But we didn't ask to be born and we are treated like chickens, scratching for ourselves whenever we can.

So, I also take a break to be a child while she scrubs away.

Instead of working like a mule, I try to catch a few shrimps in a bucket, and treasure these moments with Mamma at the river. For Mamma, it is like a day out; it would be more convenient for her to do the washing at home where she keeps an eye on her latest arrival. She sits in the shade, scrubbing the clothes, and making music with a corn stick as a brush.

But the amount of water that we have to carry to give her that pleasure is enough for a boat to cruise on down to the Sea of Galilee.

One day she tells me to read passage one to four from the book of Job. There was a man in the land of Uz, whose name was Job; and that man was perfect and upright, and one that feared God, and eschewed evil. And there were born unto him seven sons and three daughters. His substance also was seven thousand sheep, and three thousand camels, and five hundred yoke of oxen, and five hundred asses, and a very great household. So this was the greatest of all the men of the east. I look for it, and she makes me read it to her even though I can't pronounce some of the funny words. Every morning and night, she does the same thing. It is simply a part of our lives. She will leave the Bible open on the bed at the back of her new baby's head, with Psalms 117. Praise the Lord, all ye nations: praise him, all ye people. For his merciful kindness is great towards us: and the truth of the Lord endureth for ever. Praise ye the Lord. I memorise some of the scripture and I know it off by heart.

I'm sure that she loves us all, even though she knocks the wind out of us if we don't obey her orders. Nevertheless, she tries to keep us clean and tidy in spite of her many difficulties.

"Look at you all!" she cries in despair, when we return after a session under the ripe mango tree. "You look like a picture I could paste on a wall."

The stains of the mango juice run down our hands to our elbows and weave patterns on our clothes. We wipe our hands on our clean, clothes that are ripped because she has no time to mend them, and skip with wisps home. We roast sweet potatoes, yams, and sweet corns on log fire when they are in season and have a feast.

~ 6 ~

One morning Marjorie fell off a Sweet Sap tree she was scaling to pick some fruits and broke her right hand. Mamma was cross when she looked at her hand and told her off for being so reckless. Papa was gentle with her and took her to Spanish Town Hospital. He was told that her hand was broken and it was put in a plaster. She couldn't lift heavy things for a while, so she got some rest, but soon she's back to her old boisterous self and doing what we do best.

One morning I wake up with severe sore throat and can't swallow my spit for days. The pain is terrible, and I'm frightened as bloody saliva drips out of my mouth. I lie in bed staring at the ceiling in the dim lit room, my teeth making noise. I'm shaking and my body is burning, then the next minute I'm freezing. Mamma gives me water to drink, but it runs out of my mouth. My parents will have to sell a treasured goat to raise the money to take me to the doctor. But that will be the last resort. They will try an old-fashioned remedy first, such as salt vinegar to gargle my throat. If that fails and they see that I'm slipping away before their eyes, then they will take me to the doctor.

I am delirious in the night. Mamma wipes my face with cold water,and I cry while they fuss over me.

"Never mind, Valerie", Papa said, stroking my face. "I'm going to take you to the doctor, I promise."

I cough and pus gushes out of my mouth. He wipes my mouth and says: "Good God, Sadea, look at this! Me a tek her to the doctor, because she keep us up the last two nights. I can see that she is sick."

Mamma snaps at him.

"So you a tell me that me no see that she's sick?"

"I never said that", says Papa, "but I notice you turn doctor with all the home remedy that you trying, and I can see that she's getting worst. I'm going to borrow some money from Brother Hessian and use Betty and the three kids as security". Mamma glares at him and clapping her hand says: "Lord me God! Me don't want to lose that three dropper goat!"

Papa face moves, and he arches his brows as he stands up before her and says:

"Well, Sadea, we can get another goat, but we can't get another Valerie."

Mamma's eyes widen, and she say,

"Our first Pikny going to die on us, she can hardly stand up. If she dies I will stop praying. Look how me bruise up me knees every morning and night praying to Jesus. Lattie, you are right, take her to the doctor."

Eventually, in the early morning when the stars are still glittering in the sky, he gets me ready and plonks me on Hanna's back. There is no moon shining, so I can barely see, even though my father is armed with a bottle torch like a wise man following the stars. I'm very weak and hold on to the rope halter for dear life. I can hear owls screeching, and the rustling of frogs leaping through the leaves in front of us. There is a moment when I see a star shoot across the sky, but I have seen them many times before and anyway I'm too ill to bother now.

Hanna stumbles and I fall off her. I can hardly scream as it hurts so much. I blink rapidly, and my eye lids match my heartbeat. Papa scoops me up and puts me back on Hanna's back and says

"Never mind, Valerie, I know that we have a hard life but I hope that life will be better one day."

I say to myself that I will die before that day come. I don't know how I find the strength to hold to the rope.

Papa is walking just a jack horse length away, but he keeps talking to me, and I can smell the fresh earthy scent of dawn. I tell him that I want to wee, and he lifts me off Hanna's back. I can hear the wee gargling into the soil, but I cannot see it as it is still dark. He puts me back on Hanna's back, and the sky starts to burst into an orange glow as we troop along. The lush grass on the banks is inviting, and she is eager to crop some, but he rushes her on, waving a stick that he has carried since we set off.

When we arrive at the doctor's surgery there isn't anyone else in sight. Papa don't know the time but he reassures me as I wince with the pain; he wipes away all the bloody stuff from my mouth and Hanna starts to graze some grass again. I sit on her back trying to be brave, but feeling like a lamb awaiting slaughter. I can barely stand, the pain is so bad. He helps steady me, as I have reached the stage when I don't care if I live or die.

But I'm scared of what the doctor will do to me. My body is twitching. Papa wipes the sweat from my face, and says, "Never mind, daughter." The waiting room is dark even though the sun is shining outside. The ceiling is flaking and the walls are grimy. Even the chair that I'm sitting on is squeaking.

He holds my hand.

"Never mind, Valerie," he said,

"You will see the doctor soon and he will give you something to make you feel better."

I look up at him and he kisses my head. Just beside him I glimpse a lizard swaggering up the wall. I gape at it and grasp Papa's hand. I hate creepy things. Then the door creaks and flies open. A tall man walks in carrying a baby, followed by a fat woman with a blanket and feeding bottle.

My nerves are getting the better of me and I'm worried that the doctor is going to hurt me. Then suddenly a lady comes out of a room, wearing a stiff white apron. "Who's first?" She asked.

Papa puts his hand up before I can blink and we are following her into the doctor's room. She gives us a prim smile and leaves us to it.

"Hello," The doctor says cheerily.

"How-do," Papa replies.

I keep my mouth shut. It is too painful for me to speak.

"And what can I do for you?" The doctor asked.

He explains that I'm unable to eat or drink because it is painful to swallow.

"How long has this been going on for?"

Papa stutters. "Two… two weeks, now."

The doctor's eyes are bulging as he gets up from his seat. He is a tall, well-built man who towers over me. I notice his hands. They are big, with long fingers. His coat is dazzling white and I'm terrified of what he is going to do to me.

"Open your mouth! Say aah! And again! Well done! Goodness…!" He turns to my father. "It's very bad, she's got tonsillitis. I will give her an injection… it's all right young lady, it won't hurt, I promise. Just a needle prick."

My heart beats double and I'm sweating as I cling on to Papa. He tries to reassure me as I glance around the room which itself is quite primitive, but there are some shiny instruments of some kind on the table. I watch him draw out some liquid into a syringe.

"I'm just going to inject this into your bottom."

I'm frightened to the point of running out of the room. I feel as if I'm going to die, and I don't want him to see my floral panty that Mamma made for me. When he pulls up my dress I feel ashamed and give out a scream before he sticks the needle in my ass. "Take her back if she is not feeling better." He tells Papa.

Hanna looks up and brays when she sees us coming as if to say, 'Where have you been?' On our way home he buys me a bottle of cream soda, and a slice of sponge cake. I grind my teeth and bite a small piece of the cake, then sip the soda and it tastes wonderful. By the time we get home, the sun is old in the sky, and I feel parched and donkey- travelled. Mamma tells me to go to bed, but I sure don't need any Persuasion.

The zinc roof is cracking in the afternoon heat as I drift off to sleep after my harrowing journey. I'm woken by my sisters Marjorie and Icis when they arrive home from school. There is an explosion of "I want this and can I have that!" After two weeks I'm back to my normal boisterous self and I soon wade back into the swing of things and Papa doesn't have to take me back to the doctor.

My parents are looking forward to going to Crawl Pass for the coming cane season. A week after we arrive, I'm attacked by a swarm of bees that is hiving in a hag plum tree. My body and face become swollen like a piece of dough pumped up with yeast. Mamma and Papa fuss over me and I scream, while they pick out the stings. They dab vinegar all over me, and I smell like fried fish sprinkled with scotch bonnet peppers.

The following morning when I wake, my eyes can't open. I'm scared that I'm going blind. I'm in agony and I just want to curl up and die. There is no mention of taking me to the doctor, and I know that if they do, I'm on my way out to meet the angels.

After a few weeks, there is a swollen lump on my left foot that grows larger and larger, until I can't walk. Then it bursts and the grimy sting swims out. I'm left with a gaping hole on the top of my foot; all I can do is crawl around.

School is a million miles away from my mind as I drag myself around. I realize now what life is like for Harry, who was born without any legs. He has to drag himself around. But he manages to sit and break stones all day long and sells them to the Parochial Board to put on the roads. When he finishes work he crawls back home. It's an amazing sight to watch him creeping up and down the hills with padded gloves to protect his hands. Some days the rain is pouring but he still crawls along the road, like a fish having a swim. So I will get by, just like him.

Icis has to do more work since my foot becomes septic. One morning when she is chopping some wood to make the fire, she nearly chops off one of her legs with the machete that I have used so many times. She bawls when she sees the blood pouring from her leg.

Icis has a gaping wound and Mamma bandages her leg with a piece of old embroidered white sheet. I think, wow, she is very lucky, as I know that sheet is only spread on Mamma's bed on a Sunday.

Although it is old, it is beautiful and I wonder why she doesn't use a piece of it on my foot when the swelling burst.

Neither of us is taken to the doctor. Our legs are infected and rotting away. Both of us are stuck at home, crawling on our hands and knees, with the ever present gingery flies. I don't know why, but at last they decide to take us to the doctor. They must have had enough of the unpleasant whiff that we carry around. It is terrible that we have had to wait so… long before we can get some medical treatment.

Papa decides to take us to the doctor in Old Harbour. He puts us both on Hanna's back and we ride to the main road. I sit at the front and Icis behind me. I have to hold the halter. When Hanna is going downhill we are sliding forward. I try to grip her flank with my good leg, but it doesn't help and

Papa shouts, "Stop!" He shoves us back as far as we can go and we carry on further.

We pass a few people who gape at us. Is it the first time they have seen two people riding a donkey? Or is it our legs, maybe, wrapped up in old clothes and surrounded by flies? I'm ashamed and wish for the earth to open up and swallow us. I close my eyes to help shut out the shame. But it doesn't go away, and from that moment I know that being poor is a crime.

The sun beats down and our ride is uncomfortable. Icis has me to hold on to, but I only have the rope on the headcollar. We have never sat glued to each other like this before and it is a pain to have her breathing down my neck and clinging to me like a leech. But she is my sister and I have to put up with it.

It is a relief to reach the main road. Papa helps us down off Hanna's back and we both sit on a big stone. Then he ties Hanna at the roadside to graze and goes across to the little shop to ask Mr Walker to keep an eye on her until we return. The truck turns up eventually but it is difficult getting us into it. Another man helps him to lift us up and then we hopscotch to the long wooden seat.

When we reach Old Harbour, we wait in a dingy room full of sick people. The pong is dreadful – sweat and rotting flesh. I shove up my mouth and my top lip covers my nose. Papa doesn't mention money, and that leads me to think it is a place for 'poor-arse' people.

Icis whispers, "Look at that boy's face, his face is black and blue, and his bottom lip is split in two." We are shocked. I nudge her and tell her to shut up.

At last we go in to see the doctor. He asks loads of questions and Papa cannot answer all of them. Well, he is not the one with the rotting legs. The doctor is a small man with bushy eyebrows. He has short hands and has to turn up his coat sleeves. He is not gentle, even though he promises not to hurt us. I scream as he cleans the rotten flesh. He tells Papa we have worms in the sores. I'm petrified of worms... what am I going to do? I feel my stomach roll over and I throw up.

The scornful look on his face when he sees our horrid legs makes me feel ashamed. We have the dreaded needles that we fear, but after a few shots and tender care from the nurses at the clinic, it works. It is quite a while before we can hop around, as our legs heals slowly, but gradually we slide back into our chores again, and wrap ourselves in the binding web of what I think is our destiny. The scars are with us to this day and will be until our last.

~ 7 ~

One morning after we have finished all our tasks, I'm having a bath in the bathroom behind our house. The bathroom is made from corrugated zinc, and a piece of Hessian sacking draped loosely for the door.

Icis creeps around the corner and hammers on the zinc, "Hurry up; I'm going to be late for school!"

"What's new?" I say to myself. "I never see you in a hurry ever, if they have a snail race you will be the last one to slither past the post! Well too bad, sister."

I deliberately take my time just to get my own back on her. I can feel myself getting angry. "What did she do this morning to be late?" I ask myself. I have fetched three pans of water, swept the kitchen, made a raging fire, and roasted four breadfruits so she can get to roll her long tongue. While she only crawls up the hill with half a pan of water, saying she have belly ache. I feel that taking a bath is the only time that I have for myself, and I have earned it. I'm not going to allow her to put a stopwatch on me. 'You selfish, slimy bitch,' I growl under my breath.

However, she is determined to harass me and comes back after a few minutes and does the same thing again. This time I meet her with a calabash bowl of my bath water. I chuck it into her freckle face and she loses her breath for a moment. I'm delighted that I did it and she never does it again, but she sticks her tongue out at me many times since that morning. I threaten to punch her in her face and give her nose bleed if she does it again, and that puts a stop to her blackmailing me.

One morning Tootsie Pie, Marjorie and I wake up as night is saying hello to dawn. We set off down the hill. I look around and Icis is crawling behind us while Marjorie walks like a young soldier and strides past her. When I say she is lazy, she *is* lazy and skiving. I don't think she is cut out for the sort of grind and she does her best to get out of everything that means some grafting.

We clutter around the water hole with other children, and stumble to scoop the water in our pans. Then we honk the pans onto our heads and climb back up the hill. On my return home I pour the water into the drum and turn the breadfruits that are roasting on the hissing log fire, and then skip down the hill with the pan pressing under my arm, making a popping sound. But Icis will be still crawling like a snail in sand.

I hate her for being so mean to us, but especially me because she knows that I'm the *older* one. I'm always doing so much more work than her, and it makes me mad when I see what she gets away with.

Anyway, one day her luck runs out, and Mamma catches up with her and gives her a good spanking with the old strop - her trademark.

When we see it, we know that Mamma is around and when we see Mamma, we know that the strop is sleeping like a cat somewhere.

Mamma tells Icis, "I'm going to spit on the ground and if it dries up before you comes back, then you will get some more."

I thought, 'Yes!'

I never seen Tootsie Pie move so fast; she runs down the hill like someone put pepper on her ass. She is going faster than the Rio Minho River after a tropical storm. I'm delighted and roar with laughter until my stomach aches. I'm sick of my parents and family saying how willing I am. It is only through fear of Mamma's belt, or whatever else she lays her hands on, that makes me appear enthusiastic.

We have to walk a long way to school, and I'm not allowed to leave Icis and Marjorie if I'm ready first. But as soon as I get out of our mother's eye corners I run as fast as I can and leave them behind, because if we are late for school we will be punished. So I cannot win. I do love school and enjoy the days that I attend. But anywhere in this world, there are children who get a buzz from bullying others. They think it's great, but they are cowards.

For a long time I endure bullying by a group of girls. They force me to join in rounders and hide and seek, even though they can see that I have a sore toe that I bucked on a stone; and I'm walking lame. I refuse because I'm frightened that I will hurt my toes again, or they will step on it spitefully. But still they won't leave me alone. So I decide to do something, even though it's four of them against me. I grab onto one of the hands, I don't know whose, but it turns out to be the gang leader's finger. I yank it, she screams out loud and the rest of the gang stop and stand with their mouths open.

"You are hurting my fingers. Let me go."

The rest of the group look on. I'm under pressure from those girls who bully me whenever I attend school. I'm told that Jane-Dan's little finger is dislocated, or worse, broken but her parents can't afford to take her to the doctor. It has stuck out from that day like a fan. They think I am a soft touch, but they got a surprise at my reaction and they were shocked. I don't get into many scrapes; they are few and far. Just because I'm lame don't mean that I'm useless.

One day I go to school with a new reading book that Mamma bought for Icis and me to share. Icis and I were in the same class at the time, although I'm one year and seven months older than her, but she is brighter than me. I decide that I'm not going to let her read the book that day, so I sit with my best friend Loris Berry and we have an enjoyable time reading it. Icis was vexed and she calls me a jack horse. That makes my blood boil over, as I don't have a tail, or four legs, and I don't bray. But yes, she is right, because I often feel like one when she worms her way out of tasks. She threatens to tell Mamma and she does so with delight on her face, and I get the full blast of my mother's wrath showered on me.

"You do that to your own sister?" she storms. "Do you prefer your friend more than her?" she barks. "I cannot afford to buy two books. The both of you comes from the same backbones and the same belly, so you have to share it with each other."

As she rants, she pulls out a wattle from the kitchen wall and she lashes out at me, but I duck. It misses my eyeballs by inches. However, I get the next shot and it sends me hopping like a kangaroo. I'm stunned.

"Do you know how hard I have to work to get the money to buy that book?" she asks.

"Yes, Mam," I said, nodding my head like a puppet.

"Promise me that you will not do it again, right?"

"I promise that I will not do it again. Please don't hit me again." I'm still friendly with Loris Berry, but I'm too ashamed to tell her what has happened to me when she wants to read the book with me. When it is reading time, I give Icis the book and do without, or sit with her as Mamma said.

The time is coming up when the family will be going to our father's small farm to harvest the sugar cane, not to read books. We arrive at Crawl Past in the early hours of the morning as usual. Pappa wastes no time and starts cutting the canes while us girls load up the donkeys and head for the main road several times before midday.

Mamma is cooking lunch in a huge, black iron pot that has three legs, and I can smell it from a distance. The smoke is bellowing and blinding her, so she wipes her eyes with the end of her dress.

I can't wait to get my teeth into the Green Gungo peas and Corned Pork soup. Papa says "Sade that was lovely." The dogs whiff and sniff the ground and fight each other to claim their share of the leftovers.

We have a cool drink of lemonade. But Papa is still sitting down.

He looks dead beat. "I could just go to sleep, I'm just flogging a dead horse every year" he says. "The money I make from the sugar cane isn't much, it is peanuts. By the time I pay for the truck, and the cost of hiring one or two men, there isn't much left to buy new khaki pants. It is just from hand to mouth." Eventually he gets up and starts taking his hanger out on the sugar cane. I just keep my distance.

Papa builds a kitchen onto the two rooms to provide a little comfort when it's raining. There is only one small window in the whole house, as originally it was a one-bedroom farm building, before he started to add more rooms. I used to think how strange it is to have one window in the house. I have thought about climbing through it many times, but I decide not to just in case I get stuck.

We sit in doors and fan the smoke with our hands, and wait for the fire to burn down. Mamma counts the plates that she lays on the ground in readiness. She has to, or else she will miss someone out. One dumpling, one peg of breadfruit or whatever else there is, and then she says the magic words.

"Dinner is ready." For our afters we have some Cow Boy pineapple.

I love when they are in season as they are juicy and sweet. The mongoose loves them as well. It is annoying when they ravage the best ones.

Crawl Pass is a change for us. It's like going on an adventure holiday. It is a pleasure for me personally, because I don't have far to fetch the water from the spring. The water bursts out from the bottom of our land and I wonder what will happen if the land slides away. The spring water is crystal clear and never runs dry.

Papa says, "I could be a rich man if I have the knowledge and facility to bottle and sell the water. When a man is poor you are just frigging poor."

It is still there at this moment, bubbling up from beneath the ground. It's a quenching hole for herds of animals and people cluttering around filling their pans with the crystal water...

When the cane season is over we go back home to Bois Content. But Papa gets restless and wonders what else he can do to make a better life for the family.

~ 8 ~

Mamma has a baby, our brother Dudley, but I didn't realise that she was having a baby. I'm only told that the airplane brought him. So I'm very confused because I only see airplanes miles up in the sky, and nowhere near our house. I pray for him to grow up overnight, and take some of the responsibilities because he is a boy. Papa has a big smile on his face now he has a son. "This boy will carry the Hancel's name for ever," he said. But I'm worried that I will get less food and more work to do.

One night, when I am tucked up in bed, I hear my parents talking. I raise my head off the pillow and listen. Papa seems vexed and his voice sounds angry. He says, "I want to immigrate to England to make a better life. They need people to go over to work, and help rebuild the country after the war." But Mama doesn't want him to go.

"How the hell do you expect me to cope with all these children that we hatch up like chickens?" she says.

Papa is trying to explain to her.

"After I save enough money, I will send for you and the children." But her voice becomes stronger and I don't need to strain to hear what they are saying any more. She tells him that there is no way she will join him, because she isn't going up in the sky like a bird.

"It's only birds should fly up there, I watched enough John crows riding the wind and saw how they land on the ground, blasting up dust, and flapping their huge wings. I'm not a bird and I don't have wide wings. I'm staying on the ground, where if I fall I can get up and walk home."

She tells him she won't be able to stand the cold weather, as she is not an Eskimo. She is afraid of what she heard – that frost could eat off people's fingers and toes and she certainly doesn't want that happening to her. I must have fallen asleep and missed the end of their conversation. I often hear my father talk about going away, but his dream seems to melt away like the snow and ice that Mamma fears and warns him about.

One day I hear Papa telling Mamma, "I have enough of this grind; no wonder some people end it with a noose." Mamma glares at him.

"Don't talk like that, me no have no black frock," she says.

"Well I'm sorry that me open me mouth." Papa's face is burning. He's so vex that he starts to stutter. He picks up his machete and stabs a piece of wood and walks away. I am frightened.

Mamma has a cousin called Miss Edna who lives in Money Musk. She doesn't have any children and she's very fond of me. She is always begging my parents to let me come and spend some time with her. I cannot believe it when my parents agree that I can go. I am excited and look forward to the change and some refined living.

It is August 1951 when Papa and I set off early one morning to Old Harbour. He says, "Valerie, it is going to be a long journey to Money Musk."

It is very hot, my palate needs showering, and I'm dying for a pee. I tell Papa, but he tells me to cross my legs. "It won't be long now," he says. When we get off the bus, I rush behind some bushes and relieve myself. Papa showers the ants and worms as well. When we arrive I am surprised to see a plantation with lots of workers. Miss Edna works for some Bakra white people in a house on the huge plantation which is called Bullpen. The owners cultivate bananas and they have acres of banana trees waving their long leaves.

However, there is a surprise in store. After a few days, she gives me a list of jobs to do. I was kidding myself, thinking I was going to have long, lazy days. Nevertheless, the jobs don't include carrying water on my head or loading sugar canes, but doing housework: cleaning, washing pots, and doing errands. The work isn't as exhausting as it is at home. Miss Edna's room is big with one window. There are two chairs, a wardrobe with curtains for the doors, a dressing table and a double bed. The floorboards look like glass, and they creek when I walk on them.

After a few weeks Miss Edna sends me to school, but I don't enjoy it very much because there is a lot to catch up on. Most of the children are bright, and I feel like an outsider – a wandering sheep that has lost its flock. The white children's parents take them to school in Jeeps. They are nicely dressed with pig tails flashing when they run. The boys play cricket. The Indian girls have long black hair that they sit on. The Chinese children are small with slit eyes and their parents speak Chinese language. I don't understand when they speak. Some of the black children speak Patois, and still they don't understand when Valerie the country girl speaks. They must think that I came from the moon.

Some days I feel lonely. I'm hungry for some laughter from my sisters and brother. I miss my family and the animals. One day I cry buckets, but I brighten up again when I remember the things that I would have to do at home. I have a cold shower; we don't have such luxury at home.

Miss Edna gives me a bottle of cream soda, and some ice cream. I can hardly believe it. I'm not accustomed to treats, but I lap it up like a cat licking cream. I have to get up at the crack of dawn and polish the floor with... guess what? A good old coconut brush! I push and shove until I can see my face gleaming back at me, but the odd bee waltzes in, following the fragrance of the beeswax. I love the aroma of the wax, but I'm terrified when a bee whirls into the room.

I have trouble reaching things in the high cupboards in the kitchen and it annoys me. We don't have such fancy things at home. One day I drop a china cup and break it. I am slapped for it. Worst of all, Miss Edna tells me that I'm not allowed to use the mosquito net that night. I am horrified and the mosquitoes have a feast of my blood, and the next day I am covered in bites. I catch fever and become very ill. Miss Edna rubs Bay Rum all over my body and wraps me in two white sheets, so that I can sweat it out. I'm shaking and my teeth are clapping deliriously. I'm feeling weak and just want water to drink.

Thousands of mosquitoes breed in the trenches that carry the irrigation water to the banana trees.

I'm shocked to be punished because of my clumsiness. I had never held a china cup in my hands before. It was very beautiful and I was just admiring it when it slipped from my hand. At home when we drop a tin can or an enamel mug on the ground, they spin around like a gig until they stop, and are ready to use again.

But she needs the cup to serve Mr Hanson his Blue Mountain coffee. She is worried that she will get sacked if she uses a white enamel mug to serve him. But she has to. When he sees it he glares and says, "What's this? Where is my cup?" Miss Edna starts to stutter.

"The cup has broken; it fell by accident when the door was opened," Mr and Mrs Hanson's faces turn crimson. Mr Hanson taps the plate with the knife and says, "These cups have come down generations, and you have to take care in future. If it happens again you are out of a job." Miss Edna blinks her eye lashes, and the blood drains from her face. "Don't you think you'd better get going?" Mr Hanson says. She walks away frightened to the kitchen. I feel it's my fault.

The following evening Miss Edna sends me to a shop in Alley for some groceries. The sun is sinking in the distance, and the sky seems to be on fire. Twilight creeps in and daylight turns into night. I can hear footsteps behind me, but when I look around there is no one.

But the sound of heavy boots continues and I'm very afraid. I wish I could fly off the ground like a bird. The footsteps become louder and louder, then I hear a man's voice saying, "Where are you going? Little girls are not safe walking in the dark."

I screamed. "Go away leave me alone you monster."

"Monster? Good lord, I'm a fairy god father. I take care of children, especially little girls who walk in the dark." I can't see the face of this huge figure dressed in black clothes. I scream aloud.

"Leave me alone!"

He laughed and laughed.

I begin to run fast. My heart feels like it's going to explode, by the time I get to the canal bridge, I'm breathless. When I reach home I tell Miss Edna about my frightening experience, but she doesn't seem concerned. I get the impression that she thinks I'm making it up, because I don't want to walk so far in the late evening. But I'm worried that it will happen again and that she still won't believe me. I keep getting nightmares that night.

Her husband's uncle Andrew (well I think that they are married, but it is some years later before I realise that they are living a sweetheart life). One evening, they decide to go crab hunting. I'm very excited about it. I have seen land crabs run backwards into their holes many times as they see me coming. Uncle Andrew makes three bottle torches, then he lights them with his Havana cigar that is always in his mouth between his broken teeth. We glide out into the black night to the mangrove bush. He is in front. Miss Edna is stepping lightly behind, and I'm fighting to bend back the mangrove branches that threaten to dig out my eyes in the swampy creeks. Suddenly there are hundreds of crabs scuttling around.

I freeze when I see Uncle Andrew and Miss Edna diving down and covering the crabs with the hessian bags, then dumping them into another big bag. I'm there for the adventure and excitement, holding my torch to dazzle the crabs' eyes. I certainly don't want to touch them, with their claws that look like scissors. Uncle Andrew puts the bags in the rusty handcart and I can see the claws poking out of the bags like shears, ready to slice off his hands. But I'm keeping my hands safely by my side. I keep jumping backwards every time I see that something dramatic is about to happen. I will cherish the memory forever.

When we arrive home, the moon is creeping up in the sky, but the stars were already twinkling before we set off. Uncle Andrew starts a roaring fire, and plonks a huge tin pan precariously over the flames. The crabs are still in a fighting mood and are trying to escape. He drops them into the pan, and after a while they just simply lie still. Miss Edna and Uncle Andrew invite some friends to join us. We sit under the moon and stars eating. I have never eaten so many crabs before. He pulls out a bottle of Appleton rum, and some Red stripe beer, they drink and get merry. I have lemonade.

But I'm worried about my tongue that is on fire from the scotch bonnet peppers that he dropped in with the crabs. That night I sleep sound until Miss Edna stirs me from my slumber. I begin the day fresh from the adventure of my life.

That morning, the workers prop up the banana bunches with crook sticks and cover them with blue plastic bags to protect them from insects.

However, that afternoon it begins to rain heavily, thunder is clapping loudly and it scares me. The nearby sea is a frenzy of froth, with pounding waves.

That night the rain plays Rumba music on the corrugated roof. I bury my head under the sheet, as I'm terrified of thunder and lightning, but I can still see a blaze of light flashing in the room.

Somehow, I manage to fall asleep but I am awakened by a flood of water pouring in the bed. "O my God," Miss Edna says, as she pulls me closer to her. The roof has disappeared in the wind and I'm frantic and confused, but there is nowhere for us to hide, as it's too dangerous outside. The screeching sound of the zincs scares me. We are soaked and I begin to cry.

When dawn comes, we rush outside; all the banana trees are lying on the ground. The Hanson family are devastated. The workers salvage some of the bananas. I eat bananas for breakfast, lunch, and dinner. Ripe bananas will become my favourite fruit, but the experience has left me with a fearful memory of what a tropical storm can do.

A few days go by, and my father comes to visit us. He is talking to Miss Edna in a low voice, but I realise that he don't want me to hear what he is saying, so I edge closer. I can hear him telling her that our house has been battered by the hurricane, and Mamma has had a new baby the day after hurricane Hatty flattened the island. My heart skips many beats when I hear him telling Miss Edna that they want me to come home to help. With my few pieces of clothes hastily packed I reluctantly walk with my father to Alley and wait for transport to take us to May Pen.

Papa is quiet and I'm not in a talking mood either. It is very hot and I'm parching for a drink. I feel beads of perspiration running down my face, and I wipe them away with my hands. The asphalt is melting like butter under my sandals; I have to waggle my toes. Papa is lucky... he has proper shoes on his feet.

When we get to May Pen we wait for a bus to take us to Old Harbour, then another transport from Old Harbour to get home. I'm almost panting like a dog with thirst, so Papa buys me a ginger beer and a meat patty. I enjoy it and could eat another one. However, there is fear in my mind, but I try to keep calm. On our way home I can see houses with no roof - it was terrible. I'm not geared up for the destruction that I see as we walk into the yard. I have to skip over the debris that is scattered dangerously all over the place until I reach the veranda.

~ 9 ~

The walls are still sound, but the roof went with the wind. I walk calmly inside where Mamma is sitting on the bed with my baby sister wrapped in her arms. She is rocking and humming a song. I bend down and kiss the baby. I feel bewildered and confused. It is hard to grasp, because when I left a few months ago I wasn't aware of any changes in my mother's appearance. They tell me all kinds of hilarious stories and I believe what they say.

She is a beautiful baby with dark curly hair, and a small dimple in her right cheek. The shock of the hurricane must have sent her rushing out into the world to our nearly broken-down house. They have named her Evelyn after Mamma's mother. Mama says that she died early. My grandparents never lived long and that's why I don't know any of them. I feel a little envious of other children, who have grandparents.

I help with everything that my parents are doing, salvaging zinc and board to fix the roof. They tell me to be careful as I trip on the rubble on the ground. It is good that Papa can do the repairs himself, but he gets us to pass him things. However, when the rain starts pots, pans and even the baby's bath are set out to catch the water that is tumbling down. The zincs are all damaged and need replacing.

Mamma says, "Brother Lattie, look how you frig up the roof. I can see the stars! I will have to bring in some banana leaves tomorrow night to spread over the children, because I don't want them to drown while they are sleeping."

Papa gives her a cut eye look. I can see the frustration on his face when he snaps back at her and says, "Tomorrow morning, I will give you the frigging ladder and you can bung all the zinc holes yourself." He is furious; they are like two wild cats fighting with each other, but after that I never hear her say another word before I fall asleep. It takes him some time to fix the house. He says he doesn't have the money to buy new zinc for the roof.

The sugar cane season is here again. The night before we leave Papa says, "We will get up before the first cock starts to crow and before the first person starts to chop up their firewood. We will make our smoke curl up with theirs." We set off in an exodus on foot to Crawl Pass when the stars are still twinkling in the sky. Mamma tells us, "Walk good, mind you fall." But Marjorie falls and she begins to bawl. Papa lifts her up then looks with the bottle torch at her leg and it was bleeding.

"Sadea, can you find anything to bandage her leg?" he says.

"How can I find anything in the dark? Take off your shirt and cut a piece off with the machete," Mamma said.

"My shirt! So me fe walk half naked and catch cold?" Papa hesitates, and then does what he is told, but Marjorie is still screaming.

"I think we will have to put her on the donkey," he says.

"But there's no room," Mamma says.

"We just have to give Valerie and Icis some of the things to carry," he says. So they tie two bundles and plonk them on our heads. Papa lifts Marjorie up and puts her on the donkey's back.

"Don't fall asleep," he says, "It will be day light soon."

Hanna is laden with both our worldly possessions and Marjorie. Hanna is an amazing animal, to walk through the thick mushy clay in the dark. But she gets stuck again and her legs burp as she splash-splashed in the mud. Marjorie falls off Hanna's back and screams with fright.

"Hanna is going to step on her leg!" Mamma shouts, "Get her out quick, Lattie!" Papa pulls Marjorie out. Hanna struggles and frees herself. Then she sticks up her ears and flashes her tail as if to say, "I have freed myself again, clever Hanna."

Marjorie is covered in mud and everything is a mess. She is still crying but he puts her back on Hanna's back. He leads his flock until night says good bye and a new day emerges.

When we arrive at Crawl Pass we are excited and run around to see what is available to scramble for. The Mangoes on the trees are turning red, while the branches groan under the weight. The avocado pears hang low and some of the branches are propped up with sticks, like old ladies stabbing the ground for support.

But Papa has caught cold and fever; he's shaking like a dog with mange. Mamma says she can warm water on his body. He cannot cut any sugar cane because he's weak and coughing from his belly bottom, but she nurses him back to health with home remedy. When he feels better he says that his enthusiasm for growing sugar canes is running low and he feels worn out, so some of the sugar cane spoils.

When we return to Bois Content, he becomes restless and tells Mamma he needs a change. After a lot of discussion they decide that the whole family will go to his sister in Old Harbour Bay for a while. But it takes a lot of shouting and losing of his temper before Mamma agrees.

Eventually, we all join Aunt Mary and her husband Deacon, who is a fisherman. They live in a three-bedroom house with a veranda. They don't have any children of their own.

Deacon is a tall man. His complexion is dark as coal, and he has a sunshine smile. A fisherman all his life, he has battled with the Caribbean Sea many a time. Papa watches Deacon and his friend, Brother Harrison, going off fishing in the early morning. They get up before the crack of dawn. I hear him say he wants to smell the sea and feel the warm water in the early morning. He watches as they push their canoe into the sea and slowly disappear out of sight. He has his dreams and hope that one day he will be off with them, fighting the waves while the stars still twinkle in the sky.

Mamma is shocked when he tells her his intention. She rants and raves and says he must have gone mad, because he can't swim and she isn't ready to be a widow in the prime of her life.

"You can't swim and you want to be a fisherman? Let me tell you something. If anything should happen out there, you will be the first one to drown."

Papa doesn't seem worried one bit; if he is, he doesn't show a tinge of it. He simply wants to be on the ocean riding the waves with the rest, and experiencing the excitement of pulling in a catch. He sees it as another way of making some money, and although it's dangerous, it is different from the gruelling work of cane cultivation.

Aunt Mary makes jacks for the men to take for their lunch. Jacks are flour dumplings with butter, and a little sugar for good measure. She rolls them into round shapes and fries them slowly in coconut oil. I'm awakened by the frantic noise that Mamma is making. I think she is going mad, because Papa is about to go off fishing for the first time with Deacon and his mate. The way she is bellowing, I think she is already in mourning! We never go back to sleep after they leave, as Mamma starts to pray to God to guide and protect them, and the commotion continues for quite a while. We go to school that day feeling worried about him, but Mamma can't hide her fear: she has misery written all over her face.

She persuades Aunt Mary to go with her to the shore and wait until their boat returns. Aunt Mary isn't very happy to go, as she never waits for Deacon to return from the sea, but she decides to go with her in the end. Mamma can be very persistent when she wants to; she is scared that something will happen to our father. Aunt Mary sees the canoe slowly coming towards them into the shallow water. Mamma lifts up her dress high, and wades into the sea, bobbing up and down like a grasshopper in her eagerness to greet Papa. He is surprised to see her, but he is more interested in the amount of money he will get from the sale of the fish as a crowd of people swarm around the canoe.

We quickly get used to eating roast, fried, steamed, and escabeched fish. The only time that Papa is not full of enthusiasm to go fishing is when huge swells are forecast at sea. Then he has a lie-in until the sun scatters over the house and mixes with the sea breeze.

Aunt Mary's house is only about half a mile from the sea. The yard is sandy, so nothing seems to grow except thorn bushes. When it rains, the yard is like a shallow sea. It frightens my sisters and me, as it takes so long to evaporate, and smells very fishy.

I begin to secretly miss our home, with its lush countryside, the humming birds that zip around from flower to flower and the crickets and toads that chatter through the night. But in other ways I am bursting with joy, because I don't have to fetch water and do lots of things. Aunt Mary has pipe water flowing in her yard, so things are much easier here.

Mamma is getting uneasy and ill-tempered sometimes. She is missing her own front door and tells Papa that she wants to go home. She says if he isn't ready to go she will leave two of us with him, and return home to Bois Content. He is very angry with her because he wants to try out something new, even though she says he is the first one the sharks will eat because he can't swim.

"I'm the man, I wear the trousers," he says, "I'm going to give fishing my best shot, so do what you want to do." He is fuming. She tells him, "If anything should happen to you, I don't want to know." He is determined to let her sweat for a while. But on the day she decides to leave, he can see how she is struggling down the lane with all her belongings, and his heart melts. He has no choice other than to go along with her decision. He packs up reluctantly with a face like thunder and returns home with the family.

On our return, the house seems dead. But we bring back lots of noise from Old Harbour Bay, and soon it is alive again. Perhaps all the fresh fish that we have eaten over those restful months has given us a new zest of life. I don't know if Mamma will return to buying and selling in the markets of Kingston, where she sleeps under the stars; covering her tired body with a hessian bag.

I'm not looking forward to carting any more artefacts on my rested head. I wish I could find a bolthole and disappear out of sight but that is only a dream. To be rebellious and disruptive would cause the strap to sting my body, and anger to fill my parent's hearts. I'm expected to be thankful to have been given life, to be the person who I am, taking whatever destiny throws at me.

I begin to notice things. Little things that I never thought of before, like who's getting taller and who's getting fatter. Suddenly I realise that Mamma and her sister, Aunt Bertha, look the same. They have put on loads of weight. Their backsides are dancing every time they take a step.

One day, Aunt Bertha comes to visit us. She isn't living far away. I'm in the kitchen, where the walls are made from bamboo. There are little gaps that I can peep through and secretly listen to their conversation. Auntie Bertha tells Mamma that she is expecting twins.

They are laughing, and are both in a happy mood.

"That's why you're so huge!" Mamma says.

I'm smiling silently inside, but I have to keep a straight face, like a judge summing up a case. However, I know that they will tell us what Mamma has always told us before: an aeroplane brings the babies for the mother. Perhaps she honestly doesn't know what to say to me and my younger sisters. We are children, and children are to be seen but not heard.

One night, not many months later, I'm awakened in the dead of night by some commotion in the next room. As I slowly gain consciousness, I can hear strange sounds. There are exclamations of "Oh!" and other unusual, monstrous sounds coming from Mamma's bed room. I lie there, looking at the glow of the lamp. Suddenly I hear a crippling shriek, followed by the whimpering cry of a baby. My two sisters are sleeping soundly while I'm absorbing the shock. I fall asleep again and dream about what I have heard.

Mamma usually rouses us with her call of, "Wake up! Wake up!" But that morning it is Papa who is blowing his trumpet. One by one we rise like flowers blooming into a new day. I walk into their bedroom and stand by the bed, expecting to hear the usual list of jobs to do. But when I gaze down at the sheets, our freshly delivered baby brother is sleeping peacefully beside my mother. He has a funny face. She doesn't say who brought him or where he came from. That morning, I cannot embrace my duties because I know that I will have more work to do.

Papa must have been happy when Mamma had a son but he will have to be a tough one to follow us girls. However, the little fellow dies this evening and Mamma is bawling. She says he had three toes on one foot and one hand and his top lip was split in two. I am not too sad. I couldn't have coped with a three-lip brother. Mamma picks up the baby off the bed and holds him in her arms. She prods him, raises his eyelids, and he start foaming froth from his mouth. She lifts his left hand and it falls limply out of her hand.

"He's gone, Lattie. He's really gone."

"Lift up his head and see if it drop limp", Papa says.

Mamma has a wild look on her face and she pulls off her head scarf, her curly hair falling over her forehead. Sweat is running down her face mixed with shiny tears. Papa takes the baby from her arms and wraps him in a white sheet, and Mamma holds her head in between her hands and says, "Help me Lord."

He stands in the room staring around. The blood drains from his face. He puts his arm around Mamma's neck, his hand shaking.

"Sadea, I'm going to make a drink for you," he says after a while and leaves the bedroom.

He comes back with a glass of lemonade. She takes a few sips and starts wailing again. Aunt Bertha comes and comforts Mamma. She brings some dinner for her. Mamma tells her, "I can't eat it now." Aunt Bertha just says,

"Look at the salt lines on your cheeks, let me get the face flannel and some cold water to wipe your face."

"Bertha, my baby is dead. Only one day he had in the world. I feel like I'm going mad."

"I know," Aunt says. "He's gone to heaven."

"Heaven? What is God going to do with him up there?"

"An Angel, Elsaida, he will be an Angel".

Papa is busy making the coffin and singing the hymn *Abide with Me.* Mamma names him Jonathan Hancel. The next evening the Wallace and Hancel family gather in our garden and Papa and Brother Hussein stand stone-faced as Mr O'Conner the minster commits his body to the ground. Mamma shakes like she has fever and Papa puts his arm around her. I never cry. I am just sad. But I'm glad that I will never have to get up in the night and feed him and wipe his you know what. Mamma cries and cries all the time and I have to give her a hug.

Papa is busy cutting down some cedar trees, assisted by Uncle Man. Eventually they build a platform and hoist the logs up off the ground with lots of muscle work. They are drenched in the perfume from the ceder planks. Dripping with sweat, they pull the huge whip saw with all their strength. I have never seen a saw so long. They take it in turns: one plants his feet on the ground, while the other stands on a platform pulling his heart strings with the effort, looking like Nelson standing on his column.

I stand and watch with amazement, and feel sorry for them when I hear the sounds they are making as they rip the saw through the planks. I don't know why Mamma always sends me with Papa's lunch whenever he is working. She ties it up in a freshly starched, bright-coloured tablecloth and plonks it in my hands.

"Hold it good," she says. "Don't throw away the gravy."

Then I walk as quickly as I can with the steam seeping through the cloth, and my brow dripping with perspiration. When I arrive, Uncle Man and Pappa look as if they have had a shower in their clothes. I feel sorry for them, as it is hard work pulling up and down the long saw. I don't understand how they manage to saw these planks manually. I look up at them and think: what a way to make a living, surely there must be an easier way? It seems so tough and laborious, with their clothes ripped to rags, and tiredness dimming their eyes.

Finally, they stop and sit on one of the planks, and have eaten the food I brought before I even finish wiping the sweat from my face. By the time I get home I feel as if I have done a day's work with all the walking that I had to do. When I get back, Aunt Bertha is at our house talking to Mamma while Mamma scrubs some clothes in the tub.

Aunt Bertha is so big with pregnancy that she looks like a barrel ready to burst. What I don't know is that a deal has been sealed. Mamma has agreed for her sister to have her babies at our house.

One evening, Aunt Bertha comes to our house. When she arrives, she keeps walking up and down on the veranda. Then she sits for a while and gets up again. Mamma sends us to bed. That night I am disturbed from my sleep by some awful noises – noises of panting, and groaning – in the next room. I can hear Mamma's voice echoing loudly, speaking words of encouragement, but I hear another voice, one I've heard before. It is Miss Rosalinda, the midwife from Bella's Gate. Some people call her the Nana.

I lie there, not moving a muscle, determined to enjoy the experience. No one knows that I'm awake. I keep still and tell myself not to turn, just in case the bed squeaks and gives away my secret. I'm lying there with my eyes wide open. But I fall asleep at some point because the babies are taking so long to come.

I wake up again and remember that I was waiting for my new cousins to be born. I listen and hear a monstrous sound.

"I can't do it," a voice says.

"Yes you can!" another replies.

"Come on, Bertha! I can see your baby's head. Go on, big push; like when you are constipated!"

Then I hear a deep groan and the cry of a baby.

Some time goes by before I hear Miss Rosalinda giving encouragement again.

"Miss Bertha, this one bottom is coming first, so don't push until I tell you to, yes?"

"Lord me God, I'm going to die! Please help me, Nana!" Aunt Bertha screams

"I'm helping you," Miss Rosalinda says. "Right, come on now - push, push, push! That's it! Well done."

But I don't hear the baby cry. There's nothing but silence. So I wait and wait until they give him his first beating. Finally it gives out a loud cry. I think how many times a day their shitty bottoms will need washing.

I close my eyes and snuggle down to sleep again, thinking back on what was the experience of my life.

~ 10 ~

The secret that Mamma held from me about where my brother Dudley came from didn't last for ever.

I learnt it the midday of the Sunday that she had my three-lip brother. We didn't go to church, as the pain of loss was stabbing her and she was screaming out, so she couldn't plait our hair. I decided to hide under the cellar and listen to all the commotion until I hear the baby scream. So I know that no aeroplane brought our twin cousins, but I keep it to myself. I make them think that I'm a fool but I'm wiser than they think. No one knows to this day that I heard what was going on in the middle of the night when Aunt Bertha was saying "I can't do it, please help me."

The following morning we go into the bedroom and Aunt Bertha is sleeping in Mamma's bed. The babies are beautiful, a boy and a girl lying beside her. The dusky pink skinned girl was named Yulda, and her brother Busha has almost white skin. Brother Hessian is quite white and Aunt Bertha is dark like my mother. The babies are like coffee and cream. There is some sort of ceremony before Aunt Bertha comes out of our house, where she has stayed for nine days after giving birth.

I find it strange that history has repeated itself for me, as Mamma had the same sort of ritual when she had Dudley. Papa kills Billy, a black and white ram goat, and cooks him with lots of spices, rice, peas, and vegetables. They drink rum and throw some to the ground to feed the ancestors that have passed on. Brother Hessian and Papa blow horns and knock drums and they dance: everyone is so happy.

Aunt Bertha dances with Yulda, and Mamma dances with Busha. The babies have their first dance, their first ray of sunshine, and a wet cross mark with rum on their forehead. That will let them sleep when they get home. Then Aunt Bertha and Mamma sit on the veranda and talk. Aunt Bertha goes home that day. Mamma carries Busha and Aunt carries Yulda in the evening sunshine, while Brother Hessian's smile gets wider as he walks behind their mule, loaded with Aunt Bertha and the babies' clothes. When we reach their house Mamma prays and we sit around for a while, and then come back to our house.

One day, Papa buys a piece of dense wood land. It's full of thorns, stone water holes that catch water when it rains, and there is a cave. There are also twisting tracks, and loads of bird nests. We look forward to going there, because there's a lovely view and we can see the sea in the distance. He cuts down some of the trees, and sets fire to the bushes, before planting corn, gungo peas, cassava, and sweet potatoes. We help drop the grains as he slices into the ground with a pickaxe. When it rains, the plants sprawl out in heavenly bliss. I watch the gungo peas grow and blossom, and the root vegetables burst out of the soil and peep up at me.

One day, as were walking through the bush, we hear a goat bawling. We think it is tangled in some wisps, but when we get closer we realise that it is giving birth. Icis, Marjorie, and I watch until the two kids come out. We don't want to leave them, but eventually we reluctantly walk away.

When we arrive at our Dad's property, we lap our dresses between our legs and hop over the barbed wire fence like butterflies, but we never breathe a word about what we have just seen. With my sisters I have watched a goat giving birth, and I've stretched my ears when Yulda and Busha and my three-lip brother burst out in the world, but I keep that particular secret from my sisters. If they want to know where baby comes from and what's going on at night, then they have to sleep light like me.

As we walk over towards the black mango tree, we are met by the aroma seeping from the baking wood that Papa covers up with bushes and dirt to bake into charcoal. Sleepy smoke is still swirling out in the air. The wood that is already baked lies still, black and glistening in the sun.

He says, "Come on, girls, give me a hand."

We stoop around the charcoal pit, picking out the coal from the black dust. However, as we squat around the baked coals we find charcoal that is still alive, and hot in the dust, ready to blister our fingers.

Papa packs the charcoals in long cowrie bags and ties them with wisps, ready for Hanna to carry to the main road, where the truck picks them up, and for Mamma to sell them at Grass Yard Market in Kingston. He makes a huge fire so that we can roast corn, and cashew nuts. When we finish eating we scoop water from the stone holes, and sip it from the Calabash bowls that Papa makes from the gourds. By the time we finish picking the charcoal we look like coalminers.

He packs and ties three bundles of wood with wisps, then plonks them on our heads with a grass cottar. We walk back home in the late evening sunshine. Then the sky becomes cloudy and dark and suddenly the rain is blasting our skin. When the thunder and lighting starts, I half close my eyes, with my clothes clinging to my skin.

Mamma is very concerned, when she sees the huge piles of wood that Papa has perched on our heads. She is also worried that we will catch fever from getting drenched in the thunderstorm, but worse still, end up with huge balls growing between our legs. I'm surprised when I hear her remarks, but I am too tired and rain-washed to care if anything will grow anywhere. All I know is that I wish my sisters and I don't have to carry those bundles of wood like we are carrying the cross of Calvary.

Mamma is blazing, and she tells us that our father is going to give us a hernia.

"Listen to me," she says as she rubs us down with Bay Rum, "Don't carry anything that you can't put on your heads. Throw it on the ground and take some out." She is busy fussing over us.

When it is dark, Papa hasn't come home, but that is nothing new, as he often comes home late. But Mamma is worried and says to us, "I'm wondering what has happened to your father. He might have collapsed and the crows ate him."

My heart starts to beat like a Bongo drum, and we sit there with our ears propped up like rabbits until we hear the dogs, Buster and Hickla, greeting him. He clears his throat to signal his arrival. We rush to the verandah as he wipes his feet on the straw mat. He smiles and cuddles the bunch of heads on the dimly lit verandah, then walks inside.

Mamma meets him with her razor-sharp tongue, before his bottom touches the chair.

"Lattie, you going to give the girls hernia. Those bundles of wood is too heavy for them to carry, they will stop them grow." Papa never answers or gives a reason for being late, and that makes her more furious. I am glad that he is home safely, although he is late, but Mamma cannot contain herself and rips into him like a tigress. He sits and washes his hands and feet, while we stand around chatting. It turns out that he stopped down at Teacher's shop while the rain beat down, and watched the men playing dominoes.

We can't wait to get a bite of his dinner; this is something that we look forward to when he comes home. At the end of his meal he cuts up one dumpling or whatever in equal pieces, and gives it to us. The little pieces are delicious, so I hold onto the taste in my mouth as long as possible.

Saturday nights are memorable when we are waiting for Mamma to return from Kingston. We look forward to the treats of grated coconut cakes, candies, or mint balls. But Papa is looking for his special treat also, as Mamma always brings a huge, hard, dough bread home. It is well known that he cannot resist the smell of freshly baked bread. He waits for a while, and then creeps into the dimly lit room. I can hear the sound of the chain creaking that holds the basket up on the hook in the ceiling. Then I hear the paper ripping, and think, yes, that's him ravaging the bread! He plonks the basket on the floor, and hack off a hunk of the bread.

We have mice in the house, so that's why Papa hangs the basket in the ceiling. He hangs it down, and bites into his favourite treat.

There's no way that we could reach up there to pinch a slice. But there is one mouse that can reach up there… and we all know who that is.

One night, I am lying in bed listening to the rain falling like pebbles on the zinc. I say my prayers. Pray for Mamma, pray for Papa, pray for God to bless me and make me a good child, Amen. Then I say a second prayer, 'This night as I lay down to sleep, I give the Lord my soul to keep, in my little bed I lie, heavenly Father hear my cry, Amen…' when suddenly I hear a squeak, then this almighty bang. I jump up and look around the room. The shade lamp is flickering on the table, and there he is, the big rat that brought the basket crashing down. He stands for a moment recovering from the shock, and hoping that he haven't woke up his clan, then dives to the floor like an eagle. I slide back down, and watch him cut a hunk of the bread. I snuggle under the sheet and wish that he'd seen me; maybe he would have given me a slice.

Mamma sleeps like a log through all the commotion, and so do the rest of the children. On the Sunday morning, when she goes to fish the basket down, she gets a shock.

"The rat has got to it before us," she says as she cuts wafer thin slices, while calling out our names. The can of bush tea is welcome to dip my bread into, but it just gets lost in my mouth and my palate is yawning for more. Then she reminds us to brush our teeth, though we don't have a toothbrush. So we make our own from a special stick that we chew on, and call it chew stick and it does the job every time.

"Hurry up!" She shouts, "So that I can comb your hair for Sunday school."

I love it when she doesn't plait my hair on a Sunday, but just leaves it loose to blow in the wind. We live near the Baptist church, and we can watch people walking into the churchyard as Mamma ties bows in our hair. Then she watches us walk away, lively, up the lane.

Mr O'Connor is the preacher that Sunday, and part of his sermon is about children. He says that children are a gift from God, and parents have a duty to guide and protect them from harm and danger to enable them to enjoy their childhood. I nearly shout out to tell him that we aren't protected from hard work, that our childhood is blighted since we were born. But I have to bite my lips, and hold my breath, which nearly kills me by the time he finish his long sermon.

"What did you all learn today?" Mamma ask inquisitively when we return home.

I'm the first to shout out that children are a blessing, and parents should guide and protect them from harm and danger. "But we are not even protected from the rain at nights," I tell her. The rain comes in at night through the leaking zinc when we lie in bed, and I often hear the raindrops tip-topping into the buckets that Poppa sets to catch the drips. Mamma seems speechless. It takes a lot for her to close her gab. When she gathers herself together she says, "Go and take your clothes off."

I never got an answer from her to this day. I go off in a huff but dare not show it. I fling my treasured shoes across the bedroom, until the rage subsides. All I need is for her to give me an answer, to talk to me. Who knows, maybe any old Anancy story will satisfy my bravery to question her in the first place.

When I come back outside, I notice that her dress is bursting out at the side seams, and I wonder if it is because I am beating it too hard with the clapper stick at the river. However, I soon realise that our dumplings will be getting smaller, and we have to work even harder, when she starts to send me to the shop to buy salted cod fish. I watch her roast it on the fire and eat it by herself without giving me a crumb. I'm also shocked when I see how often she is spitting in the old condensed milk can, and I wonder where all that fluid is coming from.

Then one morning I am awakened by a new alarm clock... Papa. "Valerie, wake up my little angel, it's time to get up," he says in a low soft voice that I never knew he had.

I stretch and rub my sticky eyes, then reluctantly crawl out of bed like a long slivering snake sliding off a piece of wood. After a while I am buzzing around like a bee from flower to flower. I sweep the kitchen, light the fire and watch the smoke spiralling up through the thatch roof while the four breadfruits sit quaking in pain on the fire.

Then I walk up the slope behind our kitchen and pick some lemon grass to make the tea.

I am stretching to reach the leaves, when I hear a baby crying. I stop and listen to make sure that it isn't Bubble mewing and, to my amazement, it isn't. I drop the leaves and run back to the kitchen, and turn the breadfruits with a piece of stick and at the same time listen in case I hear the little mite cry again, but it has shut up its trap.

Then after a while Papa comes outside flashing a big smile. "Come inside, all of you," He grins, beckoning with his hand. "Come inside."

Everybody runs inside, not knowing that there is a surprise waiting for us, except me. I marvel over the baby like the first time I set my eyes on a chicken cracking through an eggshell; I had stood there and watched the unfolding moment until it tumbled out, damp and squeaking.

We gather round the bed, pushing for space, as Mamma cuddles the baby in her arms. They name him Samuel, and we are all excited, especially Evelyn, who bops up and down on the bed like a ping pong ball. Mamma doesn't try to conceal the fact that the airplane didn't bring Samuel. She simply keeps a silent tongue, maybe because she is exhausted.

I have forgotten the breadfruits on the fire with all the excitement and they burn, but I don't get into trouble. What would we have to eat? I sigh with relief when Papa rescues them. He lays them on some ashes from the day before. Then with his strong hands, he peels the black skin away, without the skin breaking once. I could not believe how quick. He finishes peeling them, and then counts the enamel plates just like Mamma does, laying the slices on them one by one.

~ 11 ~

When Samuel was three months old, Mamma goes back to buying and selling fruits. I'm nearly eleven now, and growing into shape, and I become a mother to my baby brother. I can be sound asleep, but as soon as he starts crying I wake up too. Papa wakes up sometimes, but other times he is sound asleep after a hard day working like a dog. So I warm the mint tea that lies sleeping in the black pan, as Samuel bellows.

Sometimes he won't settle. Well, it's just water and sugar I give him. I wish I have two melons as huge as Mamma's to plonk into his gob, but all I have is two little buttons sprouting up on my chest. I bond with him so much that I feel as if he is mine. I often feel like a real mother and wish I could grow up fast, and have my own children to put all my skills into practice.

Icis begins to take an interest in him too, maybe because they resemble each other, with freckle faces and light brown skin that they inherit from Papa's Irish father. We lay fruits on the floor and watch Samuel crawl towards them, and puncture them with his new pegs, until the juice runs out like a dripping honeycomb.

But it is a shock when he starts to talk. We watch him bounce up and down, as he struggles to get words out. It is so difficult for him to express himself, but we absolutely adore him, and he's my favourite brother. He grows into a fine boy with a stammer. He often makes mother's blood pressure shoot up, because he skips school to go diving into blue holes hunting for crayfish. Mamma threatens to take out her breast that he loved so much when he was baby, and calls out his name to God, to show him some sign that will make him slow down. She wants him to come to his senses, because she fears that he will end up early in a grave.

Icis is excelling at school; she shows all the signs of being an intellectual scholar. Although I'm seventeen months older, she aspires to the class above me and sends my confidence in a downward spiral. I feel conscious that my younger sister is doing so well and I'm thrown aside like an old barrow without handles. Still I suffer from lack of school attendance while helping out at home, and I have to watch my freckle face sister go off to school some days. I try to comfort myself by giving myself little treats of dry coconut with sugar.

On my way to the river, with the wash pan balanced on my head, I throw stones at some ripe mangoes, and watch them fall to the ground. I have a feast in the long grass before I ramble down the hill. I put the mangoes in the stream to keep cool, and then compel myself to wash the clothes. But I'm not alone; I meet some other children who are in the same situation as me. I hang some clothes on stones to dry, and then jump in for a playful splash with the other kids.

The shrimps dive for cover as we fish for them, but I manage to catch a few, and plonk them in a Butterpan of water to take home. I walk wearily up the winding hill in the fading sunshine, while long dark shadows with hints of evening mist creep among the hollows. My day's work isn't finished until I have ironed Mamma's clothes, the most important of all her long pocket bib that she goes off in to town fresh as a daisy. That night I am very tired that I sleep sound until I hear the wake-up music playing.

Miss Alma and uncle Buy Sam have repeatedly asked Mamma and Papa to let them adopt Evelyn.

"Sister Sadie" Miss Alma says. "Our house is dying for the sound and laughter that a child brings." Mamma is angry.

"Although we have so many children we are very proud, and I feel that we will be giving our child away." Mamma's face looks like raging bull. "I carry me child around for nine months and bear pain to bring them into the world, so I have no intention of giving her away while I am still alive!" I couldn't believe what I heard. So it's not the airplane that brings them the babies.

Miss Alma prays to God to give her a child and he answers her prayer. One day she tells Mamma that she's having twins and isn't well. Mamma sends me to their house to work. I ask myself, when is this going to end? Here I am, thrown from pillow to pole, and home from home, doing the same jobs that I am sick to death of. I think of running away again. But where to you fool? A voice in my head answers. "In the woods, up at Parade, under the stone caves, where the rat bats roost." But I tell this voice in my head that the smell would kill me, and carry on, hoping for a new day, a day that will bring me joy when I can walk away and hold my head up high.

Miss Alma and Uncle Buy Sam are on top of the world when their little boy and girl burst into the world, but I am vexed when I am sent to help with their donkey work and wash shitty nappies. Uncle Buy Sam is a District Constable, and often goes off to court in Old Harbour, and Miss Alma is left on her own. Anyway it is one mouth less for my parents to feed for a while, as some days they wonder where the next meal is coming from; it's always a struggle to make ends meet.

But Aunt Bertha always shares things with Mamma and vice versa. Mamma stalks the young bunches of bananas, and scratches the soil from the young yams and sweet potatoes to see if they are ready. Pappa warns her not to dig them so early, but she takes no notice of him. Sometimes she hears a voice calling out.

"Sister Sade, tan good, hold the dog."

"Ho," she says. "Come mam."

As Aunt Bertha walks into the freshly swept yard, with a basket sitting steady on her head, containing a bit of this, and a little of that, Mamma thanks her and lifts up her hands in prayer to God, that Aunt's store basket will never be empty.

That evening, after Aunt saves our lives, we play until darkness sweeps in. Once in a while Aunt Bertha goes to the river, flashing a sunny good morning, and telling Mamma that the huge water tank that Brother Hussein built is running low.

"I'm only going to take the whispering out, and leave the talking," she says to Mamma, who racked with laughter, but it takes me a long time to get my head around that proverb.

Aunt Bertha's husband is a farmer. He is a tall brown man who smokes some of the tobacco that he plants; he is always joking and smiling. He farms coffee and chocolate, and we sometimes go and help out. I hunt for the low trees, and leave the high ones for Icis who tip- toes to reach the laden branches that are perched on the ridges. However, she gets into trouble for breaking some of the branches. My heart is beating for her. She isn't used to picking them like me; if she were then she would use the wooden hook to bring the branches close to her.

It is October, and the rainy season has started, but we carry on picking the beans in the rain until the sun comes out again and dries our clothes. Brother Hussein is busy poking sugar cane into the squeezer, and flashes the mule with the cowskin strop tied to a stick, as it goes round in a circle. We watch the juice run down the bamboo gutter and into the huge copper pots, where the juice is boiled until it turns into wet sugar.

When we are parched with thirst, we return for a drink of cane juice, and take a few licks of the wet sugar which is filled with rum as none of the wicked stuff has been extracted out.

Then Icis, Majorie, and I stagger back with our eyeballs dancing in our heads, to pick some more coffee beans, truly tipsy, and it can be dangerous on those ledges, but we survive. *(Looking back now, we were drinking rum from the day we took our first breath, as they used the wet sugar to sweeten bush tea, and lemon ale. We also used to wash the pans with our tongues, as nothing was taken out of the concoction.)*

Aunt Bertha is busy with her family and still having babies, just like Mamma. But Aunt Bertha is lucky and doesn't have to go to Kingston to sell fruits and clucking chickens, like her sister Elsaida. She never lies down under the moon and stars, waiting for morning to break, when Kingston comes alive, and the customers start bartering with the country folk for the best deals. Mamma says that sometimes she doesn't sell much and she has to leave the goods on the ground, barely making enough money to buy the essentials to bring back home.

The only market that Aunt Bertha goes to is Old Harbour when she feels like it. Brother Hessian pads Marco the mule, and packs the hampers to the brim with food. Like a jockey, she mounts Barite, and they disappear down the hill into the early morning sunshine. I secretly watch the turning sun, and guess what time she will return home, then sneak out of the lane to meet her.

Sometimes she gives me a mint ball, that I let no one know about, and the pudding pan of fish that Mamma asked her to buy. That evening the aroma of fish is everywhere. As Mamma cooks, the whiff seeps out into the yard and beyond. I wait bolt-eyed for my share, while the rest of children run around playing with the feathers of the fowl that Mamma killed the Sunday before. By the time dinner is ready they complain that their heads feel dizzy. I wait patiently for my fish. I love the heads and they say if you eat plenty of fish heads it will make you become brainy. However, I will have to await the result of that one!

Papa comes home early that Saturday evening, and must surely smell the whiff that drifts into the air. I see him taking unusually long strides. We all eat happily and wish there is more to eat. But this is a one-off. Mamma has to dream up something new; being creative is one of the things that she has to do. She often says, "I will have to make some fashion today." Then she grates a few coconuts, bangs a salt mackerel in it, some scallion, tomatoes, a scotch bonnet peppers for good measure and turns it into a delicious meal. I can guarantee that you will beg for more if you are lucky to catch the feast.

I'm growing out of my clothes like a pea pushing out of the soil fast, especially around my chest, with my melons growing. I secretly wish when my baby brother is crying that I could satisfy him with them, like Mamma can, in the middle of the night when he wants to curl up in her arms and nuzzle on her breast. But I'm only his substitute, not his adorable mother. I remember feeling maternal, and being filled with motherly love for him, as he sucks my undeveloped breast through my night clothes until he falls asleep in my arms. Then I would reluctantly put him down.

No one knew these little secrets during all these years; I kept them to myself and wrapped them safely in my heart. The burden is easier to bear now that I have shared it with you; that part of my life you can understand only if you have had the joy, or sorrow, to experience it. I have been there and done it and it wasn't always exciting.

The next day I sit behind the house in the shade, and wash my brother's shitty nappies with my mouth touching my nose as he sleeps in the crib that Papa made when they knew I was on my way. It has been a hot day and the washing dries quickly. I watch the sun turn around the house, setting the sky on fire until sunset.

As darkness falls I leap for the bottle of fireflies that I caught the night before, to use as a torch, although they aren't as bright as the oil filled lamps that flicker in the rooms. But I want to be different, to show how I can invent something new, and less dangerous. I have a terrific time catching them as they zip about in the dark, lighting up the night with dots of twinkling light.

As I walk up the lane in the dark I can hear the truck's horn blowing down the road, and I wait excitedly for Mamma to arrive, and watch her climb down off the truck, like a monkey off a tree. She is surprised to see my new lamp, but much too tired to make a fuss over me, or indeed the fireflies. I feel disappointed but I'm not the only one needing her attention. When she reaches home she washes the baby with the milk from her leaking breast. I watch her face curl up as he latches on to her nipples, while she eats her dinner at the same time. She looks like a woman who has been to Mars and back, tired and dead beat. So, I make her a cup of mint tea to soothe her tired nerves. She drinks it and belches several times. Then she says, "Thank you, my daughter, you are such a good girl." I feel great and smile when she compliments me.

~ 12 ~

If we are lucky, Mamma buys material to make us new clothes. I love it when we get something new. It makes us feel good. For weeks before Christmas all I can hear is, "Leave that; don't pick this; that's for taking to Grand Market." At Christmas time she takes the best fruits to the Grand Market: grapefruits, oranges, and tangerines tied in neat bunches and sleeping in boxes to Kingston.

That Saturday evening she returns home looking like a deflated balloon, saying that she met a bad market, and didn't sell very much.

"There were more sellers than buyers," she said. "The Kingstonians had a feast. It grieved me to watch them taking my goods away that I couldn't sell, when I think how many hungry-belly children I have back home that need food."

Papa is up early to silence the pig or goat that we have lovingly fed all year, while we watch them quiver into a silent world. However, I won't complain when I get the meat on my plate. I intend to suck my bones until they are white. Mamma gives us sparklers for Christmas.

They are my favourite; I'm fascinated by their flickering illumination as I hold them in my hands. However, clappers scare the shit out of me, and balloons hurt my ears, so I never manage to blow any up. We have a whale of a time before we have our Christmas dinner, with port wine that Mamma only buys at Christmas time.

When Aunt Mary visits us in the New Year, I hear Mamma telling her she is in the family way again. With a surprised expression on her face, Aunt replies: "What a way you and Lattie hatching up the children, like fowls hatching up eggs!"

Mamma racked with laughter, as Aunt Mary continues talking to her. I listen to their conversation, while pretending that I'm busy doing my duties in the kitchen.

Before long she is filling up all the space around her, and I have to make way for her when we meet up in the doorway. Still she never breathes a word to us, so all I do is watch the size of her belly as it grows larger and larger, and wonder if she is having twins.

However, from what I hear, Mamma was expecting twins but she lost them when she tumbled down the hillside with the basket of fruit on her head. She tells Aunt Mary that all the fruits rolled away and she lost the babies. I cannot believe what I'm hearing. I secretly worry that I will have to look after more new arrival(s) when she buzzes off to Kingston.

All of a sudden our mother starts to get modern and goes off to see the doctor, wearing one of the new frocks that she made on Aunt Bertha's hand sewing machine. I say to myself how life changes; normally they only go to the doctor when someone is at death's door. Some people snuff it on the way, and then the bawling and wailing starts. The women band their bellies to ease the grief, and the men drink rum, sing songs, and play dominoes until morning comes.

When Mamma walks down the hill her belly swings from side to side, and I figure out that something fantastic will be happening soon. About two weeks later, she and Papa go to Spanish Town, but he returns home on his own. When I quiz him to find out if she ran off and left the lot of us, he starts to beat around the bush, but I wasn't having any here- we-go-round-the- mulberry-bush stories. Will the volcano erupt in me if he says the aeroplane brings this one again?

Two days later Mamma comes home with a bundle wrapped in her arms. There she is… smooth and pink with a mop of light brown hair, sound asleep. Mamma slowly walks into the freshly swept yard, as the six of us shove to get a glimpse of the sleeping beauty, which they name Hyacinth. Icis and Marjorie are also doing a good deal of work, but with the family expanding like a bush fire out of control, we have more and more to do.

My education comes to an abrupt end. I am fourteen and I have to leave school a year early as I started a year early. I'm so far behind the other children in my class. I leave without any recognition that I have ever been to school and I wasn't happy.

Still I have my dreams that I wish will come true, but they are just dreams floating in my head like a butterfly in a garden. I begin to nag my mother to send me to Mrs Tool, who is a dressmaker a few miles from where we live. Sewing is one of the things I like from an early age. I am always getting in trouble for cutting up old clothes that Mamma wants to patch and mend.

Papa wastes no time when he realises that I have a passion for taking a piece of old rag and making it come to life. So he decides to give me a cedar tree that he planted when I was younger. I think it is a strange thing to give your daughter.

Then he says, "We'll watch it swell into a huge tree just like the ones that Uncle Man and I saw down at Breadnut Bottom." He says it with a grin on his face.

"We'll cut it down, and saw it, me and Uncle Man, and sell it to the lumber yard men, with the big Leyland truck. Then I can buy you a brand new Jones sewing machine so that you can learn to sew."

I say to myself what a strange way to get a sewing machine and stand there stunned, as if I have gob stoppers in my mouth. Then suddenly I start jumping up and down. I'm absolutely delighted with joy. Arrangements are made with Mrs Tool to teach me dress making. Mrs Tool has a sewing machine that she pedals and I can't wait to have a go on it. I start to learn how to hem dresses and pants by hand, but hate it when the needle pricks my fingers and I have to suck the blood.

One day I get into trouble when blood spurts onto a white dress that I am hemming.

"What must I do?" I ask myself. "Everywhere I go I get into trouble. Mamma will be mad when she hears, and stop me from going." I am so frightened; I almost wet myself as my nerves get the better of me. I'm so glad when she doesn't tell Mamma what happened, and my heart starts to beat normally again. I don't like the fact that she cuts out the garments when I go home, and never shows me what to do. In the mornings when I arrive, neatly tied bundles are looking at me. I watch the game for a while, but I can't stand it any longer, as my feet never touch the machine and she never shows me how to cut anything out. So how am I going to learn?

I tell Mamma and she plays holy hell and before I know it she has stopped me from going. I could kick myself for being so stupid, but I don't know what else to do, because Mamma is looking like a hawk for signs of improvement from me.

"I have to pay for you to work for her. Look how I'm struggling to find the money every month" she moans. "We have lots of things here that you can stay home and do."

So it is back to the grindstone, but I am determined to learn and I'm sure that I can teach myself if no one else will. I continue to cut up our old clothes, and make outfits for the rag doll that I'd made myself.

Uncle Eddie's ex-wife, Miss Merry, lives in Spanish Town, and runs a bar and restaurant in a lively part of town. She tells

Mamma about a top class dressmaker she knows. She encourages Mamma to make the sacrifice to let me fulfil my dreams. She tells Mamma that I can stay with her for free; all she has to find is my keep. I'm very excited about the proposal; a girl from the country going to Town is a big thing. No more snake-twisting smoke spitting in my eyes, and getting up at the crack of dawn to fetch water. I begin to daydream and holding my breath, until I nearly get a heart attack while Mamma makes up her mind. When she finally says yes, I want to jump up with joy, but I don't allow myself to do it, just in case she changes her mind when she sees me looking happy.

~ 13 ~

I was put on a truck that is going to Kingston, with a cardboard box holding my clothes. Mamma asks Miss Zelda, a market trader, to keep an eye on me until I reach Spanish Town, where Miss Merry will collect me. It's hilarious as Miss Zelda has one eye and a backside like a tub.

She almost squashes me to death every time the truck takes a corner. The journey seems to take forever, and my throat is on fire. Any way we arrived safely.

Miss Merry says she was scanning the trucks that arrived. She hugs me so much that I think she is going to break my neck. We walk up the packed street, in the sizzling sun, and I have the box with my cloths on my head. I hold it there until we reach her house. She gives me a drink and some finger licking food that soon stops my belly rumbling. I only had a mug of black tea and a slice of bread that morning. I sit down and celebrate the moment that I jumped up and down for in secret.

In the background I can hear the juke box playing a Sam Cook song, *Don't know Much About History*, that I usually sing. I don't know about town life, and although I want to get away from my unbearable existence, I wonder how I will cope crossing the busy roads. I can see that I will need eyes in the back of my head to cope with all the cars, trucks, and country buses that are laden with food and people like bees clinging to a honeycomb.

Anyway, I soon find out that I have to watch the handcart boys that tear up and down the roads. The carts run on old motor car wheels, and the boys are dressed to kill in their ripped bottom trousers that shows their dancing ass. They are busy rushing around, looking for jobs in the crowd. I'm used to walking on the road behind Hanna for miles, with just the sound of leaves rustling, and the birds flitting from tree to tree singing songs that only they know.

Anyway, I listen to the songs that the people play from the juke box, and watch how they break up their bodies to the sound of rhythm and blues. Miss Merry comes and tells me what to do. When I hear all the rules I think I have jumped out of the frying pan and into the fire again. But at least I don't have to carry water on my head, so my brain will get some rest. All I have to do is turn a tap and there is water flowing. Flick a switch, and my eyes dazzle with the glow of light, and there is no smoke to make my eyes drip raindrops.

That night when I go to bed, I roll from edge to edge and laugh to myself when I find myself alone in a double bed. I think this is heaven and drift off to sleep, until Miss Merry wakes me up in the morning. She tells me what she wants me to do. I get out of the bed like a jumping jack, and start to clean the restaurant until breakfast time. But when I see the amount of food on my plate, my eyes pop out of their sockets. After breakfast she punches a tune from the juke box. When it starts I realise that it's a song I love called *Stand By Me* by Benney King.

"Monday morning, we will get up at dawn," she said. "Lunch time is a busy time, when all the children arrive at the same time to buy their lunch."

I hold my breath and wonder if she is going to talk about what I came here for. Then all of a sudden she puts her hand on my shoulder and says, "The first thing I will do tomorrow morning is take you to Mrs Steven, and we will take it from there, but you will have to find your way home."

I get excited and can't wait for the next day to come. That night I can't settle; a million things are rolling in my head.

When we arrive I am very nervous, but Mrs Steven is very nice and soon puts me at ease. She is a tall lady, well spoken, and dressed very elegantly. My eyes are already fixed on the young Indian lady who is ramming the sewing machine. She makes it look easy, as the fabric slides through towards my unblinking eyes. Miss Merry and Mrs Steven talk for a while, as my eyes feast on all the beautiful children's dresses in the showcase.

After Miss Merry leaves, Mrs Steven takes me under her wing and shows me what to do.

"This is Nema," she says. "When she first started she couldn't use the sewing machine, and now look how fast she can sew. You will be okay. Most of these dresses were made by her. She is my rock: I don't know what I would do without her."

I stand and watch as Nema labours her love into the fabric and creates beautiful dresses every little girl would love. I dream of the day when I will be able to sew like her, and watch a child dance around in a dress that I have made, while her mother tries every trick in the book to get it off her back.

The day flies by, and I pack my brain with all the information I'm given and walk home to Walks Road, skipping around the street peddlers that sprawl out on the pavement, and dodging the traffic. Miss Merry says she was worried in case I lost my way, but I had remembered the landmarks that she showed me. I am used to walking through the bushes without any signpost, so I find my way, with all the signposts.

She doesn't know how much I enjoy myself walking home and soaking up the town atmosphere.

When I arrive home I take off my blue chambray dress and hang it behind the door, while I inhale the aroma from the kitchen. When I sit down to eat my dinner, Miss Merry said, "I want to hear how you get on." So I tell her. I can tell that she is impressed when she hears everything I had learned.

"Well done!" she says.

I'm so surprised that I nearly fall off the chair, as I'm not used to praise, only exploitation.

Well, it isn't long before Mrs Steven tries me on the electric machine. I must admit that I was scared, as I am not used to electricity, and I'm frightened that the machine will gallop away with the fabric. Every time I touch the pedal it goes burrrr! like a drill, and makes me jump like a dog when you step on its tail.

"Take your time," Mrs Steven says. "Just a small touch, you will soon get used to it." So I lift up my toes in my shoes, and flick it like a peacock's feather until I can hear it grumble, and practise until I get it right. I am so delighted that I feel like I am floating on cloud.

Then I start to sew things up, and I'm bursting with excitement when I see the beauty of the designs gazing into my face. Mrs Steven is very pleased with my progress, and assures me that I am doing fine. It's amazing what her assurance does for my confidence; it's just what I need, someone to make me feel special and wanted.

At weekends I help Miss Merry in the restaurant, frying fish, clearing the tables, and washing the pots. On Saturdays I have to go to Spanish Town market, to collect the basket and the few shillings my parents send for me with Miss Zelda.

The basket is blazing with fruits and foodstuffs. I plonk it on my head and walk up busy Street, soaking up the culture and the crowd of people that stroll along. When I get home we have a feast, and I pretend that I am sitting under a mango trees again. Occasionally when I collect the basket it isn't full, but then I know that there are a lot of mouths to feed, so I take it as it comes.

The weeks go by, and I am enjoying myself on the sewing machine. Nema gives me lots of tips and encouragement. One Saturday I go to collect the basket in the pouring rain. The streets turn into rivers and I walk through the flood water, until I reach the market.

"Hello Miss Zelda!"

She looks at me with a thin worried smile and says, "How are you, my child?"

"Fine. I'm mastering the machine very well, and because they see how clever I'm getting, they are giving me work to sew."

"Well, my dear child I don't know how to tell you this," Miss Zelda says in a low voice.

"Tell me what?" I asked.

"Your parents haven't sent a basket this week, they told me to tell you that they have nothing to send, as things are very hard at the moment."

"What am I going to do?"

"Well, they said… you have to come home." I cannot take in what she is saying to me. Suddenly I thought everything was going my way, and now this. I burst into tears, becoming hysterical with the shock. "How could they do this to me? Why can't they give me a chance to do something that I want to do so badly? I wish I was dead."

Miss Zelda looks at me, and I can see the sadness in her eyes as she wraps her arms around me, and I bathe in my tears. Before I can compose myself, a small group of people gather, craning their rubber necks for a bite of the news. It is like someone has just died, and it is me; I have died inside. It is a terrible shock, I feel let down and I truly wish that I were dead, because it would be a way out where I can be with myself, not my plight or destiny. I walk back in a daze, sobbing softly in the rain, but no one notices the pain on my face.

When I arrive home, Miss Merry hollered out, "What's the matter with you child, why are you bawling? Somebody trouble you? Where is the basket with the food?"

I open my mouth to tell her the news, but nothing comes out. Not a sound. After a while I get my voice back and tell her the bad news.

She hurls her hands in the air, claps them together and says, "Lord me God! Well, you have to go home. I can't keep you here and feed you. I have already contributed by giving you free board. I have to buy everything here; I haven't got fruit trees like your parents. You will have to let Mrs Steven know. You can't just fly off like a bird out of sight without telling her."

"I don't want to go back to the country," I tell her. I'm trembling with the shock and confusion. I feel ashamed; how am I going to tell Mrs Steven? She seems so well to do, she'll never understand.

That weekend goes very quickly, as I agonise over my dismal situation. It is a beautiful night, the sky is blazing with stars and an alien moon; but I'm too sad to enjoy it. On Monday morning I drag myself through the morning rush, with a look of death on my face, and a rage in my heart.

When I reach the shop I take a deep breath, and then tell the sorry story. Mrs Steven is very surprised, and so is Nema. I can see the shock on their faces, and they watch the blood drain from mine.

"Do you really have to go back? Can't your Auntie help out?" Mrs Steven asks.

"She's already helped by allowing me to stay for free, so she can't afford to feed me, as she has to buy everything."

I stand there trembling, as my clothes are dripping from the rain and I have lost the chance to give birth to the creativity that is bursting in my head. I'm devastated by the bad news.

"If they ever change their minds you will be welcome to come back," Mrs Steven says. Suddenly there is a glow of sunshine, but I feel as if I am going to pass out.

"I'm so sorry" she said, and walks over to the machine that I made my first stitch on. I reluctantly say goodbye and walk out into the sunshine to return to my destiny.

When I arrive home the room is hot, so I open the window and let the humid air in. I want to breathe in the fume-mixed breeze of Spanish Town for the last time. That Monday night I let in the moon shine and the scent of flowers for the last time, as tears rain down my face. I am consumed with anger and smash a bottle of my cream soda on the tiled floor. I stand there, trembling, with a piece of the broken glass in my hand and murder in my eyes. My heart is broken, just like the shattered fragments of glass on the floor.

I expect Miss Merry to come rushing to my room, but she never moves a muscle and I feel so abandoned. I sit on the bed with sadness choking me. I manage to calm myself and eventually fall asleep. Then, with the sunrise, I wake up to my judgement day, and pack my few belongings in the same cardboard box that came with me three months ago.

Miss Merry wishes me well and says she is sorry that I have to go, but there is nothing she can do to ease the shock and anger that I feel. The sunshine has vanished from my heart, leaving me weary and … sad.

PART TWO
GROWING UP

~ 1 ~

With the light gone from my eyes and the spring from my step, I walked to Wellington Street, and joined the line of people waiting for transport, in the blistering sun, with the short memory of Spanish Town bobbing up in my mind. Storm clouds were gathering and I knew that it was going to rain. I had nowhere to shelter, and no one to share my thoughts with and I felt sad.

There were people grumbling as they waited for the bus, when they saw that everybody was going to get soaked to their skins. I could not believe that so many people were afraid of rain. I didn't want to get wet any more than they did, but I wasn't going to kill myself to dive for cover. As far as I was concerned, I felt as if I were already dead.

Then suddenly the cloud burst. I had nowhere to shelter and stood there, watching the water gushing down the road like a swollen river, with my box falling apart on my head. My imagination began to run wild. I tie a dress around the box and chucked it back on my head. I was soaked and my badly worn shoes were slipping from my feet. I held my spirits up and waited for the stampede that was to come when the transport arrived.

When it came, I pushed and shoved until I could touch the hand of the man that was pulling up an old lady. I held on to the box on my head, and planted one of my feet on the floor, as the other one feet fought for a space.

When the truck reached Old Harbour, I hopped off like a grasshopper with my worldly goods on my head, and watched the swarm of people trying to sell something to those still on board. My eyes caught a woman selling fried fish and cassava bread, but I didn't have the money to buy one of the fish bones; never mind the cassava bread. So I found an empty space under Mr Sing's shop veranda and wait for one of the old clapped-out Morris Oxford cars to take me home.

I had to say a prayer, when I saw ten people packed in one rusty old car like sardines in a tin. I saw a passenger sitting in the driver's seat, and I wondered where the hell he was going to sit to drive the car.

"Move up," The driver said in a loud voice as he slid one of his cheeks onto the edge of what should be his seat, and revved up the clapped out car. Its belly was pulping with the weight. By the time it crawled away, everyone was baking in the car.

"Lord have mercy," one woman bellowed out. "I don't think I can stand this until I reach home, because this woman with her big backside is going to press the shit out a me!"

I sit there with my ...ass squashed to pulp, and barely able to breathe, listening to the conversations around me. When the car started to climb the hills, I wondered what I was going to do with my life now I going back home.

My mind was in turbulence, as the car crept towards Cole Beck kicking up cloud of dust that made it look like a misty morning. As it crawled up the hills and around the twisted bends like a snail, I close my eyes and pretend that I'm asleep.

By this time, the smell in the car was overpowering, but I held my breath and grind my teeth. I felt like a lost sheep wandering home and crying silently inside.

When the car reached teacher Thompson's shop, I knew in my heart that there was some reason for wanting me back home. I begged the driver to blow the horn when he hit Shop Hill, hoping that I would have an audience when I got out of the car, but there was no one in sight. The lane was silent, with just the leaves flitting from the trees, and the birds singing overhead.

When I get to the gate I cleared my throat and called out, "Hold the dog!" The two scraggy dogs crawled out and growled softly, wagging their tails as I walked into the yard. It was hard to hide the anger that is boiling inside me. Then Papa walked on to the verandah.

"How you do daughter?" he asked, as I lowered my bottom onto the edge of the veranda. I noticed that he had a smirk on his face.

"What's the problem?" I asked, and a smile spread, over his face. He didn't say anything.

"Papa," I said, "I have some news for you all. I won't be around for ever. One day I will have to go and make a life for myself. I'm not going to pack sugar canes and do donkey-work for the rest of my life."

I was wondering where Mamma was, but I was so vexed that I didn't bother to ask. Then all of a sudden she rolled out of the room, and my eyeballs nearly popped out of their sockets.

"How are you? I'm glad to see you," she said, and slid her arms around my neck. I nearly died from shock with the gentle touch that she gave me; the only time that that she touched me is when she lashed me, or when she was plaiting my hair.

My sisters and brothers were excited to see me, but I wasn't in any mood to join in their funfair. I was too upset. Mamma was pushing out all over the place, and the only way that I could miss her size was if I was blind.

Within weeks of my return, Papa took her to Spanish Town Hospital. I thought to myself they had started to go up in the world, going to hospital. I was glad of it though, as I had enough disruption when she and Aunt Bertha were bawling and groaning to deliver their babies. Even though they never knew that I was awake, and clawing the bed with my fingers when I heard how they were groaning to let the aeroplane drop out the babies. I played a long letting them think that I am a fool. But I was well aware, of what was going on and been awake most of night, recording the lessons of life. I was fourteen.

Mamma returned in a few days with a light-skin baby girl that they named Hyacinth. She is beautiful and I couldn't restrain myself from touching her tiny fingers, and watch as she gripped mine. From that day we formed an affectionate bond.

Mamma didn't flap up her mouth about where the new baby came from, but I was vexed that it had taken me all that time to figure out for myself where they came from. Now all the younger ones were as smart as me, and it had taken me all those years to realise what was going on.

I was boiling with anger and no one knew how I felt. I don't think they realised how much their behaviour had affected me and the rest of children. I was growing up into a young lady, and my mother never told me about the changes that would take place in my life, only stressing that I shouldn't let any boy touch me. I was puzzled as I didn't know what she meant.

One morning I got up as usual, the rain was chucking down, I ran like a gazelle to the kitchen. I was chopping up firewood with the old machete that Papa abandoned, when I suddenly felt a rush of fluid between my legs. When I scrutinised my legs, I discovered that I was oozing blood. I was shocked and couldn't understand where it was coming from, as neither the machete nor the wood had grazed my legs. I was frightened that when Mamma found out she would flog me, thinking that I had let a boy touch me. I was delighted that I had on a rainbow dress, and mopped up the blood that was seeping.

The following day when I realised that it was not going away I sneaked up to Aunt Bertha's house and told her what was happening to me. The look on her face made me fear it was something terrible, as her jawbones suddenly dropped to her bosom. Then she said I was a young lady now, and I have to go and tell my mother.

I started to zigzag back down the road. Mamma was busy packing up foodstuffs in wooden boxes that Papa made for her. I seized the moment to break the twenty-four hour news to her. Her eyebrows arched and she stared at me, as I stand paralyzed with fear.

"Come with me," she said, and turned around like a sweeping tornado. I thought she was going to grab me up in her arms, but there was no such luck. She just said, "Come, come," In a hurry and we sprinted down the lane.

"I will have to cut up one of my white sheets and give you to use, you have to keep them clean and white. All I have to tell you don't let any boy touch you. If you let them touch you, or breed you, then you would have to go and live up at Parade under the stone caves."

I was shocked and I began to cry. She certainly knew how to stuff me with fear. Can you imagine that? I sprinted off down the lane so fast that by the time I reached the shop I was breathless.

"Why you have to run so fast every time you come to the shop?" Bedward the shopkeeper asked. I wanted to tell her why, but I would feel such a fool to tell her the real reason. So all I did was shout out the items that I wanted while I marked time, as Mrs Bedward took forever bouncing the paper bag with the flour on the counter, measuring the gill of coconut oil and the quarter pound of salt fish. I sprinted back home just in time to see the last bubble of you-know-what and I began to breathe normally again.

~ 2 ~

After a few weeks, we all went to Crawl Pass like a herd of elephants. I tried my best to be a part of the world I knew, but lost the will for toiling in the heat. It was the same old story. My legs were buckling behind the donkey and I'm exhausted. I was fed up, and just didn't want to be part of it. But I had no choice.

The heaviest burdens I carried were the ones that I didn't do with a free will and there were many of those. The ones that broke my spirit were the ones I detested the most. I felt as if I was held to ransom. But I carried on, nursing my dreams in my heart.

One day, after we returned to Bois Content, I noticed that Mamma's belly had grown huge suddenly. I knew for sure then that she was having a baby. I was sixteen years old, and she could not fool me any more with her Anancy stories that she told us for years. But I had to tread carefully. Why can't she just tell me the truth? I asked myself. I used to dream of the day that she would let me touch her expanding stomach, just to feel close to her, but no such luck.

One afternoon the sun was blistering hot, the zinc roof was cracking like logs on a fire. Mamma looked like a heavy pregnant cow. I watched her slide and shuffle to her side to get comfortable. I looked at her and to my surprise she returned a motherly smile back.

"I am praying to God that I never have any more babies," she suddenly said.

"Why?" I asked, trying to hide the shock and concern that I felt.

"Because I'm feeling weak and tired".

"I'm forty-seven years old," she tells me. She has had a hard life from the day that she was born. So I don't think she had much sympathy for our plight. She had been busy producing a clan of us and never seemed to have any time to scratch her head.

Mamma said, "I'm parching for a drink of lemonade, come go and buy some sugar and a piece of ice for me." She seemed to have a fancy for lemons, but I had to keep my trap shut or else I might lose one of my teeth from her left hook.

As I set off to the shop, she got up and spat on the ground. "Straight there and back before that dries up!"

I was served by a man I had never seen before. "What is your name he asked?

"Valerie," I told him.

With a dazzling smile he said, "A lovely name for a lovely girl.

Where do you live?"

"Old Walk Lane." I pointed in that direction.

"When are you coming to the shop again, Valerie?"

"Don't know," I said, irritated by his interrogation.

"My name is Eric," he said. "I'm going away to England soon. I would like a nice girl like you to be my pen friend… you know someone to think about."

I thought it was a bold way for a total stranger to introduce himself, in such an upfront, articulate way. However, I was only sixteen and as green as the bananas on the trees and forever being told not to let boys touch me. He was just a fellow with wandering eyes, and a trap that flew open easily.

Mrs Bedward sat under the Pomegranate tree, scrubbing cloths in her washtub. I thought he must be her relation, but I was too shy to ask and sprinted back down the lane, remembering the spittle drying on the ground. Gasping for breath, I reached home just in time to see the froth succumb to the shimmering heat. My close encounter became a passing moment. A few days later I was busy scrubbing the floor, when Mamma called.

"Valerie! Go and get me some sugar so I can make lemonade; my throat is burning." She gave me the money. "If they have any ice, get a pound."

I flew off like a kite in the wind, gasping for breath when I reached the shop. Eric was stocking the shelves.

"Who is chasing you?"

"No one," I panted. "One pound of sugar, please."

He looked me over. Shabbily dressed in an old frock, with dirty straw die hands and knees from scrubbing the floor, I felt embarrassed, knowing I looked as if I had just blown in from a refugee camp. Again he mentioned writing to me from England our mother country, as we referred to it then. I suddenly realised Mamma hadn't mentioned the spit, but I know the rules; my life could be made hell with her spit watch.

Eric's words rang in my ears. I'd never met anyone so ambitious. Excited and flattered, I was out of breath when I got home. Mamma was shelling gungo peas surrounded by the fowls.

"A who you a run from?"

I dropped the paper bag. She has been sending me out with a warning not to let the sun dries up her slobber before I got back and never noticed that when I came back I can hardly breathe. All this time!

I decided to tell her about the man at the shop, who said I was a lovely girl. But before I could tell her about his plan to go to England, she glared up at me with her eyes bulging out of their sockets.

"What man? When I send you out, you don't stand up chatting to no boy, do you hear what I say?"

"Yes Mamma."

"Lord me God!" she said, springing up and scattering peas all over the floor, giving the chickens a feast. "If you ever let them touch you, I'm a going to turn you out of the yard with your bundle, and you can go to the woodland and live under the stone cave with the rat bats!"

She changed her clothes and stormed off up the lane like a goose on the run, while I stood there in shock. I never moved a muscle until she returned; she must have erupted like a volcano while she was there, as she came back much calmer.

"Well," she said, plonking her hands on her wide hips, "I told him you were far too young for him, and he should not talk to you and eye you up again. I'll tell you again: when I send you out and boys and men want you fe stan'up and chat, you run home. You hear me?"

"Yes, Mamma."

"An' you don't care what they say, you just run, because all them want is to get them wicked ways with you. Then when they breed you, they turn round and say they never touch you." She pointed her fingers into my face and I shivered with fear.

I was quite shaken by her reaction, but Eric hadn't done me any harm. I only told her because I was excited at meeting someone who planned to cross the Atlantic, never believing I could meet someone so ambitious weighing flour in a shop.

I didn't see him again. Mamma sent my sisters to the shop, shielding me from the wolves. I tried to forget him and his talk about England.

One afternoon Mamma sent my sister Marjorie to the post office. She returned with a letter for me. I was shocked. I never had a letter from anyone before. I was mystified by the name on the envelope; I couldn't recall anyone named Bartley, but before I could look at it properly Mamma shouted,

"Don't open it, put it between the wattles until me finish plaiting Evelyn's hair."

I didn't want her knocking me about for a red and blue envelope, so I did what I was told. As I chopped the wood, I rocked my brain; it might be from the man I met at the shop. I was scared, remembering how Mamma had exploded. I watched her through a hole in the kitchen wall, plaiting the lost few strands of Evelyn's hair. Then she ripped into the letter, and her eyes bulged out as she read it.

"It looks like Eric's heart still a burn for you. Look how far away he is and him still boiling up for you." My head was spinning. I wanted to read my letter, but didn't dare ask. I never thought he would keep his word. Mamma held on to the letter. "Me a keep it till your father come home."

She stuffed it into the depths of her bosom, where it mellowed until Pappa arrive home. The sun was a vast orange, sinking fast in the distance and the chickens were going to roost. Mamma sat on the veranda, her face like thunder, watching as Papa yanked the food-laden hampers off the donkey's back.

His voice was weary. "Evening Sadea."

Mamma shuffled on the old wooden chair like she was sitting on thorns.

"What happen to you now? Why you swell up like that?" Papa asked.

"Lord, Sir, I don't know where to start to tell you." She fidgeted again. "Valerie got a letter from Mrs Edward's brother."

"Who?"

"From the man that she met at the shop that was eyeing her up."

"Which man?" he barked, scratching his head lividly as if a horde of lice had suddenly descended.

"The man that said he was going to England, where you always wanted to go."

"Oh!" Papa said, swinging round. "So what are you trying to do, open up old wounds? I never remember a thing about it."

Mamma refreshed his memory.

"So where is the letter? Read it to me!"

He watched as Mamma delved into her cleavage. She suddenly said to me,

"Go and light the lamps."

I rushed to light the lamps and darted back.

"No way will I let her go thousand of miles away to a stranger." Mamma's voice was raised and I knew what that meant.

~ 3 ~

Papa cleared his throat. "I remember," he said, "when they came here looking for people to emigrate to England after the war, and I had a burning desire to go, but you said you wouldn't because you had no intention of flying in an aeroplane. All I wanted was your blessing, but you didn't want to know. I was a dam fool to listen to you." He gave her a filthy look and took a sip of water to cool his temper.

He seemed annoyed, but Mamma just shuffled her ass in the chair. "What if she goes and he treats her badly? We got no money to send back for her."

Papa's comments gave me a boost, and a rebellious feeling too. I really want to explore the world, to make a life for myself. When she finally allowed me to read my letter, tears of anger welled up. She had confiscated *my* letter. However, I knew I had to tread carefully as my parents were the boss.

Somehow, I found the courage to tell them I intended to write back to him. I needed to win them over to my side so I tried to keep calm. Many weeks passed before I was given the money to buy the stamp. I walked to the post office in the heat, but I felt I was walking on air.

When Eric's reply came, my heart started to race.

"My dear Valerie,

England is very cold even though it is spring. I felt like a block of ice, and was shocked to see huge fire balls in the houses when I arrived..."

He was looking for a job, but without luck so far. He didn't paint a picture of how I imagined England would be. I knew the streets weren't paved with gold, but the Royal Family lived there so I thought it would sound more exciting.

When I replied, I told him all the latest news and that I would love to join him one day. Mamma watched me like a hawk, never tolerating any backchat. She always insisted on good manners, saying it will take us through the world if nothing else will. I just prayed for mine to take me to England.

Eric told me how much he loved me every time he wrote. I found it flattering, but I didn't know what being in love felt like, or what love was. I hardly knew him. He had found a job working in a Rochdale cotton mill for six pounds a week, but still found it hard to save the money for my plane ticket.

For two and a half years we kept writing, and then Eric told me to apply for a passport. I made myself a lovely striped dress for the occasion. It was the first time I was ever photographed, but the pictures were fine. I sent one to him and he told me he slept with it under his pillow. I wondered what it would be like when we finally got together. Every time I read his letters I seemed to find new meanings in the words.

Then one day I woke up and I was eighteen years old. It was just another working day with no party or presents. I was old enough to go away, but not old enough to marry without my parents' consent and signatures. It was hard but I kept going and hoped for victory.

Then Eric's letter came. He had finished paying for my fare, and the date of my departure would be 13th of December 1961. I was so excited that I began to jump up and down, and then out of the blue Papa and Mamma started to clap their hands. I almost died with shock, especially when Mamma jumped up and started to dance.

I began to cry, as I never dreamed that I would see my mother showing such delight for me. I knew then that I was on my way, and although she didn't say a word at that moment, I could tell without any doubt that she was happy for me. She hired Uncle Eddie's truck to take me to the airport, and as the days drew nearer my heart was constantly beating like a drum.

One thing worried me a lot. No one ever discussed sex with me. It was a taboo word. The thought of it frightened me and I wanted some advice and information. I gleaned a certain amount from other young people, but nothing specific, as we were in the same boat. I wanted to talk to my mother about sex, but it was such a dirty word that no one talked about it. It was as if they didn't do it. I plucked up my courage and asked her if she had anything to tell me before I go.

"Oh my Lord," she said, rolling up her eyes like she just got the last rites. "I don't know what to tell you right now."

I tried not to show how desperate I was for her advice. I gave her the wistful look, but it didn't work. Her brown eyes glared at me in shock.

"When you get there, Eric will teach you," was all she told me.

"When you reach over there, if he don't treat you good, write and tell me," she suddenly exclaimed. "We don't have money, but we would have to borrow from your Uncle Eddie and send back for you."

~ 4 ~

On Sunday, 13th December 1961, I woke to the sound of the usual funfair outside. The cocks were having a glorious time crowing and Hanna braying. I stored the memories in my mind to take with me. Mamma was up early, busying herself in the kitchen as Papa tied hibiscus flowers to the rope around Hanna's head. I was thrilled that he took the trouble to dress her up for my last ride to the main road.

I slipped into my new brown pencil skirt dress with six buttons on the bodice, and curves I did not know I had. Mamma prayed to God to protect me, and wished me a safe journey to the unknown.

I walked out into the yard, taking in the surroundings for the last time before I set off on my journey to England and Eric. Up on Hanna's back I felt like the queen on her throne. Papa plonked my case on his head, while Mamma stood waving until we were out of sight. Tears misted my vision as Hanna carried me along the road that we had walked so many times. When we reached the main road, we boarded the truck that takes me to the airport.

As the driver skipped around the potholes, I stood up and looked at the tropical beauty I was leaving behind. What would life be like in England? I knew that it would be cold, but not a lot else. My head was spinning and my heart was pumping my left melon so hard I thought it would explode.

My emotions were mixed; sadness that I was leaving all my family behind, and joy that I was about to embark on the adventure of my life six thousand miles away. Thoughts of Mamma rushed through my mind, as she had decided to stay behind and pray for me, saying that she couldn't bear to watch me fly off like a bird in the sky.

When I came back from my thoughts, the truck had turned into the road that leads to the airport. Papa's eyes moistened as he took my suitcase to the check-in desk. He held out his free hand, as if he was guiding me to heaven, but he knew that he was sending me off to a world unknown. I was given my one-way ticket and British passport back by the serious-looking clerk. My hands were dancing and for a moment I just wanted to turn and run. My father kissed me, and wiped his eyes with his saggy handkerchief.

After a long delay, we were told the flight was cancelled because of bad weather in England. I wondered if my family was still upstairs waiting to see my aircraft roar down the runway.

I was put up in the Sand Hurst hotel in Kingston, sharing a room with a lady name Beryl. We had only the clothes we wore, because our luggage had gone on board. We had a cool drink and freshened up, smelling bewitchingly of the lavender soap in the bathroom. I washed my panties with it and hoped that the smell would last throughout my journey.

We slept in our birthday suits, and when Kingston burst into life the following morning a bus took us to the airport. I was sad that my family was not here to finally watch me fly off into the sky.

I was nervous and frightened when the plane started to roar faster and faster down the runway then took off into the sky. The turquoise sea shimmered below my window seat. I watched it until there was nothing to see but blue sky, and drifting clouds that pass by.

I thought of my family back home, and the journey ahead. I prayed that we would reach safely to the other side of the world. We landed in New York some time later and were allowed to leave the plane. It was very cold, and with no overcoat, I had a taste of what was to come.

~ 5 ~

When the plane took off again from New York, there were people praying openly, and I said a few prayers myself, knowing that Mamma would be bruising her knees at her bedside.

As the plane hit turbulence, I gripped the sides of my seat. I was bursting to go to the toilet, but terrified that when I opened the door I would fall out into the sky. Beryl was equally frightened. She was joining her partner whom she hadn't seen for three years. But at least she knew what to expect when she and her fellow were united. I wished I could pluck up the courage to ask her about sex and things. But she was so much older than me so I felt uncomfortable to ask her.

I sat there thinking that what I hate about flying is being out of control. What makes me do it is love, love, love. What I hated was the food looking sad on the tray and the blood running from the steak as I tried to sculpture it. I could have murdered a bloody Mary, but my head and feet wouldn't allow me; so I settled for a coke. But I could say I have walked in the sky, six miles up, and what a spectacular view it was with sun shining and white cloud drifting while crossing the Atlantic. I joined the line of people waiting for the toilet and held on to the seats as the plane rocked. What I hated was all those sleepy zonked-out faces as I walked back to my seat. What I feared most was if it tumbled out of the sky like a stone. What I was looking forward to was when the plane touched down on solid ground.

When I sensed the plane dropping out of the sky I felt sick. Then suddenly the pilot said the magical words: "Ladies and gentlemen, we are about to descend to Gatwick Airport. Please fasten your seat belts.

We hope that you have enjoyed your flight and we look forward to seeing you again."

My feelings were mixed. Would I recognise Eric, I wondered?

Would he remember me? I had grown since the first time he clapped his brown eyes on me. I hoped that he would be armed with my photograph; otherwise he might miss his Jamaican princess when she walked through Customs and not into his arms.

When the plane finally landed I was very relieved. People were shouting, "Thank you Jesus," and clapping their hands.

It was Tuesday night when we arrived at Gatwick Airport. Confused and disoriented, I was unsteady on my feet and drunk with tiredness. I came down the steps from the plane like a sheep wandering to new pastures. The wind, biting my face, was the only welcome in the damp night. Walking the endless corridors I was gripped with fear of the unknown.

Other people in the queues looked just like me… all turned out in our Sunday best, but we must have looked a sight amongst those dressed in normal clothes, and they stared at us as if we had dropped out of space.

We were waiting to be questioned by the immigration officers. I came through it easily enough and when interrogation was over, they dropped the bombshell. A Mr Bartley had left a message for you.

Because of the delay, he'd had to return home to his work commitment. I was to take the train from Euston Station then to Piccadilly Station in Manchester.

I nearly died when I was given the message, and panic and fear took over my body. The delay had ruined his well-planned arrangements. I was a frightened eighteen-year-old; alone in a strange country, bewildered, exhausted and scared. The stiff bitter wind almost blew me off my feet, as I tried to read the signs telling me where to go.

I was fortunate that I had struck up a friendship with Beryl because when we arrived at Euston station the last train to Manchester had already gone. Beryl was going to Birmingham, wherever that was; it didn't mean anything to either of us. We sat up all night at Euston Station. I was shaking with fear; it would be the first time my feet had ever touched a train.

I was not used to seeing so many white people and there seemed to be lots of people living rough around the station area. There was one man who was very scruffy and dirty. I later discovered that he was a tramp. I had not imagined that there would be such people in England.

At home we would call someone like him a Nasty Man. He struck up a conversation with us.

"Like your'ats," he said, grinning at us. We didn't answer.

"Aint you cold?"

We still didn't respond but we must have appeared to be freezing, draped in our thin cardigans. Beryl gave the vagrant a mango in the hope that he would bugger off, but he stood there tearing into it like a lion with his first kill of the day. He continued talking as he ravished the fruit.

"You foreigners?"

We nodded our heads in acknowledgement but never uttered a word.

"Come with me I could get you both a coat."

We were horrified and exchanged glances, still without speaking.

"I don't know 'ow you could leave bright sunshine to come and sit down 'ere in the cold all night. I'm used to it, but it ain't easy."

I wished that he would go away and leave us alone.

"Must be bloody mad!" he declared, as he scans us with his eyes.

Then he picked up several cigarette butts and stowed them in his pockets.

"Got a light?"

"No," We replied in unison.

"No bad 'abits?" he asked. "Good gels."

There were a few trains sweeping in and out of the station and his voice was drowned by the clanking and hooting as they passed. He vanished as the station came to life with the early commuters arriving, and very soon it was bustling with people. By now I was stiff with cold, and I could hardly move.

Finally our train swept into the station; we boarded it and breathed a sigh of relief, glad to be on the next leg of our journey.

We sat close together, barely able to speak as we chugged along. Beryl was going to Birmingham and we were sad to say goodbye. We didn't exchange addresses, as we had no pens. We told each other the address we were going to and I thought I would remember, but the cold icy wind blew it out of my brain.

It was another long journey. I sat looking through the window at what I thought were a lot of factories, with my pillar-box hat pinned on my head. It was Wednesday and I was travel-weary and hungry.

As the steam train juggled along, I looked at the countryside with the leafless trees, their branches waving in the wind, and the dark sky without a promise of a ray of sunshine. I felt desperate and drew on my last reserve and sank lower into my seat. I had always been hungry for adventure, but I was so exhausted from travelling that it began to get to me. I was badly in need of a bath, too, after three days dressed to kill in the same clothes. Oh Lord… how much further?

Finally, I arrived at Manchester, Piccadilly Station, and walked out into the cold, driving rain. I kept walking until I got to a taxi stand and asked for 27 Scarsdale Road in Victoria Park, as Eric had told me.

Then the taxi dropped me off, I looked around, making sure that I was knocking at the right door. I knocked and knocked but no one answered, so then I started to shout "Is anybody in?" But there was no reply. I was very cold, and beginning to panic. Close to breaking down, I knocked again but still there was not a soul in sight. Just as I began to despair, a black lady came out from across the road and looked me up and down.

"Have you just come up?"

"Yes." Desperation echoed in my voice. "But there's no one in, I have been knocking for a while now."

She started to bang the door like she was wakening the dead, but still there was no reply. "You better come to my house, and I will come and knock again later."

She picked up my case and led me across to her open door. I was so grateful that I couldn't stop saying thank you.

"It's okay," she said. "No problem."

I stumbled through the door behind her in a state of shock. Had I been set up? What if I couldn't find Eric?

In the living room, a roaring fire startled me. I had never seen that before in a house, but I surely didn't complain. It was wonderful, a delightful welcome to a lost, frozen soul.

"Sit down, let me make you a cup of tea," she said, switching a wooden box on. I didn't know what it was; I'd never seen a television before. Then I noticed a baby propped up in a dry bathtub surrounded with cushions to keep him steady. Another toddler sat close to him looking at me with big eyes.

The woman soon returned with a piping hot mug of tea, a hunk of bread, and a piece of fried fish. I bit into the bread and fish and hugged the mug. I could feel the heat seeping into my hands.

"Well, I didn't even get the chance to ask you, what is your name?"

"Valerie," I said.

"My name is Melda." She smiled warmly. "How was home when you left?"

"Fine. I left home on Sunday, but with delays it has taken three days to get here."

"Really? You must be very tired. So you have come to the mother country, Great Britain!"

"Yes ma'am." I asked how old the baby was and she told me he was four months old and his name was Vinroy.

I thanked her for the food, feeling so much better.

"No problem, it's a pleasure," she said. She got up. "Let's go back and see if his morning has come yet."

I didn't understand.

"When you work nights you wake up in the evening, that's your morning," Melda said. I thought it strange, but I got the message in the end, and she went ahead to see if Eric's morning had arrived. After a few minutes she came back smiling, and told me that a guy had come to the door in his pyjamas. She asked him if he was expecting somebody from Jamaica and he said "yes."

"You should have seen his face. He had the widest smile I have ever seen on someone in pyjamas," she said, with a burst of laughter. "I asked him to tell me your name, and he said 'Valerie.' Well, I said, she is in my house."

I jumped to my feet trying to control the relief that I felt, and wondering what we would say to each other. Thanking Melda for her kindness, I walked out into the cold, dark night with my case, leaving the blazing fire behind and Melda and her two children looking at me.

~ 6 ~

The moment we had been waiting for had come at last, and as I walked up to the door I could see a figure standing in the hall. There were a few more heads popping up behind him, struggling for a glimpse. Eric flung his arms around me, and asked me if I was ok. I told him yes, but in reality I was exhausted and a nervous wreck.

He said, "I'm sorry we never heard the door knocking. John and I were fast asleep." He turned to the other two guys standing in the hall and said. "This is my girlfriend that I have been telling you all about."

"She's very nice," one said.

"Please to meet you," the tall man said, shaking my hand. "My name is Earl".

"I'm Valerie." I felt shy and awkward.

Eric broke in. "I went to Gatwick to meet you after finishing my shift. I'd worked the night before and I had no sleep. I came all that way only to be told you were still in Jamaica."

"I'm sorry," I said, "to cause you all that trouble, but it was because of the bad weather."

"That's quite okay," he beamed and gave me a hug. "You were worth waiting for, I'm a lucky man".

I saw a woman peeping from a room, as Eric held my hand and led me upstairs to his room. I told him that I was cold.

"Never mind, you are with me now, we are together at last" he reassured me.

The room was huge, with high ceiling and tired wallpaper. There was no rug on the floor, the multicoloured Lino had seen better days.

The ward robe seemed lost in the big room, while the dressing table waiting for the adornment of my trinkets and the two Victorian chairs gazed at me. The room smelled stale and of smoke. He drew up a chair for me and I slowly lowered myself on it as I surveyed the room, relieved that we were together at last. He held me close and kissed me for the first time. I had never been kissed before and I felt dizzy as my body started to melt. My heart fluttered like a butterfly caught in a jam jar. That first experience was spectacular, really mind-blowing, and the memory of it will never leave me. It was like my first taste of chocolate, my first trip on the aeroplane, and my first taste of alcohol all rolled into one. I wanted more but he slowly released me and said he would make some tea.

I couldn't understand why steam spouted from my mouth every time I spoke. I watched him light the fire while I drink the mug of tea and warm up my half-frozen body. Fire in a bedroom... I thought, my God, what have I done, leaving the Caribbean behind for this? My hands were shaking, and I spilt tea on the floor.

"You must be hungry? I'm going to make something for us to eat," he said, changing from his pyjamas into a pair of khaki pants. I sat motionless, watching the fire cracking, as the smoke curled up the chimney. He returned with two plates piled with sliced fried potatoes, eggs and beans.

When I had finished eating, he held my hands, stroking them, and I felt a warm glow seeping through my body.

"You are beautiful, even more than the first time I saw you," he beamed.

I smiled and didn't really know what to say to him, but I was beginning to enjoy his comments and his touches immensely...

"That was lovely, thank you," I said, trying to change the subject and pushing away the enamel plate that I was quite used to at home, but never thought I would see in England.

Suddenly there was a knock at the door, which made me jump. It was Earl. I think he just want to gawp at me.

"How was your journey?" he asked.

I told him, but I just wanted to be left alone to compose myself and soak up my new surroundings. Eric announced that he had to get ready for work.

"Work?"

Earl's face registered shock and disbelief.

"You will have to take the night off, man! How could you leave her and go to work? You must be mad. No work is better than what you have here tonight." He laughed a husky gravel laugh.

Eric smiled, but didn't say a word, and my face turned blood red. I cannot say that I was delighted; I just didn't know what was best, as I had no say in the matter.

Earl stood up and stretched his long, lean body. "See you tomorrow, Uncle."

I was dying for a wash, and felt that a bath would do me the world of good, but I still felt chilly and there was no fire in the bathroom. I took my nightdress in the bathroom with me to hide my embarrassment. When I came out of the bath, my teeth were chattering as the water wasn't very warm. I lingered for a moment to gather myself together, but there was no mirror to throw the last moment of innocence back in my face. I wondered if he would be kind and let me sleep until morning comes. I began to panic, my heart was thumping and my nerve was about to burst when suddenly there was a knock on the door.

"Yes, who is it?"

"It's me, Eric. Are you okay?"

"Yes". I gathered up my clothes and I took a deep breath before taking slow steps to his bedroom, feeling like a lamb going to slaughter.

PART THREE
WOMANHOOD

~ 1 ~

Eric had already had a bath, and was perched on the edge of the bed when I walked into the bedroom clutching my clothes. I didn't want our eyes to meet, as I felt so embarrassed to be alone with him. I could tell he was mentally undressing me. I laid my clothes on the chair slowly one at a time. His eyes were glowing and his face kicked up into a half smile, with a moustache that he hadn't had last time I'd seen him. He held out his hands as I walked over into his arms and he kissed me gently.

I tried to control my nerves, even though I felt like I was on fire, with the delicious shivers that I was getting up my spine. Our bodies met and I smiled nervously, and slid beneath the sheets.

"You can tell me anything," he said.

What can I tell him, I thought, and I raised my eyebrows. I felt uncomfortable and bit my lips.

"Valerie", he said. "This won't work if you are not open with me, so please tell me."

My heart is pounding. "I...I haven't had sex before, so I don't know what to do."

The whisper of my voice fades. He stared at me and said "Never?"

I shook my head slowly.

"You're a virgin?" he asked and breathed, "I'm a lucky man, why didn't you tell me?"

"You never asked, the subject never came up, and I would feel foolish revealing my innocence in a letter to someone I hardly know."

"I thought you might have had some, but, hay, a virgin! So this is the first time you've been kissed."

"Yes" I said and burned red, as I gritted my teeth and grinned a silly grin. "Mamma told me not to let boys touch me."

"Moms always say that, but I just assumed you might've", he sighs. "Come on, we have to sort this out right now."

"What do you mean? I thought you'd let me sleep first."

"No, Valerie, your situation needs sorting out as soon as possible. Can I make love to you?"

I think for a moment. "Yes…" I said.

His eyes were bright…with excitement. But my heart was bouncing in my chest, as he kissed me with glowing eyes and ran his fingers through my hair, neck and breast. I groaned with pleasure. He released me from his clutch and took my hand to his burning engine room. I could feel him stiff and swollen. He released me and said,

"I don't want you to get pregnant before we get married. I want our child to have parents who are married." He removed something from a packet and told me what it was. I began to freak out, as he put it on. I could feel his erection drilling and pushing into me. It was uncomfortable, but the pain was bearable, as I was getting so many nice tingles down there!

As he kissed me and I moaned with the riotous feeling that I was getting, I moved my fingers in his hair. It's soft and he smiles, and he smells nice, washed in a lovely scent. The old bed sinks in the middle and squeaks like an old cart, but it took the excitement to sweet motion, and as he gathered speed I groaned with the pleasure that he was giving me. I felt like I was going to burst with the weight of his body and the sensation that I was getting.

My mind went blank; I was very scared, as he persistently tried to burst my bubble. I was getting thoughts in my head that it would never end, but when it did and he slid off beside me, I wondered what all the fuss was about… the floor never seemed to move under the bed. But when he became aroused again I was shocked: I thought I can't do this again. I lay there helpless as he took charge of my body; he kissed me his lips warm against mine. I began to wince with the pain.

"Just one more time, darling." His voice was so calm and seductive. I began to move like a butterfly as his eyes blazed… with excitement.

"Good girl. Keep it going"

"O please…" I begged. "I'm so sore. Please," I whisper.

"Coming baby, coming." Then he squirts and I pant. My eyes blinked wildly.

"You've done so well, amazing." He lingers then eases out of me.

We must have fallen asleep wrapped in each other arms, because the next thing I knew was the first chink of dawn peeping through the window, and my frisky stallion lying beside me. I was lost under his armpit and wrapped up like a snake in a heaven. I woke up feeling like a woman for the first time.

When we finally rose I saw blood on the sheet. I gasped and freaked out. I was cut and sore. He stared and said, "Darling you've lost your virginity. Thank you for waiting for me."

He held me close and kissed my lips, neck and breast; then slowly released me. Then he pulled the thick dark curtains and let in, not the sunshine that I was used to, but the dark grey morning. It was quiet and dead outside and I felt exhausted.

He lit the fire to keep us warm and I unpacked some of my clothes and hung them in the wardrobe.

Getting to know each other took some time. It was important for us to talk and we wanted to share all our thoughts. The day went in a flash, and before I knew it night came again, but as far as I could figure out, it had looked like night all day. John was sound asleep in Earl's room to give us some privacy while we talked and whiled the day away. He was moving to his own room soon. We were used to hardships, and we helped each other out as we were all in the same boat.

That night they went off to work, leaving me alone in our cold, silent room. There was no radio or television, so I wrapped myself in the blankets and watched the embers of the dying fire until I fell asleep.

I woke several times, feeling strange; the house was serene and it was the same outside; no crickets or frogs hooting all night long. It was like the middle of a graveyard. My mind was working overtime and I felt afraid.

'Is this it?" I asked myself. The illusion of England I had in my mind didn't add up to what I had seen so far. I pulled the blankets over my head and sobbed until I heard a knock; and the key turned in the door. Eric was home and I was glad to see his face again. It was too cold for me to get up and sit in the room, so I laid there with my warm body waiting for him. He climbed into bed and snuggled up beside me, with a wide grin on his face, as if I was a ball of fire waiting for him to thaw out with. He kissed me and asked if I was o k. We talked for a while and then he drifted off in his night. When he woke up in the evening we went down to the kitchen and cooked spaghetti for our dinner.

Eric took me to the Church Pub on Stockport Road a week later.

We met a few guys from Ghana and we got talking. Ben was quite friendly. Eric asked him what Ghana was like.

He laughed and said: "It's very nice with plenty poor people. I left my wife and two children and came here in1957 to make a better life. But things haven't worked out for me well. It took me a long time to get a job and my own room.

We Africans had the same problems just as you did when we arrived in England. There were signs for room to let that said no blacks, no Irish, no dogs. We found ourselves in situations where we were being discriminated against when we went for jobs. To rent a room was the same and it wore us down after a while. We were told that they can't understand what we were saying, as our accent was so broad.

Sometimes we felt like giving up, because things were not working out for us."

Eric told Ben not to give up, but to keep trying and things would work out for him.

"You have to be determined to fight the oppressors. If I had given up Valerie would not be here sitting beside me now." He put his arms around me and cuddled me. Ben and his friends laughed, and said, "Thank you for your encouragement, brother."

They were well oiled before the night was old and told us that they went pub-crawling sometimes. Eric told Ben that if he kept on pub-crawling he wouldn't be able to send for his wife. Ben laughed and said, "It's very hard to save money from my small wages." The stories we exchanged were unforgettable.

Ben asked if we believed in God.

"Of course I do, He is the saver of mankind, and He gave up so much for us so that we can be sitting here, flapping our mouths like puppets," I said.

"O yes, to be sure, an' I thank Him for drinking this," he replied, holding up the glass with its thick head of froth. He only put it down once, and then it was gone, down the trough. Eric bought me a Cherry Bee and Ben had beer.

"I used to go to church every Sunday before I came here. Most people do in the West Indies," I told him.

"But do ye still go?"

"No. It's too cold to get up and go, and besides, I don't know if I would be welcome."

"Well now," he said in full African drawl. "I'm thinking' if ye can't be welcomed with open arms in the house of God, then where else will ye be welcome?" Then with a wink of his eye, he added, "I'll tell ye something, ye can come to my church any day."

"Do you go to church, Ben?" Eric asked him.

"Wid me hand on me heart, as God looks down on me, only the Sunday mornings when I can lift me bangin' head off me pillow," he said, with a cheeky grin on his face.

We all rocked with laughter in the smoky pub, as they lit up their *Park Drives* and Woodbines and the smoke danced around until I could hardly breathe. Eventually Eric and I left, walking down Dickinson Road with our hands wrapped around each other and love bubbling in our hearts.

It wasn't long before we were making plans for our wedding, but we didn't have much money. Eric had asked at his workplace if there were any vacancies for me. Miss Scott told him that there was a job going, and that he could bring me on the Monday morning. We were thrilled. But because of the colour of our skin, a lot of us were told that there were no jobs anywhere, even when we had been sent by the Job Centre with a card and all the information. It had happened to Eric when he was sent by the Job Centre for his first job to do moulding and to operate the machines that make plastic containers. He was distressed and could not believe it. He went back to the Job Centre and told them that there were no vacancies. The Centre insisted that there were three jobs available. This was in April 1959, but after six months he got his present job.

On Monday we got up early to get to Eric's workplace. After we got off the bus he put his arms around me and said, "You will be fine. Just be yourself."

I was a bit nervous as we walked to the office. I didn't feel at all confident that I would get the job. When I went inside the lady asked me why I had come to England.

"To work and have a better life." I told her.

"Have you had any experience working in a factory?" she asked. "No, but I'm willing to learn." I said.

She told me that there would be a job for me when I arrived the following Monday to train to do 'Doffing'. She took me inside the factory to see the machines in action. When I walked in I felt as if all eyes were on me. She showed me the different stages that the cotton goes through. I left feeling positive and hopeful.

However, when I arrived for work, I was given the job to clean the toilets and sweep the floor, although I had been promised a job like Eric's, doffing the Bobbins of cotton. Eric said to her "I thought Valerie would be doing a job like mine."

Miss Scot declared. "We will see. Not now."

I had higher hopes for myself than cleaning toilets and sweeping floors. I had scrubbed plenty at home and hadn't come all this way to do just that! I must get something better; otherwise I would not be moving up in the world.

The following week, Miss Scott came to me. I was busy sweeping up the cotton from under the machines.

"Come to my office immediately," she barked, like a sergeant major. "I want to speak to you!"

To my horror, she asked, "Why did you put banana skin at my office door?"

Her eyes were bulging and she banged the desk in her office, as if she was deranged.

I had no idea what she was talking about. I told her I didn't put any banana skin at her office door, and knew nothing about it.

"Well, I'm giving you notice to leave on Friday." She delivered her statement in a cold tone without a fragment of emotion on her face. I stood with my feet frozen to the floor, unable to move or speak as she stared at me.

"I think you had better be going, don't you?"

I stumbled out of her office feeling shocked and angry.

As I walked back I was raging. The words she said were ringing in my ears. We needed the money desperately for our wedding. I felt I was being racially discriminated against by this woman. I had no idea how to make a complaint, or to whom. I left on the Friday feeling humiliated and angry. I was crying as I didn't know if I would find another job before the wedding. Mamma was sad when I wrote and told her that I got sacked from my first job. She wrote back and said to keep trying.

However, two weeks later I found a job at another place sewing buttons on coats by hand. It was difficult because I was on piece work. I had to sew the buttons on as fast as I could. I took some thread home every evening and strung as many needles as I could for the next day. It was very hard to make £1 a day. My fingers were like pin cushions but I persevered.

Eric was saving £3 pounds a week with several people. Every week each person out of eight of us gave their money to the banker and one person got a lump sum of money, until everyone got his share. We asked the banker for an early draw, as we needed the money for our wedding. He promised that he would see what he could do.

When Eric got the money, I went with Aunt Kate and Millie who were good friends of Eric, to Debenhams, Kendal and Lewis's in Manchester, to look for a wedding dress and a maid of honour dress for Millie. I have four younger sisters and wished they could have been my bridesmaids, and that Hyacinth who was four could be my flower girl, but they were thousands of miles away. I tried on several beautiful dresses and I felt like a princess when I looked at myself in the mirror. I was bursting with excitement, but wished my mother was there to watch me try on these beautiful dresses. Aunt Kate was very kind and she was like a mother to me. She and Millie watched the shop assistants help me into the dresses, and they told me that I looked beautiful. But I wished I could hear those words from my mother and watch her eyes fill with tears.

We went several times before I decided to buy a white Chantilly lace gown designed by Mary Quant. It had a slash neck line, low back, long sleeves and full skirt. But the key to its elegance was the classic simplicity. I chose a long silk veil and a sparkling flower head dress and white satin shoes by Bally.

The day I went to pay for my dress, I carried £100 pounds in a small cloth bag, tucked in my bra like my Mamma used to do. I had never carried so much money before, but felt confident that it was safe in my bosom. When I got inside the store I pulled out the bag and paid for my dress. I was very excited getting on the bus with the huge box. Aunt Kate kept it at her house where I was going to get dressed. Eric's black suit and shirt was from Burton. The flowers, car, and wedding cake were ordered, and every thing was on track.

My parents sent us a bottle of Jamaican Rum when they returned the consent forms, duly signed, as I wasn't 21 years old. All the arrangements were made: Eric's friend Willard would be his best man, his wife Millie my maid of honour, and Mr Clark, Aunt Kate's husband, would walk me up the aisle. But I dearly wished it was my Papa walking me up.

On Saturday, 31st of March 1962, I arrived at the Church of God on Moss Lane, East Moss Side, five minutes ahead of my wedding to Eric Bartley, in my beautiful Chantilly lace dress, carrying a bouquet of roses and peonies. Millie my maid of honour helped me with my train and long silk veil. I took a moment to compose myself, because I was frightened that I might trip as I walked up the steps of the Church in my high heeled shoes.

It was magical, even though I was a bit nervous as I walked up the aisle to the strains of the bridal march holding Mr Clark's arm, and thinking that this was happening, the thing that I've dreamt about... I just wanted to savour every single second about the girl I used to be. I wished that my family could see me, but they were thousands of miles away, basking in sunshine while I shivered in the cold spring day.

Eric looked around and smiled when he saw me coming and I returned a soon- to- be his wife smile. We exchanged wedding rings and one of my favourite hymns that I requested was All Things Bright and Beautiful. It was the perfect end to a romance that had begun three years earlier when I met him in his sister's shop. We walked back down the aisle to cheers and applause.

When we emerged from the Church, flecks of snow were falling like confetti and a determined wind tried to whip my veil away as we were taking the photographs. We returned to Aunt Kate's house where the reception was held. We had prawn cocktails, curried lamb, rice, and vegetables washed down with Baby Cham. We made our wish as we cut our wedding cake. The speeches followed, and during Eric's speech he spoke about meeting me. He said life before me seemed irrelevant now. I had made him the person he meant to be. Turning to me he added "My world is a brighter place with you in it".

I hadn't planned to make a speech, but couldn't resist standing up and thanking the people who had helped us to make this day perfect. I had to put on a brave face as I looked round at the reception, thinking of all my family that I loved dearly, who weren't with us to laugh, joke and have fun. But I'm sure Mamma and Papa would be celebrating with the family, cooking a goat and throwing some rum for those that have passed on. They would be singing and dancing and thinking of us.

These are memories that will last forever of the way I felt that day. How nervous I was in the morning, how beautiful I looked a few hours later when I had dressed and saw myself in the mirror. I felt like a princess as I walked up the aisle, making a promise to be with each other until death do us part and walking down the aisle on my husband's arms.

Our first dance as a married couple was to 'Since I met you baby, my whole life has changed'. As he held me close he told me he loved me and hoped we would share the rest of our lives together. The dance floor was soon packed with the guests. Aunt Kate, Mass Pan, Millie and Willard, were busting up some moves on the floor. Man and wife we danced the night away. The celebration continued until one o'clock in the morning. We had a wonderful day, a day that we will always remember for the way we felt to be married at last.

We lived across the road on the same Street so we didn't have far to go. When we got to front door Eric lifted me up the few steps. We were laughing and very merry. We stumbled up the stairs to our room and he swept me up into his arms and kissed me. Then he twirled me around and we were laughing like two kids. We talked for a few minutes and I asked him to undo the buttons at the back of my dress. He took my garters off and helped me to get off my dress.

~ 2 ~

Three months after the wedding my period was six days overdue. This was unheard of. I was always regular as a clock. So I decided to go to my doctor, who tested my urine. It was positive.

"You are expecting a baby," he said. To be honest I was shocked and pessimistic. I couldn't believe it, but Eric was excited when I told him. I had terrible morning sickness and my breasts were tender and large. I couldn't stand anything fried or the smell of fish. We kept the news of my pregnancy quiet for ten weeks before we told anyone. I stopped feeling sick after three months and it was a huge relief. We decided to ask Aunt Kate to be the baby's godmother. She was delighted and said yes. We thought it would be a nice way to say thank her, for having let us use her lounge and living room for our wedding reception.

I enjoyed most of my pregnancy while I worked, but the thing that I loved most was learning to knit bonnets, booties, cardigans and mittens. It was relaxing, and I was excited when I had knitted a few inches and showed it to Eric. However, at seven months, I started to bleed. I was terrified that I was going to lose my baby. The doctor told me to rest, and things settled eventually. However, they kept asking me if I had twins in my family. I told them, "Yes, my Aunt Bertha had twins. Uncle Eddie's wife died in childbirth, with twins, and Uncle Gee's wife, Sister May, had a boy and girl." But my mother miscarried her twins. I asked myself what chance would I have, if I had two babies at once when it's so hard to find somewhere to live at the moment? It scared me so much.

The doctors at Ancoat Hospital transferred me to Withington Hospital, where they were better equipped. When the doctors at the Hospital examined me, they decided to send me home and let nature take its course.

The winter of 1963 was terrible. There were mountains of snow and freezing fog, I couldn't see my own hands. It was difficult to keep warm, and I was terrified that I would fall and lose our honeymoon baby. Eric came with me to the antenatal clinic. By this time I was going to the hospital every week. The frozen snow looked like glass, and I was scared to walk on it, as so many people had fallen and broken their bones. When the snow started to melt we were relieved.

Aunt Kate invited us to their house, as they were going to have a party to celebrate her fiftieth birthday. I didn't really want to go, as I felt like a barrel and was sure that all eyes would be on me. Eric was all for it, and told me that I looked beautiful. When I got dressed he kept saying "You look wonderful, you are glowing." His comment boosted my confidence as I looked in the mirror at my huge bump. We went off down the road with him holding my hand as I wobbled along.

When we arrived at Aunt Kate's house, their Blue Spot radiogram was already blasting out blue beat and rock steady music. Some people were already jamming to the music. I didn't think that they noticed my belly in the dimly lit room. Aunt Kate gave me a chair to sit in. Eric was soon chatting away. I sat there dancing on the chair, until I couldn't bear to sit any more. So I stood up and began to rock to the music. The room came alive when they saw me dancing. Eric's jaw dropped, when he saw me jamming to the music. He held me close and we danced the night away, hoping that it might help to get things going. When we were leaving they wished me good luck and hoped that I would have my baby soon. We walked the short distance home talking and feeling happy in the crisp frosty air.

When we arrived home we could not get into the house as Mr Branton had locked and bolted the door. He told us when we first moved in that his front door was locked and bolted at 8 p.m. We thought he was joking until that night when we found the door would not open. We knocked and knocked until finally he came to the door with a face like thunder, reminding us about his house rules as if we were kids.

Eric told him a few Jamaican blue words that he knew he would understand. I thought he was going to punch him. I was glad to get inside as it was freezing, but it wasn't much warmer inside the house. We were upset so we sat up talking for a while, but with me being heavily pregnant, we knew that it will be difficult to find a room somewhere. Eventually we went to bed, but I couldn't go to sleep.

I went out to the shop on the Tuesday while Eric was sleeping and saw a 'Room to Let' sign in a window of a house on Birch Lane, Longsight. When I knocked, a white lady came to the door. I told her I came about the room to let.

She said, "It's gone."

"But the sign is still in the window." I raised my hand and pointed to it, but she was already closing the door on me. I stood there for a moment, so shocked I could hardly move. Then I gathered myself and walked to the Post Office to see if there were any rooms advertised in the window.

There were a few rooms to let, and I was drawn to one that was on Beresford Road. I went home and waited for Eric to wake up, and we went together. It turned out to be a black family who owned the house; we were relieved when we saw how they greeted us at the door. They didn't seem bothered about the fact that I was heavily pregnant.

They had two other couples living in two of the bedrooms and their three young daughters occupied the third bedroom. Mr and Mrs Jones lived in the front room downstairs. There was one living room and we would have to share the kitchen and toilet. They said we could have the room beside them. We didn't have any furniture to move, as the room was furnished. We were delighted when we were told that we could have the room. We went home and told Mr Branton that we would be moving on the Friday. He kicked up a fuss saying we should have given him four weeks' notice, but we couldn't wait to get out.

My baby was almost a month overdue, but the doctor said that I must have got my dates wrong. I knew that I hadn't seen any period since the 26th of May 1962, when I had an unexpected visit as I sat down in a white skirt having my lunch at work! So I was sure about the dates. I became worried and felt unattractive, but I tried to focus on the forthcoming event. In my mind all that was important was the welfare of our baby and everything else took the back seat. The waiting became boring after a while but I kept on the move – tidying our room and packing the baby's and my things ready for the moment. Despite heartburn, I began to comfort-eat and would polish off two apple turnovers washed down with cream soda at times.

On the Friday morning, we left behind the smell of fish that raked the house and made me vomit like a volcano. Ugh! Gwen, Mr Branton's wife, never cooked anything but fish and rice; as long as she was cooking fish she was happy. If a batch of fleas jumped on her face her expression would remain the same. We left her standing at the door and walked out into the rain.

~ 3 ~

By the time we reached Beresford Road, it was chucking down.
Eric knocked the door a few times before Mrs Jones came
tearing down the stairs shouting, "I'm coming, I'm coming!"

"Oh I'm sorry, were you knocking long? Only I was
hoovering the girls' bedroom and didn't hear."

"That's quite all right," Eric said.

"Children," she said, and sighed with a weak smile. "They
always make a mess. Please come in. What a terrible morning
to be moving." she said.

Eric proudly carried the two suitcases inside with the few
clothes that we owned, and some bags. I pushed what everyone
always seemed to see first through the door and wobbled
inside. Mrs Jones was still standing near the door as Eric
proudly brought in our baby's cot. The way he held it, like a
piece of china, made her smile.

"That will be rocking with joy soon," she said.

Our faces lit up and we laughed, but the way I was feeling
made me think that she might be right. My stomach was
feeling tight from yesterday and I felt that something was
going to happen soon.

"I better leave you all to get on with it. Please make
yourselves at home". She turned on her heels and ran back up
the stairs like a gazelle springing about in Africa. The stairs
were bare, except for the piece of lino running down the
middle, which was dangerous in my condition.

I was dying for a cup of tea, but I didn't have to persuade
Eric to find the kitchen. While he was brewing the tea I got a

twinge that made me think something was going to happen soon. When he returned he said to me, "Here you are my darling, this will warm the baby up as well."

"It's warm enough where it is, that's why it's in no hurry to come out," I said, returning his smile. I felt really tired, and I knew that he was knocked as well after just finishing his night shift that morning. He went to bed and he never moved a muscle. But I could only manage a doze, as I kept feeling that I wanted to pee. I had to move around the bags and cases on the floor, so as to get out of the room, and I was worried that I might fall. In the evening I got up and cooked some Corn Beef and rice with salad for our tea.

That night, after half a dozen "See you," and "Will you be all right?" he reluctantly went off to work. I couldn't sleep. I was getting more uncomfortable through the night, and I knew now that our baby was on its way because the pain was coming often. I wondered if it would arrive before its Daddy brushed the last blob of cotton off his pants.

The house was still, and my room was black with not a flick of light to let me see what might greet me. I remember the shade-lamps that flickered in our house back home, and wished that I had one. I wanted to call out, but felt embarrassed to let anyone know that I was in agony.

I was praying for the morning to come when my husband would return home. Even though I was frightened, I hit on the idea of counting backwards to pass the time. I started to count... one hundred, ninety, eighty, and so on until the next pain sliced my back. By the time Eric arrived I was begging for help, he took one look at me and rushed to phone the ambulance.

They took me away, driving like racing drivers to Withington Hospital. I was full of anticipation, nerves and excitement all at once. The room that I was taken to had clinical white walls and strange looking gadgets that scared the hell out of me. I gripped Eric's hand tightly, as I got another stabbing back pain. I wished he could stay with me, but it wasn't the done thing in those days. It wasn't like today when your partner can stay and support you through the experience of child birth. I was frozen with fear, and felt like I was about to be left in a torture chamber.

"Please look after my wife," Eric said to the midwife. She assured him that they would take good care of me. He kissed me softly and reluctantly walked out of the room. I could tell that he wished he could stay by the way he lingered beside my bed.

The birth was long and very painful, and even though I was given gas and air to ease the pain, it made me see three of everything. I was in labour all day and well into the night, taking deep breaths as people inserted their lubricated hands into my love tunnel. The contractions were strong but my water was still intact and I was told that they were going to break it. It was terrible to be on my own not having Eric to comfort me. I was stabbed by the most intense pain around my abdomen and back and thought my head was going to explode. When the crunch came, I thought they were going to slaughter me when my legs were yanked into two slings, as *my* body was invaded by the doctor and midwife.

I was frantic and freaked out completely. For some reason, in the middle of all what was going on, I remembered how Papa used to draw the goat's legs up and tie them before slitting their throats, and ripped the skins from their bodies. He had a licence to butcher animals. I was terrified, and screamed out loud that I wanted my mother.

"Ooohh! Get my mother! Get my mother please!"

The midwife turned around and looked at me calmly.

"Where is your mother?"

"In Jamaica!" I shrieked. Holy Moses, she was five thousand miles away!

"Well," she said, "your mother can't help you now, my dear," and she walked off. That remark upset me even more; I was very frightened and felt that I was going to die. My heart seemed to miss so many beats in that few minutes, but she came back to me in no time.

"Now young lady," she said. "I want you to push very hard, but only when I tell you to do so." She looked down on me with a mischievous expression on her face. "Now listen to me, just like when you... you know, go to the toilet." So I pushed and pushed until my head felt like it was about to explode. I thought, "O my God: Eric is not here to howl with delight when he can see the baby's head." But I couldn't push any more. I was too exhausted. They were talking to me, but I barely could see them, even though my eyes were open. It was weird. The doctor took over and suddenly I felt a sharp snip and my world seemed to open up. Within minutes she pulled our baby out with the help of some forceps. It's the most wonderful experience that any woman can have. That moment when you hear your child cry and they lay your baby into your arms is unforgettable.

After a while I was being stitched up, and I could feel every prick of the needle going into my love passage, it was so... barbaric. I had a brain storm. That's the end of me. It will be no good after this trauma, being stitched together like pieces of cloth. I won't able to pee, walk, sit, or hold my baby. I am deformed now. Then suddenly I throw up before I could ask for a bowl. "Take some deep breaths," the nurse said as she held a bowl to my mouth, but I kept vomiting for a while and heavy sweat rolled down my face. Then it began to fade away and I got the chance to inspect my baby.

The nurse told me she was a big girl, topping the scales at 8 lbs 6 ozs on Saturday 2nd of March 1963, at 9.45 p-m. She had a mop of black hair. I counted her fingers and I could see how her fingernails had grown away from the quick. Her skin was visibly dry, and the folds on her legs and arms were cracked. I knew then, as I had known all along, that she was overdue.

I was excited and disoriented after my twenty-four hours labour. I must have fallen asleep and later woke up to find our baby lying in a cot beside my bed. I bent over and took a sniff of her. It was an unforgettable smell: so new, sweet, and fresh. I couldn't wait for the nurse to help me to put her to my breast. She latched on like a leech, and the tickling feeling was amazing. It was wonderful to hold my own child in my arms, giving her that bond that I had watched my mother and Aunt Bertha give to their children.

Her father arrived with a bunch of flowers and sunbeams in his eyes. The smile on his face took my breath away when he kissed me. He was delighted and gently lifted his daughter into his arms. He kissed her and wept with joy.

~ 4 ~

I could hardly walk to the toilet as my downstairs was very painful and the wound stung when I peed. I was examined and told that I had a wound infection: a haematoma. I had to bear the pain of the needle being inserted in the wound to aspirate the blood out a few times. As the days went by the stitches were taken out, but I was still very sore and uncomfortable.

"What are you going to call her?" the doctor who had delivered her asked me.

"Maureen," I replied.

"Really? That's my name, what a coincidence. But she could easily be called Gorgeous." There was an echo of laughter around my bed as she checked Maureen and me over before we went home. My little mite didn't like it one bit and she let it be known by screaming. We had stayed in hospital for eight days, after the birth.

Eric came in the afternoon to take us home after he had some sleep. We took a taxi, but it was a very uncomfortable ride for me. It was nice to be home with our baby and they were all cooing when they saw her. Three of the ladies were mothers so I wasn't short of advice. Mrs Jones' cousin Zelma was always popping in; she was a young single woman, who shared the children's bedroom, but boy she was hot! We often thought of throwing cold water on her. She made me felt uneasy when she flashed her legs in the mini skirts that barely touched the end of her drawers. But she was nice enough and we had many laughs, especially when Eric went off to work. Without her I would have been so very lonely. But I kept my eyes on her as she was very attractive and was on the lookout for someone to pull. I felt that I didn't look my best, even though I had a new pair of breasts gushing with enough milk to feed another child. I was unable to slip into my nice dresses that I love and that made me feel weepy.

The Jones's children were delighted to see our baby, especially Annabel who was seven years old. She wanted to hold Maureen every time she came into the room, but she had to make do with propping herself up on the side of the baby's cot sometimes. The kitchen was small with a few open shelves for storage, and far too small to accommodate so many women. We were paying £2.5s. in old money for the room per week, but if we wanted to cook or bake, we had to pay an extra two shillings for the gas. Ten pence is small change today but in 1959 to 1960 it could buy a loaf of bread, a bottle of milk, and some margarine.

There was hassle when everyone wanted to cook at the same time in the small kitchen. We were bumping into each other and forever apologizing. It was really difficult because there was no fridge and I had to resort to storing food in our room. Lots of items simply walked, never to be seen again, and the funny thing was even the landlady had nicked her tenants' things. However, Mrs Jones was a nice enough person: she was a stunning looking woman with big brown eyes, light skin and talked with a high-pitched voice. Her voice became higher especially when she was cracking jokes. Her husband Moses was a tall handsome man and equally funny. He loved to make Guinness-punch with eggs, condensed milk, rum, and have it with his Sunday dinner. It was a standard joke when we heard the beating and banging in the kitchen we knew that Moses was mixing up his poison.

One Sunday I was cooking some beef in my Dutch pot, which is a heavy, cast-iron Caribbean cooking pot. I heard the cover drop – it makes a distinctive sound – so I rushed into the kitchen and there was Mrs. Jones, with a piece of my hot beef poking into her mouth! Her tongue was sliding in and out of her mouth like a dog on heat as the meat was burning it. I caught her red-handed and I was furious! The beef was to last us for a few days. With rice and peas it was meant to be a treat for us that weekend. When she had composed herself, she said she was just checking to see if it was burning, but I was fuming. I knew she had done this before to the other tenants. Our room was beside the kitchen so I could hear the women talking and laughing. The smell of the different dishes seeped into our room and tormented our taste buds We knew that we had to move, but where to? It would be no better.

I thought of my childhood and how it was, and I desperately wanted Maureen's to be different from mine. I hoped that she never would carry water on her head, work in the blistering heat like me and get a better education. I had held lots of babies in my arms before her, but this time the feeling was different because she was mine. I had my own princess now, even though I was a bit nervous when I was washing her hair, in case the water would get into her nostrils and drown her.

She was christened at the Methodist Church on Dickinson Road in Longsight, when she was twelve weeks old. She wore a beautiful christening gown made from lace and satin. I remember how difficult I found it to hold her as she let out a gurgle – much to the amusement of the vicar. She was wriggling and seemed ready to slip out of my arms.

When the service started and the vicar was leading the prayers, I could see that Aunt Kate was having a jolly good struggle to keep Maureen in her arms, as she wriggled. She was like a slithery eel, and the silky dress that she was wearing didn't make it any easier, but Aunt Kate managed to keep hold of her. However, it was a different story when the holy water at the font touched her head. She screamed and I was the only one who could comfort her. We had a lovely afternoon with a few friends in our room: nothing grand, as we didn't have the space to entertain, but it was truly a joyous day.

In the crowded house, sometimes I had to wait forever to have a bath, so I used Maureen's bath in the privacy of our room. I would say to Eric, "I'm going to have a quick lick here and a quick lick there." It was amazing how we used to improvise and make do. Then I would stumble through the kitchen to empty the water outside. Having a bath was a luxury if we were lucky to have a landlord that made up the fire at weekends, and who was willing to keep banging some of his precious coal on it. There was not enough water in the tiny tank for a good soak, but we made do.

While I was at home with Maureen, I developed an interest to be a nurse. Her birth must have brought on this emotion, but I was always a caring person and used to smother my younger brothers and sisters with love when our parents were not around. I have been a nurse ever since I could pluck them off the ground. The only thing I didn't have was the uniform to make me look the part.

Money was short and I decided to go back to work. I got a job at Smith's Crisps, working six till two pm and two till ten pm packing crisps, making boxes, and screening the crisps for burnt bits down the conveyer belt. Nothing to stretch my abilities, but I thought well, I will give it my best shot.

It wasn't an ideal job, especially having a young child to cope with. We had asked the ladies in the house to listen out for her until her father came home from his night shift at 6 am. Occasionally he put her into the bed beside him and nursed her between snips of sleep. But as she grew she became wiser and she started to poke her fingers into his nostrils and tried to open his eyes. He told me that it was hilarious, as he often pretended that he was sleeping.

It was painful leaving her and I knew that I wouldn't be able to cope much longer, as most mothers in those days stayed at home and were housewives. Then I caught a cold and lost my voice. While I was standing at the bus stop one night, I decided to leave after just four months, and I never returned the next day.

I stayed at home for a few months and enjoyed my baby, and with my physical contact fully renewed, she was much more contented. When I got a chance I strolled through Anson Road Park with our adorable daughter, and watched the ducks flapping their wings around the pond, racing each other for the bread that I threw to them. Then I walked back home with her sleeping peacefully.

The room was too small to hold all the things we accumulated.

No matter how organised we were, it was difficult living in a house with nine adults, three boisterous children, and a young baby. There were no grandparents to cuddle and fuss over her, and I began to feel sad. I felt alone and desperate for some family support.

One day I went shopping on Stockport Road and bumped into Hyacinth. I had worked with her before I had my baby. She hadn't seen Maureen since she was born and was cooing and gooing over her.

"Have you heard that Ashton Barton has moved to a new place?" she asked excitedly.

"Yes I have, but isn't it quite some way from here?" I asked.

She sighed. "It is a bit of a way, yes you are right, I have to get two buses, and when I get off the second one I have to run. Anyway, it's okay once I get there." She looked at me hopefully. "Well you know what we do already, and nothing has changed!"

I took a deep breath, inhaling the acrid fumes from the passing traffic and told her that although I had enjoyed the short time that I had worked at Ashton Barton, my life was changed now and will never be the same as before.

However, I told Hyacinth that money was in short supply and I was breast-feeding as it was good for the baby and it saved us some money. "I had so much milk, it was spouting out like a hose pipe" laughing as I told her. "But seriously the poor child had to let go some times, as the milk choked her and I had to blow into her face to allow her to get her breath back."

"Good God!" she said. "Well done, I haven't got a child, so I wouldn't know what to do."

"I saw my mother do it many times" I told her. "I have done it many times to my siblings when they were gobbling their milk from the cream soda bottles with the stretched out brown teats."

"Rather you than me," she said.

I was a little startled as she was much older than me, and by no means what I would call a spring chicken.

"It was nice seeing you and your beautiful baby, and who knows… I might be seeing you soon at work. Bye-bye!" She walked away, leaving me with my newfound joy. My spirit was lifted, and I walked back home with spring in my legs and my bottom dancing with the extra weight that I have gained during my pregnancy. I am a mother to my own child now and not to my siblings and it was wonderful. Even with a bit of extra weight, I managed to get a few wolf whistles walking in the sunshine on my way home.

I heard about a child minder named Rosalyn so I went to see her. She had twin girls who were a year old. She was a single mother left on her own with very little hope, only a bag of shame that her mother said she brought upon her family. It was a terrible stigma in those days to have children out of wedlock, not like today when no one seems to bat an eyelid, and it is fashionable to have children without the stability that marriage provides.

Eric and I worried over the matter, wondering if it was the right thing to do, whether she could cope with three children. I kept asking myself these questions over and over again. Eventually we came to a decision to leave our baby with her. I took comfort from the fact that she had children of her own, and she seemed to be doing a good job in the circumstances that she found herself in. That morning when I left Maureen I'm not ashamed to say I was crying.

I returned to Ashton and Barton working as a coat cleaner, which was basically cutting the cotton off the garments that the machinist left behind. The job was a bit boring but I decided to give it go. I told myself that one day they might allow me to use the sewing machine, and teach me how to make the coats.

After a few months I was bursting to do something that I felt a passion for, something rewarding. So I decided to apply for a job at two hospitals. Nursing was one of the things that appealed to me, to help others who were less able to help themselves. I talked it over with Eric, who said that he would support me in whatever I wanted to do. Then he took a deep breath and said, "Do you realise that you will have to do shifts and its bloody hard work, and distressing to watch people snuff it?"

"O shit!" I said, and covered my mouth in shock because of his frank reply. I had never given the snuff bit a thought, but he seemed shocked by my reply and raised his eyebrows.

In those days it wasn't necessary to have GCSE qualifications, just the ability to learn and the compassion for caring for the sick and dying, though it would be a bonus to have. The only hospital that replied was Stepping Hill. I went for the interview and was asked a lot of questions about why I wanted to be a nurse, and about my family life.

At the interview I told them that I was married and had a nine months old baby. But the three people that interviewed me didn't seem fuzzed about me having a baby. I was asked to sit in another room for a while. Then I was called back in and told that I got the job. I was overjoyed. I thanked them and literally skipped to the 192 bus stop in the autumn sunshine. Eric was very happy for me, because after three months on the wards, working as an auxiliary nurse, I would be in nursing school training for three years and eventually become a Staff Nurse.

~ 5 ~

So, I had just landed myself a worthwhile job and not long after realised that my period was late. I was frantic and worried that I might be pregnant again. My husband didn't like using artificial means; he wanted to feel my warm body.

"Nothing is better than flesh on flesh," he told me, but my sexual experience was limited I was too embarrassed to discuss any intimate matters with him, never mind anyone else, even though I was a wife and mother.

The pill wasn't available yet and I never knew that there were other methods that I could use. He promised me, with convincing eyes, that he would be careful at the height of passion, and slip his you know what out. I wasn't comfortable with his plans as I thought it was too much like playing with fire. A few weeks after I started my job at the hospital, I began to feel unwell. One day I was sick and to my horror, I found out that I was pregnant again when I went to the doctor.

I was devastated and angry with myself, and even angrier with Eric when I told him that he was going to be a father again. I burst into tears. However, he seemed shocked and sorry that his technique hadn't worked. He hugged and kissed me, telling me that I would be fine once the shock wore off.

One day at work, I was standing in a room rolling up cotton into balls to be sterilised, as every ward had to do their own in those days.

Suddenly I felt queer and my head started to spin. I must have gone out like a light. When I came round a nurse was fanning my face, and calling my name and another nurse was holding a glass of water for me to sip.

"What happened?" I asked.

"You fainted," one of them answered. "One minute you were rolling the cotton into balls, and the next minute you were on the floor."

I felt such a fool and I was embarrassed. I don't know if they suspected that I was pregnant, but I kept a silent tongue and zipped up my lips. I had some bad days, but not as dreadful as the day when I passed out. The truth was that I was unhappy about being pregnant again so soon after giving birth to Maureen. I really wasn't as pleased as when I found out that I was pregnant with Maureen. It was bad enough trying to cope with one baby.

However, I was stuck with it and to my horror, my belly began to grow. I told Eric that I was going to leave the job because I felt such a fool. I just started nursing and I felt that I had let myself down.

"You are a married woman, and I will stand by you," he said.

"I can't cope." I moaned.

"But you could carry on until it's time for you to leave," he argued, while his face turned silver grey.

I shouted at him. "No, no, I can't cope! It's too much." "Most days I feel I'm going to pass out, and I have to grab the patients' beds!" I screamed at him. This was our first full-blown row. I threw a pan at him and screamed, "I hate you! It's all right for you, you don't have to cope with it, do you?" Then I stormed out of the room. Eric followed me.

"I can't understand what you are saying. You are a married woman, for God's sake. There's nothing to be ashamed of," he retorted, implying that was a passport to heaven.

"But..."

"But what?" he asked, putting his arms around me, and trying his best to calm me down. "You will be all right; we will get through this together."

"I can't cope! I am just twenty and going to have another baby so soon after the first one, plus a demanding job. I have to work from 7.30 am until 5.30 pm, and on the late shift from 1 pm until 9 pm at night. It is still dark when I'm going out with Maureen in the mornings. She sits in her pram with her dummy propped in her mouth looking at me, as if to say "Mommy, where are we going in the dark?"

"You can't keep your flaming hands off me, can you? You're always coming on to me, night and bloody day!" I stormed, and took another swipe at him, like a deranged dog.

"From the moment I took off my clothes that first night, your skin caught fire and haven't ceased." I barked.

"Do you think that because you slid this twenty-two carat gold ring on my finger, you've got a passport to breed me up like bedbugs. I had enough of them when I was growing up. They used to invade my wooden bed, and suck my blood," I fumed. "Well, I have news for you, *you* won't."

Somehow he managed to calm me down, but that night I lay on the edge of the bed like a lone bird clinging to a cow's back. I could not bear him touching me that night. I knew that I would explode into a fireball if he tried to seduce me, even with his breath.

However, I wasn't so eager to make preparations for my forthcoming baby, even though I was blooming. I knew that I was a true-born survivor and I had no choice other than to accept my growing bump. I knew that I would grow to love whatever it turned out to be, as soon as it cried.

On my day off, I went for a walk with Maureen around the park and I saw a flock of birds flying round while some took a bath in the pond. I watched them and listened to the sweet songs they were singing. It was at that moment that I told myself that while there is life there is hope. Maureen was fascinated by the birds and was pointing her fingers at them as

I glided around in the fresh air, then walked back home with my new little mite tucked up inside me.

We decided that it was better for me to give notice and leave, so I went off to the Matron's office the following morning with my nerves twitching, and my heart thumping in my chest, and told her that I was going to leave. However, before I could breathe the last word from my mouth, she asked the question that I was dreading.

"Why are you leaving when you only just started months ago? I thought it was a three-year course you were doing, not a few months sprint. Now you want to flit off like a bat down a cave because you changed your mind."

She argued and snapped as if her tongue had caught fire and called me a silly Caribbean girl. I was shocked at her outburst. Even though she might have a point, it didn't give her the right to speak to me in that manner. Then I managed to compose myself and tell her my reason in a measured tone, an octave below middle C and watched her stretch her eardrums. Then she told me that other people carried their babies and work. I stood there and couldn't get another word out of my mouth. It just dried up like a desert.

"Right, young lady if that's what you want, that's fine, but you will have to work your two weeks' notice." She showed me the door, and I walked out of her office back to the ward, and continued my shift in a daze.

However, the shame that I felt was too much so I rushed into the toilet and burst into tears. I was a broken girl with yet another shattered dream that left me feeling very sad.

The last day came just like all the days before. When evening came I walked away from the orthopaedic ward with my P45 in my hand, and took the bus home. There was a mixture of emotion rushing through my mind and I felt disappointed with myself, that the jinx had followed me across the Atlantic Sea.

~ 6 ~

I found another job, sewing at Barracuda in Great Ancoat Street. I blocked the baby out of my mind, pretending it wasn't there, which was sad. But it was the only way that I could cope with it at the time. I still have a mental picture in my head of how I felt, and I know that it will be with me forever.

However, I tried to get on with it, and took to the sewing machine. I was sewing the vents on the back of the coats. It was quite easy, and I began to enjoy it.

I was up at the crack of dawn to get Maureen and myself ready. That was until she caught chickenpox from Rosalyn's daughters, who'd had it some weeks earlier. The poor child had it so bad that she was taken to the children's hospital in Harper Hay, Manchester, and put in isolation. Her body was covered in festering bumps from her head to her toes.

It was a dreadful sight, and the doctors said they had never seen anyone so badly affected before. Of course, that opened the door for a barrage of questions from the medical staff. Had we been in contact with anyone from abroad? Then we were finally given a chance to speak I explained that my childminder's children had caught it a few weeks ago. I had some time off work to be with her during the day. Soon the scabby bumps started to dry up and she was well enough to come home.

By the time Maureen came out of hospital, Rosalyn had lost her enthusiasm for taking care of someone else's child. She was hooked up with a new fellow and wanted to spend some time with him, which was fair enough, but we were left high and dry to find someone else at short notice. Anyway, she suggested that I ask her mother, Mary, who was retired and lived in the same area. I asked her and she agreed to keep Maureen until I finished work. I was delighted.

One Saturday morning an Asian man knocked on the door. He was selling cardigans, blankets to name a few... in fact everything except the kitchen sink.

"Buy something from me, my lady," closing the palms of his hands in prayer and bowing his Turban wrapped head.

"Very, very, cheap. Look, only ten bob, very nice." He was picking up a pink blanket with satin binding around the edges.

"You take, me give you, for ten shillings," he said in broken English.

"No money," I told him.

"You plenty money," he said in drip-drop English.

"I pay next week," I told him.

"O K."

He bowed his head like a puppet and we sealed the agreement.

By this time the other folks in the house had gathered round us, and started rooting in the suitcase, and so it went on, week after week.

This door to door selling was how a lot of Asian people started their trail to the successful life that they enjoy today. Although most arrived here without a dime like myself they seemed to have the gift that enabled them to take £5 and buy a few things, and slowly build it up into a goldmine. Burning their incense, and praying to Allah and fasting were their only pastimes. I know this because we lived with two Asian brothers for a year after we left Mrs Jones house. But before we could figure out what the hell's going on, they had already turned it into a million pounds. I do admire them, as most of them work very hard and they stick together, pooling their resources in one pot.

I think what held back most of our West Indian people, and it is still going on today with our children who are born here, is that we don't stick together as much as we should, and it shows as the years go buy.

However, the Irish, Indian, and the West Indian stories were similar to what a lot of people were going through. We were told to go back where we came from in the jungle, and swing on the trees with the monkeys, or to go back to our mud huts, you're not wanted here.

"We don't want you jungle people and nig-nogs here," was a common phrase they used; the list of offensive and abusive terms was endless. It was appalling, and very distressing. The atmosphere was tense wherever we went in those days. Most English people resented us; they were worried that the men would take away their women, and the general opinion was that we were here to take away their jobs.

But the jobs that we were given was what most English people didn't and wouldn't want to do. In time, a lot of the hot-blooded men did have their wicked way with some of the women. But no one in authority ever admits that they came to our country, recruiting people to come over and work here, to clean up the shit, and rebuild their country after the war. We came and did the work that a lot of English people would rather die than be seen doing. We worked damn hard and lived in conditions that made us cry to return to our homelands. We may not have known where the next meal was coming from, when we were in Jamaica, but we were free from insults and wishing that we could paint our skin white.

~ 7 ~

In England, most of us lived in appalling conditions with the toilets outside. I hated getting up from my bed to go to the toilet. I remember yanking my knees to my chest trying to keep warm, and then waking to find them still pasted to my breasts as I was so cold. Then having to leave the spot and wade out into the snow. It was frightening, to say the least. I thought I had left all that behind in the West Indies.

I used to pop my head out of our room door and dive for the toilet and hope that no one was there. Otherwise I would cross my legs and rush back to our room and use the bucket that sat like a duchess in the corner of our room. It saved us from accident many times. Most people had one of those white buckets then, and thank God for the covers that went on top.

This was England, our mother country, I reminded myself; not a third world country. But I got the shock of my life when I had to go out in the dark, which I had feared throughout my childhood, to relieve myself. I wondered if all the houses were the same.

"You fool, can't you see that all those houses are touching each other like clothes on a line? They must be the same." That thought answered my question, but it still frightened me to go out into the black night for a shit, especially when there was a gale blowing under my skirt.

I personally never looked upon myself as being different from a white person when I was a child growing up in Jamaica. We were all God's children in a melting pot and

I didn't realise that I could be thought of as different until I came to England. Coming here has opened my eyes; my way of thinking has grown since.

I was brought up to treat everyone with the greatest of respect. "Yes sir and no mam" was the normal way of addressing someone older and wiser than yourself. To me, as a child growing up, Europeans were people that I looked up to, because they lived in huge houses, drove jeeps, rode horses, and sheltered under huge hats to protect their skin from the sun.

They rode around watching their workers toil in the sun's relentless rays. The men and women shielded their eyes with dusty hands and glimpsed their masters trotting by in shiny saddles on their frisky horses.

The working people couldn't afford much and had to struggle to survive.

I realised from an early age that West Indian people think completely differently from others. They never seem to trust one another when it comes to money matters, nor give a hundred percent to partnerships. So, with that distrust, they never seem to take as much risk as they ought to. Everyone seems to want to be the boss, to be in charge, but unwilling to roll up their sleeves to reach their goals.

I often wondered if we had a curse on us, as our race always seemed to be miles behind. I talked about this matter with other West Indians, they agreed that something positive and constructive needed to be done to change the cycle that seems to follow generation after generation of our people. I wished I could do something about it. But, I realised that it was easier said than done.

It would certainly help some of our brothers and sisters who are still suffering in the world today, just like our ancestors did all those years ago. I think it is this doubt and lack of opportunity that has held back most black people from showing their full potential. Many of us still dwell on the past, about what the British and their like did to our forebears. I believe that we have to move on, build new bridges, and get on with our lives; otherwise we will be festering for ever.

We have to cross those bridges and allow the wheat and the thorns to grow together until the day of harvest. Our people took their scars from their beatings to their graves, but they left their traditions and cultures for their children, and their children's children to follow. Those traditions cannot be washed away like the blood, sweat and tears that poured from their sun-ravaged bodies.

When I was growing up, I heard that the slave masters used to have their wicked ways with the slave women, and the men were made to watch their animal behaviour but couldn't do a damn thing about it.

When I heard those horror stories that the older people talked about the past, as they sat under the shaded trees while the sun sizzled, my heart skipped a beat. They unfolded the history that they were told when they were growing up. I didn't want to miss a word even though it was very hard to put into context. My heart aches to listen to the past, it also gives me an insight into what humans are capable of doing to each other. Nevertheless it strengthens my determination to reach for stars and live my dream.

~ 8 ~

For some reason I was late getting to work on my last morning, even though I left home at the usual time, but I suspected that the spring had left my legs, and the journey took me a bit longer to the child minder.

When I arrived at work, I found my sewing machine dressed up with coloured streamers. Pauline had her head down and the fabric was sliding through her fingers as she pressed the pedal.

"What's this for?" I asked. I was very surprised.

"It's for you, to show you how much you are going to be missed." I laughed and I said, "Don't make me cry."

At lunch time Pauline disappeared, but before I knew it, she was back again – with a parcel. The whole canteen seemed to be awash with laughter. I looked around at everyone... now what is going on?

They all clapped and cheered as Pauline handed me a wrapped parcel. I was very touched, because I hadn't been working there very long.

"Go on," they urged, "open it!"

I didn't need much encouragement and ripped open the paper. My mouth flapped open. There was a lemon blanket, two white baby's nightdresses with dainty embroidered flowers on the front, and a cream teddy bear with eyes that looked real. My heart skipped a beat as I gently stroked it. For a few moments I was lost for words; then I thanked them.

I worked for the rest of the afternoon, though I was not too enthusiastic. I knew that it was time for me to start building my nest. The girls waved as I said goodbye and I walked out into Great Ancoat Street. The weather had changed, and the evening was grey and overcast. I waited for the bus to come, with my protruding bump forcing through my coat.

As I walked home, pushing Maureen, I told myself that tomorrow morning there will be no rush, and I will have a lie-in if Maureen allowed it. Even at that young age, she played little tricks on me: Mommy having a lie-in, so I will try to get her eyes open, and shake her awake!

I was looking forward to the birth of our new baby. Every time I felt a kick I would hold the spot, wondering what part of the baby's body it was. I was well and truly bonded with my baby – I had to be, after carrying him/her around for nearly nine months. I was secretly hoping for a little boy, but of course I would be happy with whatever God had given me.

Right in the middle of all this, we moved to 5 Birch Lane in Longsight, to a huge three floor Victorian house that was painted white outside. The landlord did not live there. The room had a high ceiling and yellow pattern wallpaper. We had a very high old bed, a wardrobe, dressing table, two chairs and a beautiful fireplace.

One evening I wrote a letter to my mother and decided to go out and post it on Stockport Road. I passed the Wagon and Annecy Pub at the end of our lane to the post box. When I was coming back a white man came right up in front of me and said, "Would you like to have a bit of this?"

I looked down and saw that he was exposing himself to me. I was too shocked to speak so all I could think of was to shout "Help, help, go away you bastard." I was just weeks from having my baby, so I could not run very easily. What frightened me most was if I'd had far to go, he might have raped me, but I was lucky that I lived quite near to the pub. I rushed through my gate screaming, "Open the door!" even though I had the key in my pocket. The people who lived in the front room came and opened the door, but by this time he had legged back towards Stockport Road.

I was breathless and it took me some time to explain what had happened. Eric was furious and wanted to go and find this man. I told him not to. I said he could have a knife and stab him. I wasn't hurt, that's the main thing. Of course, I saw his penis hanging out, but he didn't get to use it on me.

I went into labour two week later. I knew what to expect this time, but one doesn't get used to pain. It was another long labour, but a normal delivery. Another little girl; she was beautiful and weighed in at seven pounds. She was quite light-skinned with less hair than Maureen. We named her Yvonne, and Matilda after Eric's mother.

The following morning the doctor came round to my bed with Sister. "Good morning, Mrs. Bartley. How are you today?"

I told him not too bad.

"I believe you are not losing too much?"

"No, not really," I told him, a bit unsure. I was embarrassed to tell him my intimate details.

"Let's have a look, Sister," he said, and she drew the curtains round my bed. "That's fine. You are doing very well, you can go home today. Sister will arrange the ambulance to take you home."

Eric was at home with Maureen. There was no way of letting him know as there was no phone in the house. When I returned with my little bundle of joy, one of the ambulance men carried her up the stairs and into our room. The nurse came for ten days and then we were left to get on with our lives as a family.

Maureen was intrigued by her baby sister and kept touching her. I had more than enough milk to feed my baby and the nurse asked me if I would like to donate some to the Duchess of York Hospital for Sick Children. I said I would – my milk would be used to feed the premature babies. So she arranged pump and containers to be delivered, and an ambulance driver to collect it every other day.

It felt wonderful to do that, because some ladies don't produce much milk. Then there are those who choose not to breast-feed, but I'm glad that I did, otherwise I could not have helped all those babies. I did it for five months and only stopped because I was weaning my baby. She was not very happy about it either, and kept searching and snuffling through my top.

Even after all those years, I still feel proud that there are some men and women walking around who were helped by my milk. I know it was an era of prejudice and racism and there were many parents who would have been horrified had they known that their infant had been given breast milk from a black woman. I was happy to do it with the goodness of my heart. Thankfully, things are different now. We now have a multicultural society and thank God things have changed to some extent. But, some leopards would never change their spots. However, they would miss out on the rainbow nations and the vibrancy that different cultures bring to our society.

~ 9 ~

We were very overcrowded in the one room. I kept Maureen in her cot and put Yvonne beside me in the bed. I don't think there were any Moses baskets in 1964, and I didn't want to put her in a dressing table drawer like a young woman we knew. I wasn't happy with our cramped life, and it was difficult to keep two young children happy in one room. So we moved again, this time to Dickenson Road, Longsight, where we had a front bedroom that was much bigger than the back room we had.

I was determined that we would have to do something to prevent me from becoming pregnant so soon again – in fact I would have been quite happy not to have any more children. When I went to get Yvonne vaccinated I was told about a clinic where they would give me some advice about family planning. My husband did not like using a condom because of the incident he had when it came off, and I was frantic, trying to fish it out. It was quite a drama. Anyway, that was the end of it. He refused to use one again.

At the clinic I was offered a 'cap'. It was a circular piece of rubber surrounded by a stiff rim. I was horrified, thinking that if I began to feel turned on, I would have to stop and insert this horrible thing. That was *after* slapping on some spermicidal cream. However, I was told I should get myself ready before bedtime. I decided to give it a try and I didn't have another baby for four years, so it worked!

I'm sure that other ladies will agree with me that it is us women who always have to take precautions while the men have their fun. But I had to hold back sometimes, faking that trip to heaven, when I was hoping that my period would come home next month.

Eric kept saying that we should try for another child, but I was reluctant because we were still living in one room. We were trying our best to save up to buy a house of our own, but our wages were small we didn't have much left over to save.

Since we had been together, we had done everything jointly. But one day, Eric went behind my back and drew out all our savings without consulting me, and bought a van. Now the amazing thing is he couldn't drive and didn't have a licence.

He told me that one of his mates at work had a licence, so he would drive the van. He apparently had it all worked out: there was a van load of them and they would pay him what they paid to travel on the bus. He would use that money to pay for the van and save some towards a house.

I was gutted and furious. In the sixties, £400 was a lot of money and it had taken a long time and a lot of sacrifice to save it. I was hurt, devastated, and I cried, that he done it without saying a word to me. He hadn't told me about it because he knew that I would never have agreed.

Then the unexpected happened. He lost his job when the cotton mill closed down, and couldn't keep up the payments on the van, so the finance company came and repossessed it. They simply asked him to sign a paper which he hadn't read properly. When I came home from work he told me that a man came about the van and said they would keep it until he got another job.

"Did you really sign the paper?" I asked him.

He nodded. "Yes."

"You will never see the van again," I told him angrily. "Never in a million years!"

He stared at me and the blood visibly drained from his face as he realised what he had done. I told him they would sell the van, and if they hadn't got their money back, they would drag his ass to court for the rest. That's how naive my husband was in those early days. Being twenty years my senior didn't mean he was wiser than I was... far from it.

So he lost the van and had to pay ten shillings a week for quite some time. I wanted to leave him before I'm charged for murder, but with two small children, my hands were tied. I wouldn't be able to pay for a room and childcare as well as feed and clothe them. I threw a pan at him but it missed, so I had to put up with it, and more or less shut up. It was a very difficult time in our marriage when I want to fucking kill him but somehow we rode out the storm.

I found it very hard to trust him after that, but we patched things up and I forgave him. However, I could not *forget* it. But we had to move on. He got a job in Trafford Park, and I was working as a machinist elsewhere. The children went to a childminder and I picked them up on the way home from work – only to start again, cooking, washing and cleaning.

The district nurse told me that we could apply for a council house, and gave me the information. We had no idea that we could have applied earlier. Advice was not very forthcoming at that time and, to be honest, we didn't know where to go for advice. When we went to find out about it we were told that we might have to wait up to five years, which seemed to be forever.

Eric was still nagging me to try for another baby. He wanted a son, but I didn't want to have lots of children. Well, one day, I was not prepared for a sex session as my cap was not in place. He seduced me... when his lips touched mine they were burning like fire and I just melted into his arms. He was so sure that I was pregnant and it that it would be a boy!

After, I made sure I used my cap, but I soon found out that I was pregnant when my red light didn't come on. Eric was delighted but I was furious. I wanted to kill him.

After a while everyone could see that I was pregnant, and we still hadn't heard anything from the council, so once again we were looking for somewhere to live with a bit more space. One Saturday afternoon, Eric went to the bookmakers to put on a bet and met Zaffa, an Asian man. They got talking and it turned out that he had a shop on Stockport Road, selling Asian fabrics. He told Eric that he lived in Didsbury, which was quite an affluent area, and he had recently bought a house to rent out at 27 Birch Lane, Longsight – the same street where I'd had to run from the man who exposed himself.

Eric asked him if it was already rented. Zaffa said no, so he asked him if he could have the front bedroom and the next room beside it. Zaffa said yes. Eric explained that we were expecting our third child and an extra room would be a great help. He asked if we could use the second room as a kitchen and dining room and Zaffa agreed to put in a sink and cooker for us. We couldn't believe our luck.

Within a few weeks it was ready and we moved in. We bought a single divan bed for the girls and they were so happy to sleep in a proper bed with more room. We bought a new mattress for the cot and prepared that for the new baby.

I was happy because it was the first time I'd had a kitchen to myself and the children had a bit more space to play. We bought a second-hand table and four chairs, so I didn't have to put them down on the floor to eat any more.

I will always remember my visits to the ante-natal clinic at St Mary's Hospital on Whitworth Street. I used to walk home to Longsight and saved the bus fare to put in the gas meter. Sometimes we were down to our last four pennies in old money. I will never forget those days.

Our baby was due on 26th December 1967. I wasn't feeling very well on Christmas Day, I was getting a pain in my back. However, I cooked a capon for our Christmas dinner. The festive season was in full swing. The girls had two *Tiny Tears* dolls for their Christmas presents, so they were having fun playing and feeding them.

I was taken into hospital after midnight. They took me up to the delivery ward, but nothing happened. The little beggar had decided that it wasn't time yet and I was taken to a ward. I was there all day and I kept walking round to see if I could get things going, but still nothing happened.

Eric came to visit me and we just sat and talked, and he kissed me when he was leaving. Just after he left my water broke. The pain started again and I was told to get back into bed. The pain carried on all night until the midwife decided to take me up to the delivery room. It was a difficult birth. I just could *not* push him out. They had to use a ventouse to pull him out – a suction method used as an alternative to forceps. Everything Eric had said came flooding back to me. He must have been psychic.

I was booked in to stay at the hospital for forty-eight hours, but I was in for much longer than that, because the baby took his time. He was born at six-thirty on the morning of 28th December 1967, weighing 8 lbs. We named him Andrew Ray Bartley. They kept me in for six days because I wasn't well.

On the day that I was to leave hospital I began to haemorrhage very badly. I had a raging fever and felt hot and then cold. I can remember the nurses pushing up the window in the room and gave me a cold bath in bed to get my temperature down. There was snow on the rooftops. When they came into my room they wore white coats, gloves, and masks. They told me if it had started at home it would have been fatal. I was taken to theatre for an operation and was given a blood transfusion.

After I came round on the ward, an Indian lady doctor came to see me. She told me the operation had gone well. My baby was kept in the nursery for three days and I never saw him. I thought I was going to die because they put me in a room by myself. I could see my grave, with the soil piled up beside it, as I was lying there drifting and fighting for my life. But I recovered and was allowed home on the thirteenth day after giving birth. The girls were very happy to see me and their brother. Eric's face wore a permanent smile. He bought me a huge bunch of flowers which was nice.

~ 10 ~

Guilt can be a terrible thing; some can live with it and others can't. Eric can't. He said to me one day that he had something to tell me. I wondered what it was. Now what had he done? He told me that while I was in hospital for thirteen days, one of our so-called friends, Lucy, came round to our rooms. She was complaining that her live-in boyfriend Buster couldn't light her fire and satisfy her. Eric told me she begged him for sex and he bonked her brains out.

I was shocked and very upset. After all, I had just gone through a very difficult birth and now had a new baby and two small daughters to look after. I felt confused and very angry that he had been too weak to say no and show her the door. I think it was put on a plate before him and probably most men would have done the same, but that didn't make it any better.

I told him I hoped it was the first and last time he cheated on me.

Otherwise I will castrate him in his sleep. He stared at me and said he was sorry, but he'd had to tell me because the guilt was killing him. He was also frightened he might say something about it in his sleep. I have no reason to think that anything like that has happened again, and I have never given Lucy the slightest hint that I knew anything. I had my children: they were what she didn't have, and what she was dying for.

Eventually Lucy and Buster parted and she went to live in London. I heard on the grapevine that she'd married a widower. I don't know whether she had any children. We had lost touch by then. I was just twenty-four years old and naïve.

I'd had no previous experience with men, so maybe that's why I didn't have a fighting match with her, but for all my youth and naivety, I knew that I was *Mrs Bartley*. I was the one wearing the 22-carat ring.

But I was not free from other men making advances and seductive remarks to me. Right under Eric's nose, some would say, "Hey man, where you find this pretty girl? I'm going to take her away from you!" I don't know if it was meant as a joke, but I felt angry. I wasn't a parcel to be picked up and passed around. I had eyes for only one man and that was Eric, the man who had helped me to fulfil my childhood dream by making it possible for me to go thirty-seven thousand feet up in the sky.

I kept in touch with the council to see where we were on the housing list and eventually, after a number of years, we were offered a house. Eric went to view it and said that the place we were living in was a palace compared to the dump they were offering us. We turned it down.

Some months later we were offered a three-bedroom flat in Hulme. We all went to view it. It was a post-war three storeys flat on the top floor. We had to climb several flights of stairs, and Eric was unhappy. He was worried about the children climbing out onto the tiny balcony and falling. We talked and talked about it until finally I won the argument, but it wasn't an easy victory as I had to show him that we could make it safe for the children. I said that if we locked the kitchen door they would be unable to climb out. He strongly voiced his concern.

"Yes, but, you can't lock them up all the time!"

"They can go out there for some fresh air if we make sure we are with them," I told him.

"In other words, we have to supervise them all the time."

He was still kicking up a fuss that he didn't want to live in the sky.

"Neither do I, but we are not turning this down just because it hasn't got this or that!"

"How the hell are you going to get a pushchair up all those stairs… three kids and the shopping…?" he stormed.

I just stood and listened as he roared like a bull in a field with anger. After he calmed down I told him that although this flat might not be exactly what we had both hoped for, it would be our first real home.

"Look," I told him, "We will have our own front door, there is plenty of room for us and we won't be sharing with anyone."

For a while he looked at me, not saying a word. "Okay," he said eventually. "You win, but the first chance we get, we're leaving here."

I found it difficult to control my emotions. I just said, "Well, hold on, we haven't moved in yet." Silently I was saying: *if you didn't take the money we were saving to buy a house and bought that bloody van, we would have our own house by now…* but my young head was getting wiser now and I knew that would only add petrol to the fire, so I just shut up my mouth.

We moved into the flat on 28th October 1968. Andrew was ten months old and just starting to take a few faltering steps. It was winter already and we could only make a fire in the living room. There were no fireplaces in the bedrooms and they were like ice-boxes. Icicles formed on the windows. However, it was home – a real home for the first time. We started to decorate the living room but neither of us had ever done anything like that before; we were both novices. We had three children, but we didn't know how to put paper on the wall!

We bought some lovely paper with a striking pattern. We didn't know that we had to match the patterns and thought it looked lovely, until someone came to visit and said it should have matched. Well, I thought, a man on a galloping horse won't notice it, and so we just laughed it off.

We struggled to put the paper up because we didn't have a stepladder. We stood on the chairs and stretched our guts out. The smell of fresh paint was divine, and the children were delighted with the extra rooms to move about more freely. Yvonne and Maureen were attending Cornbrook Primary School in Hulme.

Eric was right. It was difficult to take the baby and the pushchair up and down the stairs, but I soon found a way to cope with that. I used to take Maureen and the shopping up and then run quickly down the stairs for Yvonne, the baby and the pushchair. I would never do it any other way because the chances were that the shopping would disappear before I returned.

I got a part-time job sewing cushion covers at home to make a bit of money. I fitted it round my housework and I got a lot more done when Andrew was having his siesta. The way I saw it was that the extra money I made would help to buy paint and paper for decorating the house. I had always been very creative and was just roaring to go.

The girls settled down at School and made friends with some of the neighbouring children. Most evenings on our way from school I stopped at the nearby play area and let them go on the swings and slide. Yvonne was always a bit frightened of the see-saw but she would give it a go if I stood near her. I used to hop on the merry-go-round with Andrew and he would laugh as I sang to him *Here we go round the merry-go-round*.

But those happy moments came back to haunt me. Every time we passed the play area Andrew wanted me to stop, and then threw a tantrum to get his own way. He used to scream so much that I was worried people might think I was murdering him. Even at that age, he knew how to try and blackmail me into getting what he wanted.

However, when I said *NO*, I really meant it and kept to my word. I didn't have *my* own way all the time when I was young, and I wanted them to learn that they couldn't either.

We were concerned about keeping our flat warm through the winter months because the miners were threatening to go on strike and there was no wooded area around Hulme where we could go to get any logs. However, there were many houses being demolished in the Moss Side and Alexander Road area. Eric salvaged an old pram and went down there collecting any spare wood lying around. He must have looked a sight pushing it down the road, but at that time only the well- off had transport. He had to yank the planks up the stairs and store them on the balcony. There were lots of people who were in the same situation and it was not unusual to go rummaging in decayed houses. Some of those houses could tell a story. They were used for Blue Beat parties where all nations, especially West Indians, would hang out until the early hours.

When the miners went on strike in 1972, a bag of coal was like gold-dust. We couldn't afford to pay the inflated prices being asked – if you were lucky to find anyone with coal to sell. The wood smoke blew back into the living room and inflamed our lungs; we were all coughing and spluttering. It was a terrible time that we shall never forget. We would even burn the contents of the rag and bone man's cart if he took his eyes off it long enough!

The national coal miners' strike of 1972 was central to contemporary British history; it undermined Edward Heath's government and sharpened social conflict. The common interpretation of the strike as a victory of violence, shown to be disingenuous, legitimised the Thatcherite attack on organised labour in 1980. The miners' actions and attitudes and the predominant historical contingencies brought about uproarious events which sharpened the outcome of the strike. This was related to industrial politics more generally in the 1960s and 1970s...

We were fairly new to television; it wasn't so long ago that we had purchased our first black and white TV so we were glued to it, watching the news about the strike.

There were many rivers to cross, but our will and our children kept us going. They made us laugh at times when there was really nothing to laugh about. Only doom and gloom wherever we went. But millions of us did what we had to in order to stay warm and alive. Those were the *good old days*. Today, we can flick a switch and the fire comes on. We have come a long way, with our children, and others of that era. We will remember the hard times and how we managed to cope.

~ 11 ~

When Andrew had reached three and a half, I looked for a part-time job that I could fit around the children. In January 1971 Andrew started nursery school and I started work making ladies' dressing gowns. I had to get my head down and work hard because I had to clock off at three o'clock on the dot. Then it was a mad rush across Manchester City Centre to Cornbrook School at Hulme.

We had now started to save for our own house. We were determined to get out of that top floor flat. My dream was to be the proud owner of a semi-detached house, but there always seemed to be something else waiting around the corner to prevent us from going ahead.

We started looking around for something that we could afford... or could we? It was going to be a struggle. We didn't want to stay in the Old Trafford area. I loved the area where we had lived since I arrived in this country. You could say it was what I knew best, but to be honest, Longsight, Victoria Park, and Levenshulme were very nice areas in the early sixties. The houses in Victoria Park were big houses and there were private roads and gates to enter some of them, so they were beyond our means.

We found a nice three-bedroom semi on Beresford Road, Longsight, with a lovely garden at the back where the children could play (and there would be no Mrs Toby banging on the ceiling when they jumped up and down.) We applied for a mortgage and then had to wait six nerve-wracking weeks for their decision.

We were overjoyed when we got it. It was an exciting time for us. We had a survey carried out and everything was going our way for a change… or so we thought. We were very close to exchanging contracts when someone offered a better price and crashed our dreams. We felt let down and disappointed. But what could we do about it? Nothing. So off we went, trooping about with three children, on and off buses, house-hunting again.

Eventually, we found a house in Levenshulme. We mentioned that we had been let down before and hoped it would not happen again.

"Oh dear," the woman said in her razor-sharp Irish accent, "That's enough to give you a brain tumour! No love, we will still get all our money," she added, rubbing her hands together.

It didn't take long to complete everything because we already had the mortgage, so we moved in exactly two months later, on 13th October 1973. I was pinching myself to make sure it was really our own house at last. Eric and I simply danced around the living room while the children looked on, wondering what the party was for. They had their own party running up and down the stairs with excitement.

"Are we going to stay here?" Maureen wanted know, and Yvonne chipped in with "Is this our house now, Mam?" Andrew was five and he simply ran around the garden, enjoying the freedom. We were all so happy, just bursting with joy.

Eric got a job with a local engineering company, Fairy Engineering, as a crane driver. I got a job at Withington hospital as a nursing auxiliary three nights a week, which suited me very well. I would run to catch the 169 bus home. I made sure they brushed their teeth and didn't have sticky eyes and then one would want toast and another *Sugar Puffs*. Every mother will relate to what I'm saying.

I walked them to school, which took ten minutes. I can remember walking down the street feeling cross-eyed because I was falling asleep on my feet. I just crawled into bed, and at other times I had to sort out things for supper later on.

Some mornings it was gone ten o'clock before I got to sleep. In winter the bed was so cold, I would get a hot water bottle and cuddle up to it. I set the alarm clock for 3pm, but I was usually awake before it went off. Then I yanked my clothes on and dashed down the road. There were other mothers in the street whose children went to the same school, but I liked to meet my kids myself.

One morning I was late coming off duty and missed the bus, so when I got home the children had looked after themselves. But the girls' hair needed combing – they both had afro hair. Of course, their eyes were not looking clean, so I had to smarten them up. They were not happy because they were already late. It certainly wasn't easy trying to juggle all the balls.

However, school holidays were a total nightmare. I didn't get much sleep.

"Mammie, Mammie, Maureen hit me!"

"Why did she hit you? What have you done?"

"Nothing."

That's Andrew. "You must have done *something*."

Then Andrew would slam the door and the shouting would go on and on. They were not allowed to play in the street while I was in bed. We lived in a cul-de-sac so it was not dangerous, but it would have created a group of friends at our gate.

The following summer we had a lovely holiday at Butlins. The children enjoyed themselves. We had been once before, to Filey in Yorkshire. However, we were moving upwards all the time, and I had started taking driving lessons. I couldn't afford them every week, so I took them every other week.

Although the cost was £2.50 and I had a discount because I was a nursing auxiliary, it was still hard to find the money from £14.40 a week job. But, being a very determined person, I was going to give it my best shot.

It took me a while to get to grips with it, and I was very nervous.

I was terrible at the hill start. I kept rolling backwards, every time. So one day my instructor took me to Stockport, up a hill. I was terrified when I saw how steep it was. He told me I must listen to the engine – it talks to you, he said. Well, I started and stopped, started and stopped, until I reached the top of the hill and that was it. I learned my hill start and was proud of myself.

The first time I took my test my nerves got the better of me and it was a terrible, rainy day. I applied straight away to retake it. My instructor told me to do just what I was asked to do, but at the second attempt I failed again, this time on the three-point turn. I had touched the kerb. My instructor was disappointed and I got a lecture.

"Val, you should have passed this time, if hadn't lost your nerve. I told you, these guys are just there for you to demonstrate your driving skills. I know they are a bit off-putting, but just pretend he's not there.

Just do what he asks you to do!"

I reapplied again that same day. I felt tired when I took these tests because I had been working all night. But after dropping the children at school in the morning was the most convenient time for me to take it, and then I could grab a few hours sleep before rushing to pick them up.

We were saving like mad to buy our first car. A week before I took my third test, we bought a Ford Cortina for £450. I know it sounds crazy, but I was determined to pass my test at the third attempt. When the day came I was so much more confident and as far as I was concerned, the examiner wasn't there. He didn't need to ask me to do an emergency stop because a dog dashed out in front of me and I did one. He told me to stop and he asked me some questions.

Then he said these magic words, "Mrs Bartley, I'm pleased to tell you that you have passed your test."

I felt like hugging him, but I didn't. I simply thanked him as he handed me that special piece of paper.

My instructor was absolutely delighted. "I told you that you should have done it the second time!"

I rushed home, but I was too excited to sleep. When I told the children, they exploded with excitement. My car had been parked outside our house for over a week, waiting for me to take it for a spin. I couldn't wait for Eric to come home. When he came in I just said, "I did it."

He hugged me and gave me a steaming kiss. "Well done," he said. "Everything comes to those who wait and you have *waited* – you never take no for an answer! Will you be driving to work tonight?" he asked, with a twinkle in his eyes.

"Of course!" I said.

I reversed the car out of the cul-de-sac and they were all watching me. I told Eric I would ring him when I arrived, so that he could go to sleep knowing that I was okay on my first solo journey. A Cortina was quite a big car to drive, but I was fine and it was such a relief to be able to get home earlier to get the children ready for school.

We continue to walk to school to keep me awake. The modern phrase 'school run' was unheard of at that time. We took the kids to Southport, usually on Sundays when I wasn't on duty. They loved it, running around on the beach and making sandcastles.

We started stripping the living room and had never seen anything like it! There were six layers of paper on the wall.

The living room floor was shaking and the window frames were rotten. We put a sliding glass door between the living and the front room. At one point the house was like a building site: the kitchen had no sink – just a stand pipe. It was a blessing that the children were at school during the day. But we were deliriously happy and prepared to take the bull by the horns. It was our home and we looked upon it as a long-term project. This time we had professional decorators in to do the work.

The following summer we had a lovely holiday at Butlins. The children enjoyed themselves and of course, I drove our car. I felt so good zipping around in my car and it was big enough to carry our growing family.

We all have dreams tucked away in our minds. Eric had told me that when he arrived in England in April 1959, his plan was to stay for only five years. He had certainly never anticipated staying over fifty five years. Most people who emigrate here say that they have come for a certain length of time – maybe five or ten years.

We decided to buy a plot of land back home. Who could tell what tomorrow might bring? I wrote to my parents (Eric's parents had long gone) suggesting areas that we had in mind. We didn't want anywhere remote. My mother wrote back and told me about a piece of land at a place called Rosewell. We didn't have a clue where that was. But we went ahead with it.

PART FOUR
LIFE'S CHALLENGES

~ 1 ~

On 22nd March 1978, I was getting the tea ready; I remember it was a Wednesday. Eric had told me he was finishing work on the Thursday before Good Friday. Jokingly, I had said, "It's alright for some. I shall be working Wednesday, Thursday and Friday, and finishing Saturday morning." After tea, we kissed goodbye and I drove off to work. When I came home on the Thursday morning, I took Andrew to school and came back. It had been a very busy night at work, and I felt exhausted.

Andrew was more independent now, and he'd told me that morning that he would walk home with Phillip and Jean, Phillip's mother. I was awake when the doorbell rang. I came downstairs looking and feeling rough. The girls arrived home soon afterwards, chattering about Easter eggs and how many they were hoping to get.

"Your dad is late coming home," I said to Yvonne a bit later.

"He must have stopped for Easter eggs," she replied.

"I have bought some already," I told her. "Too many will make you fat." I carried on cooking the tea. Suddenly there was a knock on the door.

"Yvonne, see who is at the door, will you?"

As she opened it, I could see a man standing there. I was in my dressing gown and my hair in rollers. I looked like Hilda

Ogden on Coronation Street. I could hear him asking if Mr Bartley had come home yet.

"Mam!" Yvonne shouted. "It's a man asking for my dad."

I quickly wiped my hands and went to the door.

"Hello," he said. "Has Mr Bartley come home as yet?"

"No. He is usually home by now, but he might have stopped on the way." I noticed his both hands in his pockets and he looked quite nervous.

"Is something wrong?" I asked him.

He sort of shrugged his shoulders.

"Oh dear," he said. "Yes. Mr Bartley had an accident."

"Is he all right?" My stomach started churning.

"Yes… are you on the phone?"

"Yes."

"Well, could I use the phone?"

"Oh yes," I said," come in – it's in the front room."

Maureen and Andrew were in the living room. "What's wrong, Mam?" Maureen wanted to know, sliding the dividing door.

I told her that her dad had had an accident at work. I had no idea what the man was saying on the phone because my mind just went blank.

"Look," the man said, "You will have to come with me."

"Not like this," I said.

He looked at me. "Oh no. You get ready."

I rushed up the stairs. You never saw anyone get into their clothes faster. I came down looking decent and turned the stove off, then reached for my car keys.

"Oh no," he said. "I will take you."

As we approached his workplace, he said, "Oh, they are gone."

"Gone?" I asked. "Where?"

"To the hospital."

My heart was thumping in my chest and I began to cry as he turned the car around.

"He will be all right," he said. "Don't worry."

I wanted to scream, but nothing came out. It was as if I had lost my voice. It seemed to take ages to drive to Stockport Infirmary, but eventually we arrived at the A & E department. I could hear shouting and moaning and rushed up to the nearest nurse. "It's my husband," I said, "I can hear him screaming... he's had an accident."

"What is your husband's name?"

"Eric."

"Eric! Eric what?"

I was so confused. "Bartley," I said. "Eric Bartley. I want to see him".

"No, I'm sorry. You can't see him just now."

I had to be held back by Mr Buck, the man who had driven me, and two nurses. They managed to get me to sit down.

"Look," Mr Buck said, "He is going to be all right."

I was crying and shaking as he told me that he was one of the bosses and that Eric was a good worker. I knew he was just trying to make conversation to take my mind off what had happened.

Eventually, I was allowed to see him. He was drifting in and out of consciousness, screaming and shouting, "Catch it! Catch it!" I noticed his right hand was lying at the back of his head. It was so distressing to see him like that.

"Has he broken his arm?" I asked the doctor.

He shook his head. "I think he has dislocated his shoulder."

Eric was given a pain-killing injection which helped to calm him down, but what they didn't tell me at the time was that he had broken both his legs. The nurse found his wages in his pocket and gave it to me.

£44.37 – the grand sum for working one week three evenings overtime and Saturday morning.

He was taken down to X-ray when I was told that he had fractured both femurs. The right leg was a compound fracture and the bone was sticking through the skin. He had also fractured his skull and dislocated his right shoulder. I heard the doctor instructing the nurse to order four pints of blood and the operation would go ahead during the night.

Eric was himself a blood donor, and so was Yvonne when she was older. He will be getting back some of what he had given over the years what he had always considered a worthy cause.

Mr Buck had still to go home to his own family. As we left the ward he said he would take me home. I was very grateful for the offer, suddenly remembering that the children were on their own and I should be on duty. I thanked him for his kindness, but he just shrugged it off and drove off, into the night.

I stumbled in through the door and Maureen and Yvonne rushed down the stairs towards me. "Mam, is Daddy all right? What's wrong with him? Where is he?"

I told them that he was knocked down trying to cross the road. The girls burst into tears and I was crying too, though I wanted to be strong for them.

"You must be starving," I said, but they didn't answer and I knew they wouldn't want anything to eat after hearing the bad news. I didn't want any food either. I told them to go to bed, but I had great difficulty getting them to go back to their room. Andrew was fast asleep, so that was a blessing.

I didn't sleep a wink that night. I listened to the clock ticking, and tried counting one to a hundred, but it didn't work, even though I went over it thousands of times.

The next morning, I phoned work to tell them that my husband had a road traffic accident and was in a bad way. The lady I spoke to said she was very sorry to hear it, and would pass on the message to the night staff. I went next door to tell Betty the bad news. I was very distressed so she took me inside, sat me down and made me a cup of tea.

Then I phoned the hospital to hear how Eric was. I was told that he had been to theatre during the night.

"You can visit your husband at any time," the nurse said. I phoned a few friends to let them know what has happened, and the news just spread like wildfire.

I felt too nervous to drive the car, so I took the bus to the hospital. I took some clothes with me, but with both legs in traction and wires everywhere, he didn't need any. He was in his birthday suit, with a sheet to cover his modesty. Eric didn't know I was there. I moistened his flannel and gently wiped his face.

"How is he, Sister?" I asked at the office.

"Mrs Bartley, it is early days yet… you will just have to wait and see, I'm afraid."

I walked away slowly, her words ringing in my ears … *wait and see…* I could feel the tears threatening again, but they didn't come.

On the Saturday night I went to work and left the children on their own which I later realised was a silly thing to do. When I reported for duty, I was asked by the nursing officer how Eric was and who was minding the children. I was always told by my mother that honesty is the best policy, so I told her the truth.

"I left them on their own," I said. "They are quite good, they will be okay."

"Well," she replied, "We can't have you here working and your children left on their own. Anything could happen, and you would never forgive yourself. Apart from that, we would be in the wrong for allowing you to do it. It was fine when your husband was there but now he isn't… you have to go home and see to your family. When things are sorted out, if there is a vacancy, you can come back, but that is going to be a long time…"

As I walked across the car park it suddenly hit me. I had almost lost my husband, and now I had lost my job. I drove home, in a daze. There was not a sound. I dropped my handbag on the floor and slowly climbed the stairs. Quietly opening Andrew's bedroom door, I saw that he was asleep with his teddy bear in his arms. I thought how like his father he looked. I looked into the girls' room and they, too, were sound asleep. Maureen's *Jackie* magazine was lying next to her, and Yvonne had her toy frog beside her. The tears rolled down as I looked on them.

I asked myself, how could I manage? But at the time, I thought that I must carry on working. How was I going to pay the bills? Our house would have to go. I couldn't bear the thought of that, after going through so much to get it. It was incredible what was going through my mind. I took Eric's sick note to the benefits office and explained that I was no longer working. Arrangements were made for me to have a home visit.

The questions were designed to dig deep into people's private lives. It was only one thing left to ask me – how many times did my husband make love to me? Eric's sickness benefit was paid to me. After two weeks, I began to have hopes that he might pull through.

The children were afraid to visit their father. Then one day they decided that they wanted to visit him. They were alarmed by all the clinical surroundings, but glad to see him and their visit lifted his spirit.

The doctor told me that Eric's fractures were very bad. He explained they were not what they called clean fractures, and showed me the X-rays. I became frantic when I saw that there were pieces of bone missing. The bones were not setting, and he said the only way he would stand a chance of walking again would to insert steel rods in both femurs. He told me quite bluntly that his legs might eventually have to be amputated if this was not done.

I signed the forms and they went ahead with the operations. Eric was very poorly and was put into a side room. I thought to myself, that's it. He is going to die and leave me a widow with three children. I stood by his bed with cot sides raised and wiped his face. There was nothing else I could do for him... except pray. I prayed to God in silence, and then aloud. After about a month, he turned the corner and began his slow recovery.

Eric remained in hospital for five months before he was allowed home. Unable to walk, there was no way he could get upstairs, so I bought a bed-settee and he slept in the living room.

An ambulance picked him up three times a week to take him to Manchester Royal Infirmary for physiotherapy. I had to bed-bath him as well as deal with all his toilet needs: it wasn't pleasant for either of us. I had to position the two long callipers that reached his groin, before putting his pants on. Every day was a struggle and I felt worn out. It was a very difficult time in our marriage, when the vows taken before God at the altar really came into perspective. For better, for worse; for richer, for poorer; in sickness and in health... I was thirty-five years old and the going was tough, but I was doing my best to keep those vows.

Sometimes, I snuggled up beside him with my heart hammering and he had a twinkle in his eye. I often kissed him goodnight before going up to bed burning with passion as well as with rage at what had happened to us.

I prayed to God to heal his broken body and let him walk again. Every movement made the rods and screws rattle in his legs and that was a turn-off, as we didn't want to do any more damage.

He was often in pain when he returned from physiotherapy and he was very stroppy with me and the children. He was very frustrated and it was perfectly understandable. One of the children bought him a special mug. Printed across it was *DADDY CAN RUN THE FASTEST!* They thought he would see the funny side of it but he didn't, and took a dislike to it. He told me not to give him his tea in it.

One day, I made him a cup of tea and gave him in the mug without thinking. To my shock and horror, he threw it at me. I was lucky that the tea didn't scald me. I was very upset with him and told him he would have to control his temper, I was doing my best, and I was always there as if I were his slave. I threatened to walk out if he ever did it again. I was frantic with worry and furious at the same time. He took his time apologising, but he did say he was sorry. I threw the mug in the bin and neither of us said a word about it again, but I was a bit wary when I gave him a hot drink, especially when he had been for physio.

After many months of intensive physiotherapy, they told me to try and get him up the stairs at home. I was frightened as our stairs were very steep. However, I eventually managed to get him up there. The girls helped me get him in and out of the bath, but it was worth it. He was like a hippo having a long, wallow! That night he slept in his own bed for the first time in seven months.

It was a blessing to have him beside me again after all that time, and we managed to be intimate for the first time since the accident. It is said that what you don't have you don't miss. Of course I *did* miss it, but I didn't dwell on it. I'm speaking for myself now; perhaps other women wouldn't feel the same, or would deal with things differently. We all own the same bits and pieces, but we don't all use our machinery in the same way.

It's funny what can turn you off, and those rods were not the best things to keep me in the mood for love. Every time his body moved, those bloody rods would start squeaking. I would be thinking 'will he take me to the heights...?' It wasn't easy with that racket going on, and I never got used to it although it was an extra bit of excitement.

The doctors took the nails out after two years, but the plates will be there for the rest of his life. We began to experiment with different positions and so I became the stallion under the sheets because I didn't want him to dislodge anything. We both tried hard to press the right buttons to ignite the fire for each other.

Eric was a very sexy man. He always loved sex and when I wasn't in the mood (and I know a lot of women will relate to that), he would say he couldn't understand why I didn't want it, or feel like it. He never seemed to understand that I wasn't a machine, or that I just needed him to talk. Other times I wanted to be taken on a slow journey... as I was just too damned tired.

Anyway, sex was never a problem for us, and I realised that I was lucky when some women had to rub their men with antifreeze to get them going. We used to let ourselves go wild before he had this terrible accident. When Andrew was four years old, Eric had the snip, so we let ourselves go without any worries about pregnancy. We took our passion to new heights.

Eventually, I helped him to walk again, after two years. It was like teaching a child – letting go of his hands and encouraging him to take a step, I could see the fear on his face and he begged me to keep hold of his hands. It was hard, but I had to let go, so that he would build up some confidence, and after a while he was able to walk with two crutches and me by his side. It was a slow process and he walked with a terrible limp because of the loss of bone from his right leg which was shorter than the left, so his shoe had to be built up.

But you know what? He is alive and our children still have their father. It could have been worse and I thanked God for saving his life.

Even though he couldn't play football with Andrew, he played cards and dominoes with him. Eric adored his son and he had believed right from the start that the baby would be a boy. Amazing.

However, he did become depressed. When he remembered how active he was before his accident and how disabled he was now, it hit him hard. He felt less of a man because he couldn't work to provide for his family. It broke his heart and there were many times when he cried, but he was careful never to let the children see him.

Eric has not worked since he was fifty-eight years old and I know that it hurt his pride very much. So I became wife and husband; mother and father. I told him not to worry about it too much. But of course, he did. I think that if something similar had happened to me, he would have done the same for me, and been *my* rock.

I knew that our marriage was solid as a rock, because we had been through so much. I had the sense to know that marriage was a partnership and we had to work at things instead of running away from them. When we conquer these difficulties, we come out at the other end stronger people.

Eric kept saying to me that he would like to go to Jamaica and spend some time with my parents. He told me that he felt he wanted a long break after the terrible trauma he had been through. He wanted to grab the second chance in life that God had given him. I was all for it. The only problem we faced was money. I managed to save enough money for his fare. He was still not strong on his legs and had to walk with two sticks, but he went in March 1981 and spent three months there. I even managed to send the last £100 that was required to pay off the piece of land.

However, our mother had been unwell for some time because she suffered with high blood pressure. Even before I left home, the doctor had told her to eat lots of vegetables, but she loved her food and said she was not going to die looking like skin and bone.

Well, I am sure nobody anticipated what was about to happen. A few weeks after Eric arrived, our mother had a stroke. Eric said my father was like a lost sheep. She was everything to him and I knew he would find it very difficult to cope without her. She was at Spanish Town Hospital. My sister Evelyn was living in Kingston, so she was nearer and she used to take clean sheets to put on her bed. This is nothing unusual in a third world country where people have to do what they can for their relatives.

Poor Eric never got the peace and tranquillity that he felt he needed. His time to return was getting nearer but he was worried about my mother's condition and not being there to support my father. Mamma told him that she didn't think she would live to see him again. His answer was, "Well, did you know if *I* would live to visit you all when I was at death's door?"

The next day he flew back to Manchester. The children and I was glad to see him and he looked so much better with his three months tan. It was then that I realised how gravely ill my mother was and I would have to brace myself for the worst. I was still working hard on my rented industrial sewing machine – sometimes until ten at nights. Eric would often say to me, "Valerie, stop now. Switch off the machine and have a rest." I was trying my best to earn a bit extra as I was worried I wouldn't be able to find any money if my mother died.

~ 2 ~

Every time the phone rang, I felt nervous. Then, one night, 23rd October 1981, my sister Marjorie rang from Canada.

"Valerie," she said. "How is everyone?"

I said we were okay, well, just about.

She said, "Are you sitting down?"

"Yes."

"Well then," she said, "I have just had a phone call from Evelyn in Kingston... and Mamma has died."

I couldn't take it in and began to cry. "I don't have the money for the fare to go to her funeral," I said.

"If I couldn't go to my mother's funeral, I would feel really bad."

When I heard her say that, my heart lurched.

"We are all going," she said.

She meant herself and her husband and four children, and our Aunt Bertha's son, Robert. Marjorie said, "I will book the ticket for you and you can pick it up at the travel agent."

I was very distraught. We had just £150 to our name, but the fare was £650, and that was from Gatwick. My best friend Elvie lent me thirty pounds. I was surprised because I hadn't asked her to lend it me, but I was so grateful to have such a friend. She wasn't in any better position than I was, having four children of similar age to ours. She worked at the same hospital where I had worked until Eric's accident.

Elvie will always be special among the friends I have known and I will always remember the kindness she showed to me and I wish her all life's best, for she is a friend I treasure every day of my life. Peace and love, my sister; you are always there for me and I hope you can say the same of me.

The first time Elvie and I met was in the nurse's changing room in 1973. We became firm friends and have since shared each other's problems, watched our children grow up, and now our grandchildren. I know that we will continue to be more than sisters until the roll-call up yonder. I could go on for ever, but I will leave it here – I don't want to turn her face beetroot with embarrassment!

I loaned £500 from the bank, using the house as security.

When I had heard of my mother's death, Eric's nephew, Frank, was visiting from London. He suggested that I get the 5.00 pm coach to London and stay at his flat overnight. I didn't sleep that night, as I was in a terrible state.

I had to get a taxi to the underground station and then get the tube to Gatwick Airport. I only had the bare necessities in my suitcase because I was not supposed to lift anything heavy. I had had a major operation, a hysterectomy, six weeks earlier. The case didn't have wheels to pull along then, and it was a struggle to get to the Underground. Finally I reached the check-in desk at the airport. My case didn't weight 20lbs.

"Madam," said the lady, "you are allowed 44lbs."

"Yes, I know, but I have to travel light because I cannot lift the weight."

She nodded, stuck a label on my featherweight case and it was sent twirling down the conveyor belt. I felt as if I was walking about blindfolded. Everything seemed to be dark and blurred. The waiting seemed like an eternity because I had reached the airport quite early. Finally, we boarded this massive British Airways jumbo jet. No wonder we had to cough up so much cash.

The plane was soon miles up in the sky with its cargo of humans and baggage. There was nothing to see but blue sky and the cloud beneath us. The food was good, but when I cut into the juicy steak it began to bleed. I don't like rare meat, so I begrudgingly pushed it aside, feeling a little cheated. I could have as many miniature drinks as I liked. So I knocked a few of those back to help numb the pain. The discomfort of my scar was giving me hell, sitting on a ten-hour flight. I was consumed with grief. Mamma was dead, I kept thinking. No more Mamma…

The couple sitting next to me were quite talkative; they were excited about their first visit and included me in their conversation, so I tried to show an interest, not wanting to impose my sadness on them.

On and on we flew. Then, at last, the captain's voice told us he was preparing to land.

"… fasten your seatbelts, please… local time is 2.50 PM we hope you have enjoyed your flight…" As we descended from the sky I closed my eyes and prayed for a safe landing. When we touched down with hardly a bump there was a burst of applause.

I came down the aircraft steps, and a blast of heat suddenly hit me. Living in Manchester had not completely erased my memories of the hot climate, but I had become accustomed to cool, damp English weather. I walked the long passage through Customs and Passport Control patting my face.

Finally, I came through Immigration and my brother Samuel and father was waiting for me. It was a very emotional reunion. My father flung his arms around me and we held each other and cried. Then, letting go of me, he held me at arm's length and looked into my eyes.

"Valerie, no more Elsaida," he whispered. "She's gone. I don't know what I will do without her. She was my everything."

"I know, Papa," I whispered back. "I know."

It wasn't dark when we set off from the airport. I sat gazing out of the car window as my brother Samuel negotiated the crowded streets. Papa told me that the rest of the family hadn't wanted him to come and meet me. But he wanted to come.

"The drive might do you a world of good, Papa," I told him.

"Yes," he said. "I think so too."

Apart from the occasional comment, the rest of the journey was made in silence. We were all too subdued to speak.

It was dark when we reached home, and as we walked down Old Walk Lane to our house, it reminded me so much of my childhood days. I found myself literally feeling my way along the ground with my feet as it was pitch- black. My eyes were not used to that sort of darkness any more. People were on the veranda waiting for us to arrive and I had a warm welcome. They were glad that I could come.

I could not remember all the people, but this older lady clasped my hand and to my surprise it was my Grand Aunt Martha. We hadn't seen each other since I went away, so it was a joyful moment. Oh, I used to have such fun when I visited her in Dry Hill. I could pick up as many coffee beans off the ground – we called it rat cut – I would sell it to the shop and make some money for myself.

They all started reminiscing about bygone days and I did enjoy it for a while. It took our minds off the reason we were all there. But I was very tired and jet-lagged so I asked if I could lie down for a while. I climbed into my mother's bed and dozed off while the others carried on with their all-night wake. I got up later in the night and went back onto the verandah because they were singing old songs and some of the men were playing dominoes.

When I went back to lie down, the bed was laden with bodies. I found a little spot on the bed to park, knowing I wouldn't sleep again. As I sat, I suddenly heard a soft, child-like voice calling, "May... Mae... Mae..." At first I thought it must be a cat, but after the second "Mae," I experienced a strange feeling and felt afraid. I got up and went back out onto the verandah. I didn't tell a soul. I just knew that it was my mother calling "Mae... Mae." It was my second name. I have only ever experienced something like that once before – and again, I was visiting my parents at the same house.

Five years earlier, I was sitting at the dining table with my brother Samuel and my mother. Papa wasn't home yet. I was facing the window and I saw this person walk past the window towards the back door and I could swear it was my father. But there was no sign of him. As I opened my mouth to say what I had seen, Samuel said, "Me see man." It was quite a while before Papa came home, and when I told him, he laughed and said, "Oh, it must have been my guardian angel."

The next day, Marjorie, Robert and I decided to go to the undertaker's in Spanish Town. We just wanted to see Mamma; not that we didn't believe she had gone, but Robert wanted to see the coffin that Icis chose for her. He said he didn't want his aunt to get less than his mother, Aunt Bertha. Icis was livid and kicked up a fuss about it.

"Where were you all when she was sick?" she asked angrily.

"Thousands of miles away, and now you all come throwing your weight about!"

I kept my trap shut because I didn't have any money to change what she had chosen, anyway. Eventually they managed to assure her that what ever she chose would be fine. She was like a wild cat, very agitated and aggressive. I just thought to myself that she was still a bully, even after all these years.

However, we set off to Spanish Town early the next morning. When we reached the undertaker's I asked the lady if we could see our mother.

"Who is the lady?" she asked.

"Elsaida Hancel."

"Can you take it?" she asked, looking at me intently.

I didn't understand.

"Look, when I open the door, there will be fourteen of them in there."

We were all shocked and looked at each other with alarm. "No."

I thought she could just draw Mamma out on her own. It would be bad enough to see our own mother lying there lifeless, but thirteen others as well would be too much. We started crying. We had come all this way and didn't get to see her. Anyway, we would be back in two days to take her home for the funeral.

The day we arrived to bring Mamma home, I gently pulled back the sheet from her face and gazed at her. Her life had been very hard and she had grown weary, but she looked peaceful in death. She had always loved perfume, so Marjorie sprayed all most a bottle over her. We stood, with our thoughts, and said a silent prayer. Then we walked out into the blistering heat to see her being put into the hearse for the journey home.

Family and friends met at the Church of God, where she worshipped. As the family walked in behind the coffin, I could not see clearly. My vision was blurred from the tears.

Samuel sat next to me. When the hymn *Rock of ages cleft for me* began, he was still sitting down. I nudged him to get up and he stuttered, "I... I can't sta... stand up." He was completely overcome with grief, as the reality of it all hit him. He used to give his parents a lot of grief. Now he realised what he had done but it was too late. The service was very moving, but there were some amusing memories told about her which provided a lighter side to the occasion.

After the service we all walked back to Old Walk Lane. As we came into the yard, Icis started screaming that she hadn't gone to the church because she preferred to stay with Grand Aunt Martha and watch the house. She thought some lowlife might break in and have a feast on the foreign artifacts. Really? Anyway, by the time the crowd reached the yard she was shouting out, "Mamma! Papa!" with ear-piercing screams.

Everyone gathered around the grave in the garden, singing, and still she made sure she was the centre of attention. She was calling out our names now. "Valerie! Marjorie! Evelyn," and pushing past people to get to the front of the grave. When they lowered the coffin into the vault, saying 'ashes to ashes' and we threw a handful of soil onto it, she shouted out, "No dust to dust, please!" She wanted the ceremony to be in her religion, Jehovah's Witness. Our mother had not been a Jehovah's Witness, and she upset a lot of people with her rantings. She had to be restrained as the ropes were removed and Mamma finally laid to rest in the vault. As we sang, Dudley and Samuel put the cover on the vault and sealed it. Samuel used his fingers to write her name, date of birth and age.

When the ceremony was over we had something to eat and drink.

A ram goat had been killed and the meat was curried with rice and boiled green bananas. The head, feet and testicles were cooked with vegetables and made a lovely soup called Mannish Water (referring to the private parts of the goat, and also the soup is said to be invigorating for men). To drink, there was white rum, red stripe beer, dragon stout, and lemonade made with fresh limes, sugar and ice.

Finally, when the eating and drinking was over, the crowd gradually dispersed, leaving us sitting on the verandah. Icis had calmed down, but there was always tension when she was around. Evelyn was the first to leave, to go back to her nursing job in Kingston. Then Marjorie and her family flew back to Canada.

One night, I was sitting on the verandah with my father and he said, "Valerie, I wish I could see your mother. I wonder what she looks like now?"

"Papa!" I said, shocked. "Why would you want to see her now after she has been buried for five days? It would not be a lovely sight. Please try to remember her lying in peace in the church. That's your last memory of her." Tears filled his eyes. "Papa," I continued. "Think of all the hard times you came through together and the joys you both shared, especially when a new child was added to our family. I know that you had been married for thirty-nine years, and that's a lifetime, but your grieving will take a long time... there is no time limit on how long it lasts, it may be forever. But remember that we are all grieving as well, so just try and go with the flow."

My father broke down as we talked and my own stomach was turning as I cried inside, but I tried to be strong to talk to him. He wasn't going to be left on his own because his youngest son, Clement, still lived at home, and that was a blessing.

I decided to go to Kingston and spend my last two days with Evelyn. She lived not far from the airport, which was handy. We tried to chill a bit, after all the strain of the funeral.

I flew back to the UK with all sorts of thoughts bubbling in my head. I felt totally grief stricken. Eric and the children were relieved to have me safely back. I didn't know that it would hurt so much. It carried on for about two years, and then one morning, I woke up and felt that it didn't hurt *quite* so much. I still think of my mother every day, but the pain has subsided now.

The children were asking me questions and I tried to paint a picture for them so that they could imagine how it was. I told Eric that I felt like a ship that had lost its sail. "What is there to go home for, now? Mamma is not there. It won't be the same."

In a lot of ways, the death of my mother clouded our plans to return permanently to Jamaica. I felt there was no point, but my husband had made up his mind that he really wanted to go, so I went along with it for his sake. I imagine what it would be like to return to our family home and see her grave again. No more Mamma to give me the best of what she had saved for me – the biggest orange, or hand of ripe bananas. I really dreaded it.

~ 3 ~

On 4th June 1984 we sold our house after having it on the market for a year. Our daughters Maureen and Yvonne had moved to Springfield and Crumpsall Hospital to train as nurses. Maureen was studying for her SRN and Yvonne was doing RMN in psychiatry. Eric, Andrew and I moved into a rented one-bedroom. Most of our possessions were packed and shipped to Jamaica.

We stayed in the cramped room for a few weeks, until we finalised our arrangements. Andrew didn't want to come with us. He was fourteen years old and didn't want to leave his friends. However, we could not just leave him, he was still a child. But he was at the age when he rebelled about most things anyway.

Eventually we flew to Toronto, Marjorie's home, and spent two weeks sightseeing, taking in the CN Tower and Niagara Falls. Marjorie took us to visit some of our cousins, Aunt Bertha's children. She also held a send-off party for us.

We flew out on 17th September 1984. It had been twenty-five years since Eric left, and twenty-three for me. We knew there was some political unrest during the run-up to the election. I didn't really feel ready to go home to Jamaica yet, but I gave in to Eric because he wanted to go, after all the trauma and pain of his accident.

I had my fortieth birthday a few weeks after we arrived there. It was just another day as we were kept busy sorting things out. The house that we had been building for five years was still not finished. It was still without doors or windows and the kitchen had to be fitted out, so I was rushing about like a robot.

My brother Dudley had a one-bedroom house next to our land. He mostly stayed there to keep an eye on his goats, which were penned at night. He said we could use it sometimes to sleep in. It was rough and ready, more like a storage room, and I was petrified in case there were scorpions in it. I found it impossible to relax and go to sleep. At that time we were living rough and primitive.

When the windows and doors were fitted, I went to Kingston wharf with Dudley to collect our belongings. There were lots of processes I had to go through before I could claim our property, and I also had to pay charges. I didn't expect that, as I'd had to pay a lot already to ship them out.

Eventually, we arrived back at Rosewell in the late afternoon.

The huge cartons were unloaded and placed in their respective rooms. I was very tired, but also I felt that as time passed, we would get a lovely home together.

However, we had a problem with a young man, Boot, who was a nutcase, whose mother, Miss Hilda, lived the other side of us. What we didn't know was that since the roof had been put on, he had been sleeping in our house. When we went in, we found a small pile of clothes on the floor in one of the bedrooms and some Ganja weed that he smoked. Eric told him that he couldn't sleep there anymore. But Boot went ballistic. He told Eric that it was his house. He had built it, he said. When I heard this, I could feel my blood pressure rising. We had a lot of problems with him. When I remembered how I had sat all day sewing skirts and jean-pockets until late at night, and now this low-life was telling us to our faces that he built the house, I had to hold myself back from losing my rag, as it hurt like hell.

One Sunday Eric went to church and I stayed at home to keep an eye on things. There was a huge ackee tree on our land and it was laden with fruits. When they are ripe, they burst open with three black seeds attached to the cheese coloured flesh. Ackee is cooked with salted cod fish. It's the national dish of Jamaica. By adding onions, tomatoes, sweet and hot peppers, thyme, etc. you can eat it with anything and I guarantee you will be licking your fingers.

Anyway, I was watching them open one by one, but I was waiting until I could pick at least six to make this dish. I asked Mr Bob, an old man who came to visit Miss Hilda, if he could get me a long stick to pick them with. I went armed with the stick and started to reach for the ackees, when Boot suddenly appeared and began to throw stones at me.

"That's Ma Hilda's ackee tree!" he shouted, pelting me with loose rocks. "You are not to pick them!"

I wanted to retaliate, but I felt that the best thing was to drop the stick, and run inside. I was fuming, but I knew I had to retreat, because if one of the stones hit me I would be in a mess. That day, I told myself that it wasn't going to work out. We didn't need that kind of hassle. I made up my mind to go to the police and report him, because his behaviour was unacceptable. The guy seemed to have a mental problem, and he was always smoking Ganja, so he was probably stoned out of his mind. Miss Hilda told him to stop interfering with us, but her scolding fell on deaf ears.

When Eric came back and I told him what had happened, he was furious. He called on Boot's mother to discuss the problem.

"Mr Bartley," she said. "I tell him till I'm sick and tired, not to go over to your place and not to sleep in your house. I tell him long before you and your wife came. He is twenty-nine year old and ever since he was in his teens, he has given me nothing but trouble, so anything he gets now will be his own fault. All he does is walk around in his torn up trousers, no shoes on his feet, and no shirt; his two eyes, red in his head like blood, and his teeth are rotten."

Eric had sympathy for Miss Hilda, but told her that we had no option but to report him to the police, and the next day I went to the police station and made a statement, and they brought me back to Rosewell in their jeep.

It wasn't long before he was found and arrested. It was hot and I was sitting on my verandah having a cool drink when Miss Hilda appeared on her verandah.

"It's you that brought the police to arrest Boot!" she screamed.

Suddenly, she had changed her tune about him getting what he deserved. I casually put my feet up on the other chair and sipped my cool drink, taking no notice of her. She carried on ranting for a while. Miss Hilda mostly sat out on her verandah, with a cigar propped up in her mouth and a red scarf tied around her head. She lived in a single bedroom house with her two grandsons, Nicky and Pancho, her daughter Coral and her baby. Maybe that was why Boot had started sleeping in our house.

One night, after the doors and windows had been fitted, we suddenly heard the sound of keys rattling. Boot was released and trying to open the door to get in. I was beside myself. It really scared me.

Anyway, we reported him to the police and after a few days they came and took him away. We never saw him again.

My father had bought our land from Dudley's wife, Miss Mack. As soon as she heard he was looking for a plot to buy, she told him she would sell him a piece of hers. She was nicknamed the Wicked Witch.

Eric and I wanted to know why it was taking so long to obtain the title deeds to the land. For five years had she kept telling us that it was being sorted out, and we suspected that something didn't add up. Even my brother was being shifty. We wanted to get to the bottom of it.

Then came the breaking point. Miss Mack had two sons of her own, who weren't her husband's. Her husband died. She had mistreated him when he was ill and couldn't wait to inherit his land and stock. She was a lot older than Dudley and definitely wore the trousers.

It transpired that she had borrowed money from the bank using the original title, which included our house and land – the most valuable asset of all. When she defaulted, her sons told us that Dudley had to sell his cows to pay the bailiffs. It was a huge shock when we discovered the truth, and there was an almighty bust up with her and Dudley. I can see her now in my mind's eye, pushing out her double H breasts and flapping her mouth full of gold teeth. With that and her crimson frock she looked like a blazing bonfire.

Dudley had the cheek to tell me that the way I was behaving would not help the situation! We soon realised whose side he was on, and that he dared not go against mighty mouth Miss Mack. Eric and I were furious. We had to go to the title office and pay to get it all sorted out, but it was worth it. We could so easily have lost all that we had worked so hard for.

Most Monday mornings after we arrived, Wayne, Dudley's son, came with a message from Miss Mack. 'Oh, Miss Mack say she don't have enough money to pay my bus fare,' or 'She only have a twenty dollar note and do you have any smaller notes?' So I would give Wayne a ten dollar note. But I never got it back and, like a fool, I kept giving it to him because he was my nephew. After a while I woke up and realised that they were using me. How had they managed before we came? I was getting really annoyed with this hard-faced woman. She had no manners and no shame, always borrowing this and that, and no intention of giving it back.

Before we had the electricity connected I asked her if she could keep some meat in her fridge for me. When I went to fetch it for our Sunday dinner it was gone. I couldn't believe it. She started to tell me some cock and bull story about cooking it for Dudley.

"Oh, did you?" I said. "And you didn't give any to Tuggy, Uga and Wayne then?" She just stared at me with her cold eyes. I was so vexed I had to stop myself from hitting her.

How wrong I was to think that we would be happy back in Jamaica. To be honest about it, I knew before we had the doors and windows fixed that it wasn't going to work out. I didn't like what I was seeing and hearing. It was a different world to me now. I couldn't stand the laid back attitude of some people, as if they were doing me a favour by letting me speak to them. We had no lights in the house, just oil lamps. It was like going back to my childhood again.

~ 4 ~

The country seemed to run on corruption. You could get anything if you knew people in high places and were prepared to grease their palms. It made me angry and I stood fast and determine that I would not go down that road whatever happened. But of course everything took me twice as long to sort out. There were rogues who offered to fix us up with electricity from the pole outside our house, but we declined, preferring to wait and go through the proper channels.

With no power, we had no television or radio news, but travelling in a minibus packed like sardines, I couldn't help hearing what people were talking about. Some of the stories I heard were scary and I thought they must be exaggerated. Then eventually the electricity was connected and we were able to watch television. I became more uneasy as each day passed. Every day someone was murdered as there was shooting after shooting. Armed robbers were everywhere, and people like us were prime targets. We were called English, or foreigners. My nephew Wayne was nine years old and one day he said to me, "Auntie Mae, you live in this crisp house and they will think you have bags of money. If you lived in a little shack, they might not bother you."

The house was painted white inside and outside and it glistened in the sun. We were waiting to have the washing machine plumbed in and I was doing the washing by hand, just the way it was before I came to England. It seemed strange to be doing this now, but I had no choice. The water pressure was very low, there were times when no water came through the pipes at all. It was very frustrating. I had to walk down the road to a stand pipe and carry some water back on my head. I was gutted to think I was back in the hard old routine of twenty-three years ago.

We took Andrew to stay with his grandfather for a while, but it was not much better in Bois Content, and soon afterwards Eric and I made the decision to send him back to England. He was not happy in Jamaica and missed all his friends and the way of life he was used to. I had a feeling that it was only a matter of time before we would be following him, especially if we were to experience the same traumas that our neighbours had been through, because of the ruthless thugs that seemed to be taking hold of this island.

There was a shopkeeper down the road who kept a rum bar. She was robbed and shot but she survived. A woman who lived just a few houses away from us was also robbed. She jumped through a window and broke both her arms. She was robbed of her hi-fi equipment. I was worried sick by it all and could not sleep at night. One evening Eric and I were talking over the fence to Dudley about the situation. I told him we felt threatened by what was going on.

Dudley said, "Sister, all you have to do is pray to God to guide and protect you."

I told him that I was going to sell the house and return to England to look after Andrew.

He roared with laughter and said, "Sis, you only just come and you are talking about going back."

"I'm not used to this life," I told him. "When I was a child there was nothing like this."

"Well, but we didn't have anything to nick then." he said.

I said. "Greed has taken over the world." We chatted about this and that until the sun began to sink. Eric and I sat on the verandah discussing our plight. I felt very uneasy and couldn't help thinking we would be their next target.

"There's no way we are going to escape being robbed," I told Eric. "We could even be killed in this epidemic of robbery and shooting that is going on all over the island."

Later, when we were about to lock up, I suggested that we should not keep our few US dollars in the house anymore. We should hide the money outside under some stones where they would not think of looking.

"Let's put it under the washing machine," Eric said.

I thought not. "They just got to move it and they will be laughing!" But I gave in, reluctantly, and he stuffed it under the washing machine.

I always kept $2,500 Jamaican dollars in the bedside cabinet on my side of the bed. I thought if the worst came to the worst and we were held up, I could give them that and tell them it was all we had. Eric put some empty bottles behind the kitchen door so that we should hear if anyone came in there. Miss Hilda's dogs, Sally and Tug, came to us for food and felt so at home that they slept on our veranda at night. They were our night watchmen. Little did we know that in just a few hours we would be begging for our lives.

As dusk gave way to a black night, all seemed normal and calm. The fireflies were zooming around, crickets and toads were all in good voice, and the sky was ablaze with stars. But we were feeling worried and unsettled without Andrew. However, that night my body must have been desperate for a good rest, because I fell into a deep sleep. Eric said the dogs began to bark and woke him up, but I didn't hear a thing until he began to shake me.

"Valerie, wake up! Wake up! Valerie, the gunmen are breaking in!"

When I heard the word *gunmen* I sprang up in the bed and listened. I could hear the bottles rattling behind the kitchen door. Then my instinct took me over and I started to cough and splutter. I splashed some TCP over my body.

"Your chest always bothers you at night, doesn't it?" Eric said. "Yes. I don't know why."

We were making believe that we hadn't heard the vile predators invading our house.

"Shall I go to the bathroom for some water for you?"

"No, don't. I shall be all right in a minute." I could imagine him being blown to bits as he opened the bedroom door. But Eric was a determined man, especially in his own house and as he opened the door, I heard a threatening voice, "Get back! Get back inside!"

Eric didn't scream and neither did I. He was pushed into the bedroom, walking backwards like a land crab and I was bracing myself against the headboard. There were two men with masks over their faces and both were brandishing guns. One of the men told Eric to get back into bed, which he did. Then the same man covered us with the sheet and the other man stood at the bedroom door with a rifle, saying nothing.

The darker skinned man kept demanding, "Where is the money? Where is the jewellery? A long time you go away, don't tell me you have no money!"

He came back to the bed and pulled the sheet off and then tried to yank my wedding ring off my finger. At the first tug, I heard the joint make a cracking sound. I said to him, "Hold on man, let me take it off, I will give you the rings." He didn't realise that I had three rings on my finger, so when I pulled the rings off I slipped my diamond solitaire off into the bed and gave him my wedding and eternity rings. He took Eric's wedding ring as well. I told them not to shoot us, just take anything they want and go.

"Shut up!" he pointed the gun at my ear. "You talk too much."

"This is it," I thought. He is going to blow my brains out now." I looked like Hilda Ogden with my hair in rollers and he was poking them with the gun. Then he started going through our clothes in the wardrobe. When he found the money in the bedside cupboard, the cheeky bastard said, "Only this little money you have?"

I told him we didn't have any more.

"A-you me a deal with, because a-you in control. A-who this old man?"

I said, "he's my husband. Please don't shout at us, just take what you want and go."

"Me said shut up, you talk too much."

By now we could hear all sorts of activity in the other rooms.

Eric held my hand tightly. It felt as if we were passing a current to each other in support. If the robbers had shot us, we would have been discovered holding hands in death. We had been made to lie on our stomachs, but I carefully lifted the sheet to see what they were doing.

Eric never spoke. It was as if he were struck dumb.

Anyway, I remembered reading an article about being in this kind of situation. The advice was to try and talk to your capturers, soften them up, and keep some sort of dialogue going. So that was what I did for a while, but I think it only exacerbated the situation because the one who kept talking told me again to "shut up you fucking mouth." Our bed had four storage drawers and they were removing the contents. I was so relieved that Andrew wasn't with us. He wouldn't have known how to react to monsters ransacking his bedroom and the bad tempered one would have probably shot him. It was awful, staring death in the face like that. Their language was obscene and I just wanted them to get out, but our ordeal lasted at least an hour because I heard the grandfather clock strike midnight, and then one o'clock.

Eventually, the one guarding the bedroom door pointed the M16 rifle at us, shouting and swearing, saying: "some of you have to fucking die for us to live." Eric and I held on to each other more tightly. I closed my eyes, waiting for the moment. "This is it," I thought. Then I heard a stampede of footsteps. They faded quickly into the distance and then all was silent.

We lay there, clutching each other's hands, paralysed with terror and soaking in sweat. I'm not ashamed to say that I wet myself, I really thought we were going to die. My pretty M&S nightdress was soaking wet. After a while, Eric began to scream for help at the top of his voice. I could not move; the shock had turned me to stone.

"Dudley! Help! Dudley, the gunmen have been here!" Eric kept shouting and eventually Dudley came over from his house. He said when he heard the word gunmen he grabbed his pants and jumped into it, but they were back to front so he had to start again. He told Eric to get dressed and he took him to May Pen police station. I was left sitting on the veranda, shocked and in a daze.

Dudley and Eric returned in the early morning. I was still sitting where they had left me. I got dressed. The sun was beginning to peep up in the sky. Before long, the yard and verandah were full of people from the surrounding area, asking us questions about the incident.

"What did they look like?"

"Did they rape you?" one woman asked.

"No, they didn't, thank God," I said, shuddering at the thought.

"Well, lady, you are lucky, because what they do to some women is rape them and make their husband watch, then ask him if he can do it as good. So you are very lucky. God was on your side!"

I was shocked to hear all these revolting things. Someone told us that they found a shoe and a bike that had been thrown in the bushes.

People kept coming and they all sat on the white veranda ledges around the house. The walls soon became dirty, but we were not bothered about it. We were touched to think that so many people had taken the trouble to come and witness what had happened to us. They all had horror stories to tell about what had happened to people they knew. Some were ordinary Jamaicans, but most had recently returned from abroad, like ourselves.

We waited all day for the police to turn up. By five o'clock I'd had enough. I walked to the main road and caught a minibus to May Pen police station. When I arrived and complained that nobody had come to see us yet, they said they would be there soon. They didn't seem bothered and their attitude annoyed me. It was all a big joke to them. I told them that I wasn't leaving until they agreed to come and investigate. They talked between themselves and eventually agreed to come, and I got a lift back with them.

One of them had a machine gun with the bullet string on it. He told Eric: "It's one of these you need, Daddy!" We were shocked and appalled. It wasn't funny. I challenged them, saying they didn't respond quickly because they were giving the thugs time to hide their loot. I was so angry, I didn't even care if they threatened to kill us and in any case, we felt dead, even though we were still breathing. The one with the machine gun was trying to scare us, and succeeded. He said that if they had shot us, our flesh and blood would be splattered over the walls.

When we heard that, Eric and I looked at each other. It was really frightening.

The police didn't check for fingerprints or carry out any forensic tests. What they did was help themselves to whatever they could find in our fridge. They took the Dragon stout and Red Stripe beer and ate the bun and cheese. We couldn't believe it. They didn't ask if they could have them. It didn't end there, either.

There were a few ornaments lying about and one of the policemen picked some up. He said, "I will take these and when I get paid, I will bring you the money." I was shocked by that, because we hadn't discussed any value, and I was not that stupid, I realised he was stealing them in front of my eyes. But that's how the Jamaican police conducted themselves. The force was full of bad eggs. Political corruption at that time had wrecked the infrastructure of the country. Certain groups were intent on beating the system and undermining the long established democracy.

But that's how it was and they left when they were ready. That night we were too afraid to stay in the house on our own because we had no keys to lock the doors, the gunmen had taken them. A local man came to the house in the late evening with a machete that he had sharpened until the blade looked like aluminium. We were nervous. He told us that he wanted to keep our company. Speaking patois and rolling a huge gunga spiff, he popped it in the corner of his mouth where some teeth were missing. He sat there, sharpening the blade and getting high. A plume of white smoke spiralled around him. I was getting high just from the smell of it.

He told us that he would stay with us that night and if they came back, he would make mincemeat out of them. I felt very nervous when he said that. After all, a bullet can cover a distance far quicker than a machete, but his presence in the house did lift our spirits. We didn't get much sleep. He kept us entertained for most of the night. He was like a Maroon, a breakaway slave.

Nevertheless, we were still very shocked by the incident and what had happened to us. We were so lucky to have escaped with our lives. I think my preaching to those men must have reached the core of their ruthless hearts, because they didn't hurt us physically. They traumatized us, though, and caused great distress, something I will remember as long as I live. Even now, I shudder at the thought of it.

However, every morning when I wake up I give thanks to the Lord because, to my husband and me, life is very sweet. Because of what has happened to us, we value every minute of each day. We both know what it is like to stare death in the face and come out alive. We are so lucky and we do believe that God has joined us together for a reason.

We bought new locks for the doors, but after a few days, we decided to leave. We asked Dudley to take us and our few belongings to Bois Content where my father lived with his youngest son, Clement, and his girlfriend, Eileen. One day we went to Old Harbour, and while we were waiting for transport to take us back to my father's, two policemen came over and said they wanted us to go with them to Lionel Town in Clarendon to identify some men they were holding there.

I told them we wouldn't be able to identify anyone, because the men wore masks. All I could say was that the one who kept poking the gun in my ear had darker skin. He was the one who did all the searching and terrorising us. The other man had lighter skin and very hairy arms. I said we were not going with them because our lives would be in danger.

I was horrified when one of the policemen said, "Don't you think our lives are in danger as well?"

I was shocked when he said that, but I pulled myself together and replied, "You knew what you were going into when you joined the police force."

They came to Bois Content for us the following morning and forced us to go to Lionel Town. We were scared stiff. The jeep was driven at a dangerous speed. We thought the driver was doing it purposely to transfer more fear to us. He became angry because we kept saying that we would not be able to pick the men out. Eventually we got there and they took us where they had ten or twelve men lined up. The thing that struck me was they were all Indians. They stood still, looking straight ahead as we walked along. I just looked at them, but didn't touch anyone, and neither did Eric, because we had no picture in our minds to go by. The police were annoyed with us when we came out and we waited for some time for a lift back to May Pen Police Station. After a while it was obvious that they had driven away and left us. I panicked; my heart was racing and Eric had started to shake. We hadn't lived in Jamaica for twenty odd years and didn't know the area. We made some enquiries and eventually got a minibus to May Pen and then another to Old Harbour.

By the time we got back to Bois Content it was nearly dusk and Papa and the rest of the family were getting worried about us. When we told them what had happened they were shocked. I was very angry and didn't want them to get away with it. Tuggy, Dudley's stepson, offered to take me to the Commissioner of Police in Kingston. Once there, I told his Deputy about the gunmen and how we had subsequently been treated by the police.

He was a strapping man and sat in a black leather armchair listening to me. He wore a khaki shirt and trousers and there were stripes on his shirt denoting his rank. I was stunned when he admitted that he knew about corruption in the police force.

"For example," he said, "some officers live in big houses. I know there is no way they can afford to buy or build properties like that on police salaries."

To hear that from Mr Bennett, the Deputy Commissioner of Jamaica Police Force was a shock, but it was also something grand, to have heard an admission like that 'straight from the horse's mouth'. He phoned May Pen Police Station. "Grassroot," he said, "I have a lady here in my office who has been held up at gunpoint with her husband and robbed. I don't like what she's told me about your response to the incident, it is unacceptable." He listened for a moment, and then blasted the man again. "It doesn't matter where they came from. This kind of thing has to stop. If we allow these thugs to target people who are returning to the island, we have failed in our duty."

Tuggy and I shook his hand and left. I knew that we would never see our belongings again, but I felt better for having had the guts to go to the top and make my point. At the time, I was so outraged I felt that if I could face the guys with the guns, then I could face anyone. I reached Bois Content later feeling that I knew more about the Jamaican police force than I had when I had set off that morning. My father thought I was brave to go.

But I was a broken woman. I kept crying and Eric decided to take me to the doctor. When we explained to him what had happened he was shocked, but agreed that it was becoming a regular occurrence. He gave me some tranquilliser to calm me down. But we decided to leave my father's house. We were very unsettled and down. I felt that instead of making progress, at Bois Content we were back to primitive facilities. There was the pit toilet, for a start, and the shortage of water made life difficult.

~ 5 ~

Eric's sister lived in Spanish Town with her family. Her eldest son had a house in Spanish Town that he rented out to his sister Andrea, a domestic science teacher. She lived there with her husband, Vincent and their three children. She told us that we were welcome to stay with them. We took our bed that we had been held hostage in and the few things we had left, including a huge bag of rice which we had brought from England. We hadn't used much of it yet, but at least it would save us from starvation if things got really hard. Andrea's friend, also a teacher, bought our bed. We were delighted. We sold what we had left to raise our air fare back to England.

One day someone came to the door and shouted, "Is anyone in?"

I was terrified and began to shake. Eric held my hands. He was scared as well and we both thought the gunmen had returned to hunt us down. Or could it be the police wanting us to identify some more men? We wouldn't do it, even if they offered us a million pounds. We could not face that treatment again.

Eventually the caller left, and we locked ourselves in the house all day until the family returned home. What was more shocking was when we noticed that our bag of rice was diminishing before our eyes. Someone was nicking our rice and either storing it for themselves or giving it to friends. With very little left inside to hold it upright, the hessian bag was steadily crumpling to the floor. So even in his nephew's house, we were still being robbed. Who could we trust? But we just had to bite our tongues and pretend not to notice it.

One Saturday evening, Andrea and Vincent told us they were going to take us out for a spin. It was nearly dusk and the lights were beginning to twinkle. They took us to an area with a magnificent view. We stood on a rock looking out at Kingston in the distance. It was an amazing sight and quite relaxing, inhaling the sea air and listening to the tide slapping against the rocks. Then suddenly Vincent said, "This is where they dump a lot of dead people after they've been shot."

When we heard that, we said we wanted to leave. Portsmore may have been a popular beauty spot with a spectacular view, but there was a dark side to it. Eric and I just wanted to get the hell out of there. My mental state was so muddled, I even found myself wondering whether the plan had been to take *us* there and dump us. It had reached the point where we felt we could trust no one. It was a relief to get into his car and be driven away from the place, which had now lost its fascination as far as I was concerned. I was so affected by it that I was unable to sleep that night. Either Andrea and Vincent were trying to wind us up, or they just didn't think of the effect it could have on us.

That night I prayed that we could sell the rest of our bits and pieces so that we could buy our tickets to fly home. We had paid our way into hell, so it was only right that we should pay to get out of it. We held a jumble sale on the verandah, selling our things so cheaply it was like giving them away. However, we managed to raise the remaining £100 that we needed and the next day I was off, to the travel agents to pay the rest of the money. We were relieved and it was such a good feeling to have raised the money ourselves.

We could not wait for the day to come for us to leave the horrors behind and return to our children. We missed them like hell. Andrea and Vincent took us to the airport. As we drove through Kingston, we looked out at Port Royal harbour, the splendour of the Caribbean Sea and the foothills of the Blue Mountains, which rose and stood with the nonchalant grace of a woman blessed with too much beauty.

My thoughts were with Andrew; I wondered whether, in years to come, he would look back on Jamaica as a place of violence and terror or bright sun-drenched days with humming birds zipping around the Hibiscus flowers. Or perhaps the tropical thunderstorms that lit up the sky, his diet of breadfruits, boiled or roasted, at Bois Content, or the flies that he killed with the fly spray?

Suddenly the old Morris Oxford began to shake like a frightened dog. We weren't many miles away from the airport. Vincent rattled over the potholes, swerving dangerously, missing some and hitting others, but we did make it to the airport, much to our relief. After we passed through immigration, we sat like two lost sheep, watching people on the move, rushing to catch their flights to different corners of the world.

As we waited for our call to board, many thoughts were tumbling in my mind. For the last few months we had been locked in conflict – with our neighbours, the gunmen, and the police – and the situation had become intolerable, but now, for a moment, I felt some sort of peace.

God says we should forgive those that trespass against us, but I knew I was not ready to forgive those beasts, and certainly would never forget their atrocities.

We walked with dignity to the boarding gate and as soon as we entered the aircraft I said, "Thank you, Lord, for getting us this far." I had a window seat and gazed out at the tropics we were about to depart from… another dream that turned into a nightmare. I was exhausted from the traumas we had been through. I sat still in my seat as the plane tore down the runway, gathering speed, and then lifting smoothly into the sky where the clouds scudded across like snow-white cotton wool.

We were six miles up in the sky, sealed in an aluminium tube, our lives in the hands of one man and his deputy. It is amazing how you feel out of control of your life; you can do nothing but sit there and hope that when the time comes for the pilot to descend from 37,000 feet, he will bring the plane down safely. As I looked around, I noticed that most people were zonked out. Not me. I found it impossible to sleep with the racket from the engines.

Closing my eyes, which felt like they were full of sand, I twisted around in my seat to try and get comfortable, but it was impossible, the seats were crammed so closely together. I must have dozed a bit and then it was time to serve breakfast and hey, it was surprising how that little pot of orange juice and cup of coffee brought me round. Or was it the thought that we would soon be descending back to earth? Perhaps it was a bit of both, but I certainly felt regenerated.

Soon after breakfast, we heard the message from the Pilot and were asked to fasten our seat belts. I recognised the noise as the landing gear came into operation and glanced around to see a few of the passengers anxiously grabbing hold of their seats, or partners' hands. Eric held my hand and I just had my little talk with God as usual. I could see things on the ground quite clearly by now. Down... down... down... we finally hit the ground and the aircraft sped down the runway to an outbreak of clapping. I was one of them, with much relief for being back in the UK, where there was justice and where criminality of the kind we had endured would be treated by a professional police force rather than a corrupt one.

As the plane taxied in at Gatwick Airport, I was shedding tears. But they were tears of joy and relief. I felt safe now, even though I was still locked inside the aircraft. There was one thought riding round in my mind – those bastards would not be able to get near us again.

After leaving the plane, we walked down miles of long corridors.

My instinct was to get down on my knees and kiss the ground, like the Pope did, but I knew I would look foolish in the eyes of my fellow travellers. They would want to know what the hell was going on, and also I didn't want to embarrass Eric. So I just kept walking by his side as the porter pushed him towards Immigration Control.

We were free from the six months of hell.

~ 6 ~

It was 7.30 in the morning and we had to catch another flight to Manchester. We had a long wait, which was not pleasant as we were very tired, but eventually the flight was called and we were on our way home at last. It didn't take long to fly from Gatwick to Manchester. It was pouring with rain, and there was no one there to meet us.

We took a taxi to Eric's nephew's ex-wife, Gillian. She was living in Moss Side. She had not been expecting us and was surprised to see us. Anyway, she made us welcome, or so we thought, making us cups of tea and something to eat. We told her what had happened to us and she seemed very upset and was crying.

Later in the day, a guy from across the road came over. She introduced him to us as. His name was Kevin.

"Hello," he said. "Everyone calls me Kiv."

Gillian then told him what had happened to us. He was shocked and wanted to know every detail, so we ended up going over it all again. Then, when evening came, she told us that we would not be able to stay with her, but Kevin said we could stay at his house for the night. That was another shock for us, because she had a three-bedroom house; her daughter Florence had one room and there was a spare room. Even if she hadn't wanted to put us up in the bedroom, we would have been happy to sit up in the living room, we were so tired and stressed out.

We couldn't believe it. When she split up with Gavin she came to us with her daughter and we put them up in Andrew's bedroom. We had three bedrooms and three children, so Andrew had to sleep with us for three months while she sorted out a job and somewhere to live.

However, we had no choice but to accept this stranger's offer. We were just grateful not to be walking the streets with our suitcases and sleeping in a shop doorway. Well, the house was stale and smelt foul, it hit us as we walked in. Kevin showed us his bedroom, and I don't want to sound ungrateful because we truly were thankful, but the room was untidy, full of clutter, and stank of stale body odour. It was really offensive. Apart from that, we had no clean sheets, and had to sleep in the grubby bed that was so overpowering. I will never forget the smell of the pillows. It was indescribable.

Anyway, we were like two dogs and curled up together to rest. I managed to sleep for a while, but I kept waking up, thinking of what we had come to. We were tucked up in some unknown person's squalid bed and the so-called friend that we had done so much for in her time of need, had cast us off to a stranger. It was too much and I began to sob.

Eric woke up and tried to comfort me. He didn't need to ask what was wrong. "Never mind," he kept saying, "never mind."

I think I cried myself back to sleep and the next time I woke it was morning. I got up and looked across the road. Gillian's curtains were still closed. We stayed in the bedroom until Kevin came over. We never went in any of the rooms downstairs, only the filthy bathroom. We were longing to have a bath, but when we saw the state of it, neither of us was willing to get in. We were as bad as dropouts roughing it and I began to understand what these people go through when they become homeless and how easy it must be to give up.

When we went over to Gillian's house she made us a cup of tea. Eric and I were confused. In fact we felt ashamed and degraded by her treatment of us. I asked her if we could leave our cases there while we went out to seek advice.

We caught a bus to Manchester and headed for the Town Hall, hopeful that they could help us. I was nervous and so ashamed. Eric held my hand as we took the lift up. The waiting room was almost full of people, some unwashed and unkempt (as we felt), and some looking normal except for their vacant expressions of hopelessness. We went to the desk, where a large, bored looking woman sat.

"Name?" she enquired, coldly.

We told her and she wrote it down.

"Address?"

Eric and I looked at each other and told her we had no address.

"Take a seat," she snapped, with a malevolent glare.

We sat there for ages, twiddling our thumbs and fidgeting with nerves, until our name was finally called and we went to a small, stuffy room to tell the story of our lives yet again.

The woman behind the desk looked weary, and who wouldn't?

Hers was not the most envied job.

"Mr and Mrs Bartley?"

Eric and I nodded.

"Please have a seat. What can I do for you?"

There was silence for a few moments as we both waited for the other to begin. It seemed it was left to me, the woman, as usual, to do the explaining, so I began to tell her how we had sold our house and returned to Jamaica to live, but then we were robbed by two gunmen, and ended by describing the stranger's filthy hovel we had ended up in.

Then came a barrage of questions... why this? What have you done with that? Who told you that? Some of her questions were very personal and embarrassing. It was all very distressing and I felt like a common criminal. Eventually, she

223

said she would make some phone calls to see if there were any vacant rooms and sent us back to the waiting room. We had no idea of the procedure regarding the homeless and didn't know what to expect.

By now it was late afternoon and we were hungry, thirsty and tired. We chatted to each other as we waited – about Gillian and how she could do this to us, Kevin and his filthy hovel, where will we end up.

"In a dungeon," Eric said, trying to bring some humour into the situation. We smiled, but only fleetingly; we were too worried to joke about it and were soon immersed in gloomy thoughts again.

"Mr and Mrs Bartley?"

I shot up from my chair and helped Eric to his feet. Since his accident he had needed assistance to perform the simple movements that the fully mobile take for granted.

"We have found somewhere for you both and your son. It is in the area where you stayed last night – Whitworth Park Mansion, on Moss Lane East. It's a big white building. They will put you up from tonight."

Suddenly our spirits lifted and we were delighted that we had somewhere to stay. We had seen this building when we first arrived in England, and many times since, but we thought it belonged to some wealthy tycoon. It stood out because it was snow white and in its own grounds.

My nerves returned to attack me as we went into the building.

Was it going to be a dive inside? It could well be. After all, we were now a displaced family... *displaced family...* the words swam around in my mind. How had we managed to come to this? There would certainly be no VIP treatment.

We were greeted by a plump lady with short blonde hair and sky blue eyes. "Hello," she said with a smile. My name is Joy. How can I help?"

We told her our name.

"Oh yes," she replied. "Come on, I will show you the room." We followed her up two flights of stairs, moving only slowly because of Eric's mobility. She showed us the room, which was one large room divided into two. There was a double bed in one part and a single in the other. Apart from some clean bedding and an old wardrobe, there was nothing else, but we had a roof over our heads and that was all that mattered to us. We had to share the bathroom and the tiny kitchen. There were no cupboards, just a sink and a stove. I looked at the grimy bath and was reminded of the early days when we had lived in rooms.

Joy's footsteps clattered on the bare wooden staircase as she went back to her little office near the entrance. Eric and I just stood looking around what was to become our next home, knowing that our only possessions were two mugs that we had brought back from Jamaica in our cases. It was a terrible situation to find ourselves in but we tried to be strong. We knew if we didn't we would just go under.

We went back to Gillian's to collect our cases. We told her we had found a room and she was happy for us. We walked to our new abode, yanking our cases along and stopping every now and again for Eric to have a breather. Anyway, God always sends someone when you need a help. A middle aged man was walking towards us, whistling cheerfully.

"Hello, Daddy!" he said, looking at Eric with some concern.

"Hello, Sir," Eric replied.

"Boy, it a beat you, man."

"Yes sir. I am not as strong as I was."

"No, Daddy. None of us are now, man. Where are you going?"

I chimed in. "Whitworth Park Mansions."

The man's eyes widened. "A where that is? Me never hear that name before?"

I told him it was on Moss Lane East.

"You mean that big white building at the corner?"

I nodded.

"But you look like you just come from back from back a yard, man!"

He meant Jamaica. "Yes, that's right," I said.

He grinned. "Me see the tags on the suitcases. How is things out there?"

Eric and I exchanged looks. "Fine. Same old JA." We didn't want to go into any details; it was too upsetting and we just wanted to get to our room. "Sorry," I said, "but we have to go."

"Okay, Daddy. Take it easy. See you." He walked away and then turned on his heel and came back to us.

"Let me help you, man, because you a struggle."

"Thank you sir. God bless you," Eric said.

I asked the man his name.

"Vincent but most calls me Vin."

Vin carried Eric's case right to the main entrance and then walked away, whistling as he went.

I told Eric to stay downstairs while I carried one of the cases up and then I came back for the other and he followed me up to our room. I closed the door with my body and leaned against it and burst into tears.

"Don't cry," Eric pleaded. "You will set me off as well."

He put his arms around me and we sat on the bed like two lost souls. Then it dawned on me that we hadn't contact the children yet. I had a few pounds in my purse so I got some change from Joy, and then phoned Mrs Williams who had been looking after Andrew. He was out playing football with his friends, and she would tell him when he got back.

I phoned Crumpsall Hospital but was unable to speak to either Maureen or Yvonne, so I left a message for them.

Andrew came the following day. He had grown taller since we last saw him. I told him there was a bed for him and he said he would come back on Friday after school. What worried me was we had seen mice running across the room. Andrew is petrified of them, he would create a commotion if he saw them. Sure enough, they were there when he came and he was going round stuffing paper under the doors, trying to keep them out. I was afraid of them as well, so he wasn't on his own.

He stayed with us for a few nights and then went back to Mrs Williams. But we knew that he wouldn't be happy staying in a hostel, with or without the mice. It was very upsetting and my heart ached with the pain of knowing that we had a lovely house and sold it to go to hell and back.

But Eric and I kept reminding each other that we were alive and that was the main thing. We could have been killed by the gunmen. We were disoriented but believed that where there was life there was hope. So we struggled on, clinging to these words of wisdom and asking God to give us strength, and to provide somewhere decent for us to stay.

I wanted a saucepan and frying pan but I didn't have enough money to buy them, so I went downstairs and asked Joy if she would lend me five pounds, promising to pay it back when we got some money from social security. However, when we went to the social security office and told them what had happened to us, they wanted to know what we had done with the £4000 we left here with. I told them we had paid for Andrew to come home, that we had spent some and we had been robbed. They did not believe a word of what we said and after the long interview, the man told us that we wouldn't be able to claim benefit for six weeks.

We were devastated. Eric had been on sickness benefit for years and yet they even refused to help to a sick man. We left the benefit office in a state of shock and went back to our room. We were very confused. All our misfortunes seemed to be staring us in the face. We were desperate, but we were also very proud and did not want to start begging for money. Neither did we want to ask people that we knew, because we didn't want them to throw it back in our faces if we had a disagreement. When Maureen and Yvonne came, they were very distressed, and they gave us a few pounds when they were leaving. They hugged us and we all sobbed together. It was awful for us and so degrading.

~ 7 ~

We endured our living conditions the best way we could, but after a few weeks we were desperate. The bathroom was filthy and the kitchen was no better. I cleaned the stove before using it and I scoured the bath, but even after I cleaned it, I never sat in it. I just squatted and splashed the water over my body. We often gave up on cooking and went to the chippie, but we were not chip shop people. We liked properly cooked, healthy food. One day I made a pot of stew with lots of vegetables, meat and potatoes and left some for the next day. However, I had to bring the pot into our room, because the food would walk. It was a problem keeping the food fresh without a fridge and it went off a few times. I don't know how we escaped food poisoning.

We both said we could stand it no longer. I went down to the office to see how much longer we would have to stay there. They said they had no idea. Well, Eric lost it and grabbed a screwdriver that was on the desk, threatening to do himself in. I was very frightened and screamed at him, hurting himself would not help us at all. I felt exactly the same but I was trying to hold on and put a brave face on rather than give in.

Joy was very shaken and tried to talk to him, but you know, when you find yourself in that situation, it twists your guts. Suddenly we had nothing and we were totally dependent on other people. No wonder Eric flipped.

Clive and Florence, old friends of ours, came to see us and they were horrified when they saw where we were staying and began to cry. I had known them since we were kids when we used to meet up at the spring at Bois Content. Clive used to help me lift the kerosene pan of water on to my head.

Eventually, we were offered a house in Stratton Avenue in Didsbury. We went to view it, but the house was absolutely filthy inside and the huge, overgrown garden needed a herd of cows to graze it down. There were more tears, and we went back to the housing office and told them that the house was a health hazard.

The lady at the desk looked me in the eyes and said, "You are homeless. You have to take it."

I was stunned and burst into tears. I still couldn't believe what she said. We went away to think it over. Clive and Florence told us to take it. They will come and help us clean it up. They brought their friend Harry, who turned up with a machete to chop down the grass and bushes. Armed with bottles of bleach and disinfectant, we set to work.

We had never seen anything like it and wondered what kind of people lived here. Tea and coffee stains were evident on the walls and ceilings and the living room walls were covered in filth. It was horrendous.

But it was even worse upstairs. The smell was overpowering in the second bedroom. When I opened the window, bluebottles flew in and what we found in the cupboard was too disgusting to describe. I went back to the housing office, complaining that the house was still filthy after all our efforts. Then I was told they would arrange for it to be fumigated.

Our room at the hostel had been taken. In a disused garage at the back of the building, there was some old furniture. Joy told us to take what we wanted. We found a single bed that wasn't too bad.

"How can three of you sleep in that?" she wondered.

I told her two of us would sleep on the mattress and one on the base. I also found an old chest of drawers, a table with a broken leg and two rickety chairs. Thanks to the generosity of people who donated goods to charity, we were given plates, cups and cutlery for three people.

We had nothing to put at the windows, not even newspapers. We put the mattress and the base on the bare floorboards and slept on them as they were. Florence bought me a pair of pink flannelette sheets. We slept downstairs as the bedrooms smell was disgusting.

A week later they came to fumigate the house, with us inside it!

Another week passed and the smell in the back bedroom was still repulsive. It meant another trip to the housing office. A lady came to view the house, and she said she had a cold but she could still smell it. Anyway, the offensive odour was found to be in the floorboard. The previous occupants had been using the room as a toilet, and it all had to be taken out and replaced. I wondered what kind of human beings would live like that?

A month later we were given a £50 grant to help with the decorating. It was too big a job for us to tackle so we decided we would pay for some help. John, our Scottish neighbour, who was an alcoholic, said he would do the decorating for us without charging the earth. We were reluctant to give him the job because of his drinking, but I told him we hadn't got enough money at the moment and would have to leave it for a while.

I was busy writing letters to all the local hospitals to see if they had any vacancies for nursing auxiliaries. St Mary's, the Women and Children's Hospital, was the only one who offered me an interview. I was interviewed by three people, but I kept my cool and answered them to the best of my ability. They wanted someone to work in gynaecology and asked me why I thought they should give me the job. I told them that I'd had a hysterectomy when I was thirty-seven. Women are often frightened of this operation and I would be able to reassure them and tell them that I had it done and I was fine.

There was an outburst of laughter which truly broke the ice of the three-to-one interview, making it more informal.

To my surprise, I was told there and then that I had got the job. I was absolutely delighted and thanked them. To this day, I don't know where my confidence came from, because I was truly feeling at my lowest ebb at that time. But I had to be positive and give my all at that interview. When I came out of the room, I felt as if I was floating. I couldn't conceal my excitement.

When I reached home and told Eric, he was thrilled for me. It was only part time, twenty-seven hours, but it was a job and I was happy. I started work the following week. My take -home pay was £200 per month and it gave me the chance to start all over again. In time, I got John to decorate the rooms, one by one. It was money on the side for him and when he got paid, he was drunk as a skunk. I managed to buy a new bed and Andrew was able to have the whole of the single bed – base and mattress.

Every month I bought something for the house. I bought four old dining chairs for £25 and when I went home with them, Eric said, "Valerie, where are you going with them old chairs?" I told him when I had finished with them they would be old no more. I was a laughing stock for quite a while, but I had the last laugh when I covered the seats with pink velour. With their Queen Anne style legs, they looked elegant and expensive. When my friend Elvie came to visit, she asked where I got the money to buy antique chairs. I knew as soon as I saw them what I was going to do with them. I didn't have much, but whatever I did have, I wanted it to stand out, to be noticed. Like the new me... born again.

I still had my old Singer industrial sewing machine that had helped me years ago to earn extra money, so I thought I will give it go. I advertised in newsagent's windows for jobs altering trousers and skirts, repairing zips, making curtains and bridal wear and to my delight, I began to get a few jobs. I did this work when I came home from the hospital in the afternoons and evenings. Life seemed to have some meaning once again; I was so grateful to have been given a second chance and determined to make the most of every day.

I wrote to my father and told him that we had no intention of coming back to live in the house and wanted to sell it. He was shocked and said we would not be able to build a house like that again. I told him I had no desire to do so again. He refused to take any part in selling the house and my brothers said the same, so we asked Eric's brother-in-law, Mr Bedward, if he could sort it out for us. He was happy to do it for us and I told him to sell it for whatever he was offered. Even then it took a while to sell, at a low price, but we had lost so much already it didn't make a difference. We just wanted something back to make a start with.

The house was sold for $150,000 and after the lawyers' fees and taxes and (to our surprise) Mr Bedward's fee, there was not a lot left. We had no intention of letting Mr Bedward sell it for us without rewarding him, but we had not expected him to charge us agent's fee. We could not get over the fact that even our own were getting whatever they could out of us. We told the lawyer to pay him and tell him we hoped he enjoyed the money. We were sure he had never had so much money before in his life. It turned out that Mr Bedford and his wife Nina were at war over the money, because she said it was her brother's house and she should get the money.

The next problem was getting hold of the sale proceeds. We were not allowed to take the money out of the country unless we could prove it came from England. We couldn't find the papers, what with moving about and everything else that had happened. I decided that I would have to fly out there, even though I had sworn I would never return. I talked to Eric about it and he said he would not go. None of my children wanted to go with me either. Everyone was frightened. I was also afraid but when I think how hard I had worked to build that house, I felt it was my duty to go and get something back. Anyway, we needed that money.

~ 8 ~

It was eighteen months after the sale of the house I decided to go back to Jamaica. Colin, my son-in-law, said he would come with me. We managed to scrape our fare together and on a wet Monday night, 10th April, 1989, I met Colin at Manchester Coach Station. People were already boarding the coach when Yvonne and I got there. She quickly kissed us goodbye and walked away into the night.

Soon we were on our way, stopping at several coach stations during the night. I was tired and hoped that I could fall asleep, but it was the hardest thing to do. It was 7.30 am when we reached Gatwick and then we had all the usual waiting for the flight to take me back, to the country where I was born and raised… and where I was forced to beg for my life, and I had vowed never to visit again.

No one knew we were coming and so there was no family member to meet us at the airport. However, I had booked a package, so we were picked up by a rep. After travelling all night to the airport and then a ten-hour flight, we were very tired.

Montego Bay, like most of the island, had been battered by Hurricane Gilbert. It was shocking to see a light aircraft wrapped round a tree. Colin was excited and couldn't wait to see more of the island, but by the time we had snaked our way through Customs and left the terminal building, the sun was beginning to set. It made a magical scene, cloaked in floating orange clouds and gradually lowering itself out of sight. It certainly gave no hint of the greed and corruption that went on before.

The Caribbean Sea lapping gently onto the sand as the coach sped along the coastal road. There was more evidence of the hurricane as we drove on. Houses had no roofs, or had been totally demolished, and trees had been uprooted and smashed into cars and shop windows. Limp palm trees waved feebly in the breeze. As dusk gave way to the blackness of night, the toads and frogs began to croak, calling to one another as the air became still and hushed.

We finally arrived at our Sunflower Villa in Runaway Bay. Colin's friend, Benji, a travel agent, had sorted it out for us. It was perfect: three bedrooms, all en-suite, swimming pool and the sea lapping against the nearby beach. It was the end of the winter season, when all the American and Canadian visitors returned home, so it was more like a desert island.

On the Sunday morning, I could hear church bells ringing and it brought back memories of my childhood. I went for a stroll along the beach, checking out every little niche and cove as the seagulls wheeled above me. I came across a heap of freshly dug sand. I saw something and bent down. Intrigued, I scraped away some of the sand and to my surprise, it was a turtle's egg. I rushed back to Reception to tell them what I had found and a man came with me to have a look.

"Oh yes," he said. "It is a turtle's egg. They often come out here and lay them."

Well, I had only seen a turtle's egg on television and never expected to see the real thing, so I was excited. Colin couldn't wait to get out and explore. He wanted to know how far away Icis lived. I told him it wasn't very far. She lived in Discovery Bay but it was Sunday, and there was not much transport. However, we stood at the side of the road with our thumbs out, trying to stop anything that pass. We didn't have any luck and it was hot.

"Colin," I said. "I'll give it another few minutes and if we don't get a lift I'm going back indoors to chill."

Then a van driver stopped and I asked him if he was going to Discovery Bay. With a lovely smile he told us to jump in and Colin was well pleased.

When we arrived, I stood at the gate calling, "Icis? Icis!"

Eventually she came out, shielding her eyes with her hand against the glare of the sun. When she reached the gate she was really surprised to see us.

Icis hadn't met Colin before. "When did you arrive?" she wanted to know as she greeted us.

"Last night. We are jet lagged and it is so hot."

We sat down on the verandah, and Icis went indoors to get us cold drinks while Colin eyed the surroundings.

"The houses here are lovely," he said.

They certainly were, and just across the road, the ink-blue sea lazily lapped against the white sandy beach.

"Oh yes. No shacks to be found around here," I told him.

Colin's smile seemed fixed on his face. He had never travelled to the Caribbean before.

Icis drove us back to Sunflower Villa later that evening. I told her I was going to see a lawyer. I wanted to find a way of getting the money from the sale of our house out of the country.

"Oh, don't bother with that," she insisted. "All they're going to do is eat out your money."

Well, I was so vexed I didn't want her telling me what to do. We had listened to the family over the years, and where had it got us? We put our trust in my family and just got taken for a damn long ride. If it hadn't been for Colin wanting to meet Icis, she would never have known I was there.

The fact was, it was my first visit since Eric and I fled the island in 1985 and I wanted to lay low. Her husband, Teddy, worked at Kaiser Bauxite down the road from where they lived. He was an electronics engineer. But he was a guy who loved his drink. Icis said he would stop at different bars before he came home. Sometimes she had to go looking for him. Teddy offered to take us to the lawyer's office in Kingston. It was good of him.

The sun was blazing as usual and we were going round in circles trying to locate the office. Colin couldn't stand the heat and decided he would shelter from the sun in a multi-storey car park.

"Kingston is hot, man," he said. "Look at me, I'm turning red."

Eventually we found the place. It was a rather shabby looking building with its pink paint peeling off. But I wasn't there to look at that. I wanted some advice.

I was a little concerned at what he was telling me I should do, but eventually it did sink in.

"Just find someone who wants to buy a house here," he said, "and then ask them to pay you English money."

I thanked Mr Brown and told him I would keep my eyes and ears open to find out who was doing what. I could see that there might be some problems. He gripped my hand tightly and I thought he would never let go. A knowing smile broke through his greying beard and I could see beads of sweat glistening on his bald head.

"Okay," said Teddy. "We better go and see if Colin is alright."

"Why didn't he come in with you?" Mr Brown asked.

"Oh he's hiding from the sun. He looks like a red pepper."

At that point, Mr Brown let go of my hand, and boy, was I relieved. He was giving me a creepy feeling for some reason and I was just glad I wasn't on my own with him. Teddy must have been suffering from pangs of guilt because he already owed me £150. That's what he charged me to wire the house, but so far, he hadn't done a thing. We were told that he drove to Kingston to buy the stuff he needed to do the job and had a crash on the way home. No one else had been involved in the crash, so he must have drunk too much liquor and hit potholes too fast.

Everyone ripped us off, but when it comes from a close family member, it's despicable. The more I was oppressed, the more I found strength to fight back. They might have taken me for a fool, but what is not dead you don't throw away. That's where I came in. I had my life and that gave me hope. Anyway, Teddy drove us back to Sunflower Villa and then made for home... or maybe the bars.

Colin's ears were peeling and he was sore and sunburnt, so the next day we just chilled out. Icis came to see us. She was going to St Ann's Bay market and invited us. As we drove along we soaked up the views. These areas were as new to me as they were to Colin.

The market was teeming with people, but there seemed to be more sellers than buyers. I wasn't buying anything because our meals were being provided. Icis went round buying food stuff, while Colin and I looked around. One of the women selling vegetables shouted across to me.

"Lady, you come and buy some beans from me?"

I said I didn't want anything, and she turned nasty and began to curse me.

"You think because you go a England and get white man, you better than us?"

I was shocked. For a start, Colin was my son-in-law. He was Maureen's husband. I opened my mouth, but Icis lashed out with her tongue before I could speak.

"My sister only came along with me. She isn't doing shopping. I will not buy anything from you in future!" She gave the woman an angry glare. "And so what if she do have a white man? It's none of your friggin' business!"

I was embarrassed because Colin never had to deal with that kind of reception before. She was still having a go as we walked off. Colin carried the colourful basket of food for Icis to the car. "See how desperate some people can be to sell you something," Icis said.

We did stand out like a sore thumb, no matter whether we spoke or not, people knew that we came from abroad. They thought that because I was with a white man, I was loaded. Anyway, we just got on with it and went on a few trips. We were both excited, and although I was born there I don't know the places.

One morning we were picked up at our villa and taken to Ocho Rios. We transferred to a Jeep to take us to the Blue Mountains. Most people have an image of Jamaica as being sun, beaches, dreadlocks, and reggae bands. It's hard to believe that there is a place that is cold, where you can see green forests and blue haze settling into the deep mountain valleys. Most tourists don't make it to the Blue Mountains because the trip requires some effort and strong nerves to take the wild bus ride up the mountains.

All I can say is that our trip was worth the effort. It was very quiet and serene and yet there was a certain amount of activity going on with the mountain people planting, tending or harvesting the Blue Mountain coffee beans. But they were a long way from the heat and tourist bustle of the North coast. Both Colin and I were taken aback because it was so spectacular and striking.

On our way up the mountain we stopped at Dr Sangster's liqueur factory and did some liqueur tasting. There were selections of different flavoured liqueurs produced from a variety of fruits. They were rum based, of course, and by the time we left I was feeling quite tipsy. The guy who owned the business was a scientist who had come from Scotland on holiday some years ago. He took a trip up the mountain just like we did and fell in love with it. He bought a plot of land and began to experiment with the different fruits. The rest, as they say, is history.

Sugar Loaf Peak at 7,000 feet is the highest point in Jamaica and believe me, it was chilly up there. I was surprised to learn that there is a Newcastle in the mountain. This is where the Jamaica Defence Force train their men. The trip was not just pleasurable but educational as well. To think that I was born there, but had no idea that these places existed. We climbed the Dunns River Falls – 600 feet, with fresh spring water blasting down on us. It was fantastic.

So I managed to combine business with pleasure. I took Colin to meet my youngest sister Hyacinth, who lived in Ocho Rios with her two children, Brant and Sharna. Within no time the pair of them was fighting to climb into Colin's lap, so I took a picture to record the moment. I was just glad that I was able to take Colin on a few trips so that we could see parts of the island that I had never seen before.

We returned to England, not with money, but a great deal of knowledge about Jamaica. I never knew such beautiful places existed even though I had lived the first eighteen years of my life there.

Two weeks was a long time for Colin to be parted from Maureen and their baby son Warren, who was one year old while he was away.

Maureen brought him round to see me, and the little chap climbed up on my suitcase that was still in the living room. I took a picture of him climbing, not Dunn River Falls, but Grandma's suitcase.

~ 9 ~

In 1993 Eric and I went on a four-day visit to Paris. It was intended to be a romantic interlude in the most beautiful city in the world. It was a place we had wanted to visit for some time, to soak up the ambience of the city full of romance, inspiration and vibrance... and yes, we had heard that it could be just a bit outrageous!

But Eric was consumed with shock after recently being told that his falls might be connected to Parkinson's Disease (see later Chapter: Eric's Parkinsonism). It true this dreadful disease was ravaging his body at a fast pace and he was quite depressed. But I thought we could shove the matter away in a box for a few days and enjoy our trip to this wonderful city.

We travelled by coach and train. It was a long drive and by the time we arrived at our hotel it was late evening. Eric was very tired, but perked up after a shower, and was ready for dinner. I jokingly suggested we try some frog's legs, but he politely told me, "No. Thank you all the same."

We had an enjoyable meal and retired to our room for an early night... and, of course, some bruising passion. It was fantastic and we must have fallen asleep entwined in each other's arms, for that was how we woke up the next morning.

After breakfast we joined our group on a sightseeing tour. Again, it was tiring. We travelled first by coach and then took a boat up the River Seine. We visited Notre Dame and lit candles, the Louvre, the Arc de Triomphe, but when we got to Eiffel Tower Eric flipped. There were lots of steps to climb up to the tower and he knew he couldn't do it.

"Why do you bring me to a place with so many fuckin' steps?" he swore at me in his rage.

I was embarrassed by his outburst because there were a lot of people close by who could not help hearing. In an effort to calm him down, I took his arm and, instead of continuing with the climb, we descended the steps together, and sat down to wait for our group. From that day, I realised that my dear husband was being destroyed by some monstrous disease and we had a long, struggle ahead of us.

However, I was determined that we were going to make the most of our stay in Paris, and that afternoon we visited the Chateau de Versailles with its fabulous gardens. Later that evening we were taken on a tour to see the city at night. Illuminated with its beautiful lights, it looked magical and was worth seeing. There was quite a lot of sight seeing to cram into our four days, so it was rather tiring.

On the third day we went to Montmartre, the area of the city famous for its artists and street entertainers. It was a very atmospheric place; I loved it, and it seemed to work on Eric like a tonic. He was tapping his sticks in time to the music and had a beaming smile on his face. I was relieved to see him back to his old self again.

After breakfast on our last morning we went on a short tour before driving back to Calais. Eric was amazed at the number of vehicles packed into the lower section of the ferry boat. There were more steps to climb before we reached the top deck and, remembering the episode at the Eiffel Tower, I held my breath. But this time there was no ugly scene, and with smiling faces, holding hands, we went to the bar for a drink before the crossing. The sea was quite choppy, but Eric was okay. He had only one drink, because he didn't want to lose his sea legs.

When we arrived back at the White Cliffs of Dover, we took our time and let the rush of people go first. Then we slowly walked down the steps to meet our coach for the long journey back to Manchester. It had been exhausting, but we both agreed it had been worth it and, after a few months, we were off again. There was no stopping us!

Our Italian friends, Marta and Gianni invited us to Rome as their guests for two weeks. When we arrived at the airport, they were there waiting to welcome us. We didn't speak any Italian, but I was armed with a phrase book.

"Well," I said to Eric, "this going to be fun, trying to communicate!"

There was no need to worry, because Marta was a retired English teacher, although Gianni spoke broken English. He was a retired banker. On the way to their home we were chatting merrily about this and that and whenever Eric or I spoke, Marta had to translate it into Italian for Gianni so that he wasn't missing out on any fun.

We arrived at their beautiful apartment with its grand marble floor. Eric and I were made to feel at home and we were very relaxed, even though we couldn't string a sentence together in Italian between us. However, we were hoping to learn some of the language during our stay.

After a delicious meal washed down with a local wine, we sat together getting to know each other. We had first met at the wedding of our daughter Yvonne and Mark in July 1988. Marta and Gianni were friends of Mark's parents, Pamela and John, so we were not that well acquainted.

The next day, Marta took us sightseeing. We went to so many different places during our visit that I lost track, but there are some that will stick in my mind for ever: St Peter's Square, the Vatican, Trevi Fountain and the Colosseum.

We were up very early on the day we were going to St Peter's Square, to get a good place so that we could see the Pope – at that time, John Paul II. We were not disappointed.

He arrived from his summer palace in a helicopter and I was armed with my camcorder, ready for his appearance on the balcony to address the thousands of us that were waiting for him. I had a telescopic lens so that I could bring him close. It was the dream of my lifetime. How many people get to see the Pope in close-up?

It was something very special... very spiritual. The feelings of peace and holiness were all around us. I never felt like that before and just could not believe my luck. I had to pinch myself when I entered the Vatican. Emotion overwhelmed me as I saw the place where all the past Popes were laid to rest. I could not believe that there was so much history in one small area. The Sistine Chapel was the ultimate, and Michelangelo's masterpiece took my breath away, but I have to say that Paris and Rome are my favourite cities.

After a few days Marta lost her voice. Well, she had been talking at the double, what with having to translate for us all the time. But to our surprise and delight, Gianni announced that he would take over. I was up for anything, and so was Eric, and here we were in Rome, being shown around by a banker! I was ready for some fun...

Gianni took us to the business and financial centre where most of the banks were. He kept popping into some of them to introduce us to his friends. It was hilarious because Eric and I hadn't a clue what was being said. But we received a warm welcome everywhere. I was secretly hoping that we might come out with a wad of money, but there was no such luck.

We also went to a lot of villas. In Rome they are like parks, so beautiful and well kept. Some of them had fountains, and the water seemed to spring into the air with perfect timing. The scent of fresh bay leaves from the laurel hedges tickled my senses, I kept picking the leaves to sniff at them. It was so relaxing, I had to stop myself from falling asleep on my feet.

We were having great fun trying to understand Gianni's broken English, but in fact we managed to communicate very well. It's amazing what you can do when you try. He took us up the Spanish Steps and where all the designer shops were. Pasta for lunch, of course, and just enough wine to keep Gianni going with his guided tour. Eric told me he was feeling tired, but I nudged him along and he was doing just fine.

We were very impressed with Gianni. It just goes to show that even if you don't have the confidence to do something, it will come together if you try. On that day, we all learned something from each other. Marta couldn't wait for us to return and even though her voice was still croaky, she was dying to hear how we had got on with Gianni. We were all crying with laughter by the time we had finished.

We visited lots of their friends and Marta's elderly parents. Then one weekend we went to San Rocco, where Gianni came from originally, and where he has a second home. We met his family and explored the mountainous region where people go mushroom picking.

We were overwhelmed by their generosity. They made us feel special, treating us like royalty. Nothing was too much trouble. I was also enjoying myself in the kitchen with Marta, picking up some tips on Italian cuisine. Gianni had a passion for classical music and we found that we appreciated it more.

The night before we left, we went out for a meal. It was perfect. We thanked them for our stay and for taking us to all those wonderful places. Next morning they took us to the airport, we hugged and kissed each other and buried the memories deep in our hearts. I will never forget that special time with them, it was a happy time in our lives.

When we arrived home, we could speak a few words in Italian. We still keep in touch with our friends by telephone and letters. Life is full of surprises. You can have a friend all through your life from childhood, and you can meet someone in mid-life, who also becomes a friend for life.

After they had been together for some time, Andrew and Maria decided to get married in Jamaica. We planned to visit the island for a holiday as a family. I told my friend Elvie and her husband, Pat, that we would love them to join us and to our delight, they agreed.

We were quite a party. There was Yvonne and Mark and their two sons, Jake and Miles; Maureen and Colin, their son Warren and daughter Georgia; Andrew and Maria's sons Sean and Kyle; and a few friends joined us as well. As everyone said, the more the merrier. All the grandchildren were full of excitement.

Maria's sister, Debbie, lives in Sydney, Australia with her husband Anthony, their son Aaron and daughter Jenna. They flew to Jamaica a week ahead of us and spent a week in Montego Bay before joining us at Ocho Rios where we were staying at the Sandcastle and Turtle Beach Towers resort for two weeks.

My sister Hyacinth came with her son Brant and daughter Shauna, and my brother Dudley and his son Wayne. My sister Evelyn and her partner Ben flew in from Texas, USA. Our grandsons were page boys, and Georgia and Jenna were flower girls.

The wedding took place in the Sandcastle grounds among the palm trees and tropical flowers. The Caribbean Sea was lapping serenely against the nearby shore and most of us wept because it was such a romantic setting. There was a hush as Maria made her way up the aisle on Mark's arm with all six page boys and the two girls in procession behind them. Andrew looked round and his eyes were fixed on her until she reached his side. It was 4 pm and the sun was still beating down, but it was a wonderful occasion.

I had made Maria's wedding dress and those for the flower girls, and I was pleased with my efforts. I can be quite creative with a pair of scissors and a sewing machine and had made my daughters' wedding dresses also.

After the wedding feast, Alwyn, the best man, gave his speech, and the rest of us took our turns. Maria gave a speech and we were very touched when she said that Eric and I would be her parents now, as she had lost both of hers. Debbie was in tears when she gave her speech; everyone was choked up with emotion. Maureen was laughing and crying as she gave her speech. Yvonne was busy taking the photographs of the celebrations. But after that we let our hair down jamming Jamaican style, far into the night and having fun,

Afterwards, most people did their own thing. Eric, Elvie, Pat, Yvonne and I went to the Blue Mountains with some other guests. I have now been up there three times, and Eric twice. The air was so crisp and fresh as we drove up. We stopped at Roger's Shop, where we bought... what else but Blue Mountain coffee? I think that everyone who visits Jamaica should see the Blue Mountain where the coffee beans are grown, to see and touch the berries on the stalks, and smell that unique aroma.

At this point in my story, I would like to say a little bit more about the Blue Mountains, because they are so spectacular. It is hard to believe there is a place on the island where you can stand and feel downright cold, and see nothing but green forest and blue haze drifting in the mountain valleys. But this is exactly what you can see. But most tourists don't make it to the mountains. You must either rent a 4x4 vehicle or take a wild bus ride, or hike. Or all three combined. But I tell you this, it is well worth the effort.

The mountain region appears quiet and serene, but there is a great deal of activity, particularly in the coffee plantations. There are mountain villages, a botanical garden and, of course, the highest point in Jamaica. It is formed from St Andrew, St Thomas and Portland for about 40 miles from the corporate areas to the coast of Port Antonio, rising from the foothills to the highest point of 7,402 feet, with names like John Crow Mountain (6,332), Mossman's Peak (6,703), and Sugar Loaf Peak (7,000). The temperature, which drops with altitude, averages 18°C, but has been recorded as low as 4°C.

I'm just hoping, as you read my book, that you will be inspired to visit this *Island in the Sun*... Jamaica.

It was a magical day and we had such fun when the 4x4 vehicles descended the mountain. We all started singing, "... *round, round we go, gentle down the hill; merrily merrily; merrily merrily; life is just a dream...*"

We drove through Kingston and then passed through Spanish Town with its beautiful old buildings that are crying out for restoration. Spanish Town was for many years the capital of Jamaica, before Kingston was given that honour.

Then it was on to Bag Walk, where there is a dangerous flat bridge. The current is very strong and the water gushes and thunders angrily beneath the bridge. It is at a precarious point and very hazardous because only one line of traffic can pass. But of course, there are those drivers who don't value their lives or care much for others and will try to race the other drivers to get onto the bridge, sometimes ending up in the river and killing everyone. Their madness causes many people's lives to be snuffed out like a candle every year.

I was petrified of crossing the Flat Bridge and the butterflies were dancing in my stomach. After heavy rainfall, the river comes rushing down and people have to find an alternative route from the graveyard. The views are spectacular, but equally noteworthy are the potholes, like craters in places. They enabled my backside to be thumped and slapped but, dare I say, it was bloody worth it!

Threading through the villages were several hairpin bends that kept me holding onto the seat in front of me, but it was all part of the experience. We reached Walkers Wood where, among others, the famous Jamaican Jerk seasoning is made and can now be purchased in most supermarkets.

Finally, we reached Fern Gully, a picturesque, deep gorge, covered with a vast variety of ferns, and tall trees all fighting each other for the sunlight. The snake bends were wild, and I closed my eyes a few times and prayed.

Fern Gully is always cool, and quite dark, even during the day. When you reach it you know you are almost in Ocho Rios after the long descent and then… suddenly, the ink blue sea is sprawling out ahead, in the distance. The centre of Ocho Rios with all its hustle and bustle is just a mile away.

We had a wonderful day. Even so, we breathed a sigh of relief to be safely back at our hotel with the family. The holiday was memorable and the grandchildren wished they could stay longer with the family they had met for the first time. But all good things must come to an end.

Soon the group of us will take a jolly ride back to Montego Bay airport, for the long flight back to Manchester.

Andrew and Maria had arranged another celebration for their friends and family when we came back. I had already baked the wedding cake and arranged for it to be professionally iced. There was a buffet with English and Jamaican food and, of course, champagne, to toast the happy couple.

Eric and I were very happy that we had lived to see our three children married. Everything looked rosy and life seemed wonderful; it was a happy period in our lives after all the traumas of the past.

But none of us knows what lies ahead...

~ 11 ~

Obituary

YVONNE MATILDA BARTLEY GREENWOOD

Yvonne was born in Manchester in 1964. She was the second of three children, Maureen and Andrew. In the thirty-four years of her life, she achieved more than most people in a lifetime. She grew up in Levenshulme and then trained as a psychiatric nurse at Springfield Hospital in North Manchester.

At Springfield she met Mark, who was a staff nurse. After finishing her course in 1987, she went to Manchester University to study Social Administration. During this time Mark and Yvonne were married by his uncle, Father Hilary Greenwood in1988. She had her first child, Jake in 1989. After graduating, she worked as an area manager for the British Red Cross, then for Creative Support, a mental health charity. Her second child, Miles, was born in 1993, delivered by her sister, Maureen, a midwife.

Since 1994 Yvonne worked for Trafford Council as a senior manager in the Social Services Department. She had a zest for life, and was very kind and generous, always thinking of others. She had a charismatic quality which inspired people to pursue their dreams.

She had a love of photography and a knack of bringing out the essence in people, captured forever in a brief moment by a camera lens. She burned brightly in our lives with a radiance that can never be replaced.

~ 12 ~

The last time I saw our daughter Yvonne was Saturday, 17th April, 1999. I went to visit her and she seemed fine. There was nothing strange about her that alarmed me. We sat in the kitchen talking about the holiday that her father and I had returned from a few days previously.

She cooked me a pizza and after that we went into the pink room and watched the video of our holiday. She was very busy working and doing another degree and she had to juggle things all the time. She sat on the sofa with Miles nestling beside her as we talked and watched the video.

There were many moments of rapturous laughter as we watched a crab race. The children were transfixed, as the crabs were painted in different colours on their shells. Yvonne was driving on the leader up to the winning post. Eric and I had never seen a crab race before, either.

We were fascinated by them at the Jamaica Grand Hotel where we had been staying.

I left soon after we had finished watching the tape and kissed each other at the front door. The boys were fooling around beside us and I gave them kisses as well. They all waved happily as I got into my car and drove off. I gave Eric the rundown later, while we were having our tea.

I had enrolled at college some months earlier to learn how to use the computer, because I didn't want to be left behind with all the new technology springing up. So, on Tuesday 20th April 1999, I went off to my computer class and returned home after 9 pm. Nothing in this world could have prepared me for what I was about to hear.

I was relaxing in my favourite chair, tucking into ice cream and jelly, when the doorbell rang. I wondered who was at the door, I peeped and tapped on the window and I could see that it was our daughter, Maureen.

As I opened the porch, she just pushed past me and I instantly knew that something was wrong. In a split second I thought she must have had a fight with her husband Colin, but then immediately dismissed that, because she never came to us if they fell out.

"I'm smoking like hell!" she exclaimed.

"Smoking? I didn't know that you smoked! What's wrong?"

"Yvonne is dead," she replied.

"Which Yvonne?"

"Our Yvonne!" she screamed, and then burst into uncontrollable sobbing.

I began to scream as well. "What do you mean?"

I asked her again. But she just kept screaming hysterically. I began to scream again and I'm sure people could hear me from the end of our road. I just bellowed and screamed in between trying to find out when and where she was killed.

"Liverpool!" Maureen gasped out.

"What was she doing there?"

"I don't know," she sobbed.

I screamed and screamed I thought I was going to die as well. Then I phoned my friend Elvie, but I couldn't speak, my voice broken up with the shock. Eventually I managed to say the words. "Yvonne! Yvonne, she is dead," I sobbed and screamed into the phone.

"What?" she said. "Where are you?"

"I'm at home," I told her.

"I'll see you in a bit."

I started to phone my sister in Canada, but I had to stop for a moment to get myself together. Eventually, I managed to do it but I was sobbing down the phone.

"Yvonne!" I cried, "Yvonne, she is dead!"

"What?" Marjorie asked. "Where are you? At the hospital?"

"I'm at home."

"I will get back to you in a bit," she said.

She rang Jamaica and America to tell my sisters the dreadful news. They were all shocked. Eric was trying to comfort me as he sobbed.

"I'll have to go now," Maureen said.

I wanted her to stay longer with us, but she said she had driven from Yvonne's house in Romiley to tell us. She had left her husband Colin with Yvonne's children, and her own children were with her neighbour. I don't know how she drove all that way in such a state, and although I was hysterical, I worried about her driving back to Romiley. However, she said she couldn't break such devastating news to us over the phone.

"Mark and his brother Adam have gone to Liverpool to identify her," she said as she walked to the front door.

Soon afterwards, Elvie and her husband Pat drove up. They were our best friends. Everyone was in a state of shock. They sat with us for quite a while and then went home. There was nothing anyone could do, but we appreciated their love and support.

Eric and I didn't go to bed. We stayed downstairs until daylight. We just kept talking, lamenting and crying. There was no point in going to bed because we wouldn't be able to sleep.

The day after Yvonne died, Eric and I went to Mark's house. It was the first time we saw him after the death of his wife and he was devastated. I could feel his pain on top of mine sitting in the green room, sobbing and cuddling one of Yvonne's T-shirts. I didn't know what to say to him so I simply put my arms around him and we cried together.

A few days later, Mark, Maureen and I drove to Liverpool to the police station where Yvonne's belongings and car were being kept. We sat in a waiting area for what seemed like forever. There was a lot of activity going on. The policemen kept glancing over to where we were sitting, and then all of a sudden one came to us.

"Come on," he said. "Let's go."

He was taking us to the spot where Yvonne had died. I could see her car in the car park. We got into the police car and he drove off.

No one said a word. The only sound was that of the engine. My stomach was turning over. I felt physically sick and my heart began to beat so fast that I thought it was going to explode. My breathing became shallow. I could not comprehend why she came to Liverpool to kill herself.

After we had travelled for a while the policeman stopped. The name of the car park was Mount Pleasant. I wondered why she chose that car park. Was it because it has a name that's in the Bible, or was it just random?

The officer pointed and said, "It's over there." He led us over to a corner of the pavement and said, quietly,

"Here."

Then he pointed up to the building above.

I looked up and just screamed. Maureen was screaming too, but Mark stood just looking with his hands in his pockets. I called out her name, but there was no answer, only my voice echoed back. It wasn't that I expected an answer, not after jumping off the eighth floor of the car park. There were no white doves flying past. Nothing. My heart felt like ice as I sobbed in my grief.

We stood there for a while with these unbearable feelings tearing through our bodies. Then we walked back to the police car and were driven back to the station. I wanted to know where she was and the officer said she was at the Liverpool Victoria Hospital. I was numb and shaking as we were driven back to the station.

We sat in silence until another policeman walked towards us with a black bin bag in his hand. It was obvious that it contained something, but I never imagined it was my daughter's clothes. I don't know why he came directly to me as we were all sitting together.

"I must warn you," he said to me. "The contents are blood stained."

I told him to dump it, and looked away. Neither Maureen nor Mark breathed a word. The only sound was that of the officer's shoes squeaking on the highly polished floor. Then after a while he came back. This time it was with her rucksack, which he handed to Mark. When we went outside he put it straight into the boot of the car.

He drove us home and the journey was mostly silent. I was in the backseat, Maureen was in the front with him. For most of the journey I had the feeling that someone was beside me. There was also a strange smell, like stale blood. I didn't say anything. I just knew she was coming home with us, even though her body was lying in the morgue.

Mark was tearing down the motorway. I wanted to tell him to slow down, but I just bit my lip. When I arrived home Eric was sitting with Florence, a friend of ours who offered to stay with him until we returned. He was sick with Parkinson's and was not well enough to face the horror of it all. We just wrapped our arms around each other and sobbed. I felt I just wanted to go to some grey, remote area of the world and howl my pain into the void, but I couldn't as I was still trying so hard to be brave. At the time, the responsibility was as bad as the pain. I was trying to keep things going as the family was falling apart.

Mark chose Yvonne's coffin. One evening we went up to their house and he walked into the pink room where Eric, Maureen and I were sitting. He gave Maureen a brochure containing designs of the coffin.

We looked through it and saw that he had already ticked one. It had brass handles. Maureen told him that Yvonne wouldn't want brass, she would have preferred the silver.

"Well, I can get it changed" he replied.

My sister Evelyn flew in from Texas, and my sister Marjorie and her son Danny from Toronto, to be with us. Most nights before the funeral the house was full of people who came to offer their condolences and comfort us. It is in times of trouble when you know who your friends are, and who cares for you.

The day before Yvonne's funeral, Mark came to our house to pick up some drinks and other things for the meal afterwards. He was sitting at the dining table, drinking a cup of coffee when suddenly he dashed outside and sit on the garden bench. He was in floods of tears and inconsolable. We rushed out to comfort him and eventually he managed to compose himself and said he would be fine.

The evening before the funeral, we went up to Mark's house. I wanted to go to the undertaker's to view my daughter and to say goodbye. Eric said he couldn't go. Everyone except my sister Marjorie and her son Danny said they couldn't go. The undertaker was only a few minutes' walk away. Her brother Andrew desperately wanted to view her, they were very close.

As we walked down Beechwood Road Andrew suddenly stopped, and began howling. There was a huge lime tree and he propped himself against it, relying on it for support.

"Mam," he said. "I can't go in. I can't."

I told him that I had to go, and so we left him outside in floods of tears.

It was a while before the undertaker came for us. I could hear a rumbling sound while we sat in the waiting room. Then he came for us. He told me that he had placed a white net over her face, but it didn't look right, so he then replaced it with a black net. I told him that I wanted to see her face, so he removed the net. She looked at peace, but her head was turned to her right to hide the horror. I was amazed to see that she was wearing make up. I touched her and softly called out her name, I was still hoping that she would answer me.

I was twisted with pain and walked outside, feeling that my feet weren't touching the ground. Poor Andrew was still where we had lefted him, bawling into the tree which was holding him up. I tried to comfort him. We all did. Then we slowly walked back to her house. We will have to face it tomorrow again.

On the day of Yvonne's funeral I drove my sisters, nephew and Eric to their house. It's a good half hour's drive and I don't know how I did it, but God gave me the strength. All the family assembled at their house. I was wondering how the boys were going to cope. No one knows what it's like, unless they have been through the same thing as themselves.

Little Miles was five years old and his brother, Jake, was nine.

Miles trotted about as if it were just another day. He didn't seem to realise what was going on. I was so swallowed up with grief, I didn't know what to say or do. I stood quietly in the garden for a few minutes with my own private thoughts and memories.

Yvonne was unique. She was articulate, kind, caring, very stylish and vibrant. Matty was her pet name. Most of her friends called her Matty or Sunny Smile. You could see her smiling from a distance. She was strikingly beautiful and loved people, caring deeply for others. She had snuffed out her life with such a brutal force, leaving her two young sons that she adored so much. She had often said that she would die for them.

During the funeral service, Mark went up to deliver his eulogy, fishing a sheet of paper from his inside pocket. He said Yvonne was his wife, his lover, his friend and a whole list of things. He held his emotion very well. They were married for eleven years. His parents, John and Pamela, his sister, Hannah, and his brother Adam and the rest of his family were grief stricken. They all adored her.

As the final hymn, *Guide Me O Thou Great Redeemer*, was being sung, I couldn't take my eyes off the coffin, because I knew that was the last chance I had to paste that picture in my mind. Then, silently, the coffin began to slide away as the curtains closed. I suddenly screamed out her name, and Father Peter Hilary Greenwood gave me a look from the pulpit. I don't know whether I frightened him or not, but it just came out.

Eric and I were sitting in the front row but none of us could get up for a while, we were so consumed by our grief. By this time most of the people were out of the church. Eventually we got up, wrapped our arms around each other and stumbled outside. There was a swarm of people standing outside who couldn't get into the church.

Eric and I were ushered into the car and simply melted into the seats. We were blinded by our tears. As the car crawled out of that cemetery I just gazed into the distance until it reached Romiley, where we were going to have refreshments. There was a lovely spread. I was surprised because I didn't know that the Greenwoods had hired a caterer. They supplied some lovely food. As well as what we had provided there were lots of fancy things such as strawberries and cream. It was impressive.

Father Hilary had a stiff shot of Bell's Whisky, and everyone mingled sociably within the crowd. Eventually we walked back to Yvonne and Mark's house which was a few minutes away, so that the family could carry on socialising. The green room floor and back garden was crammed with flowers. The whole house was infused with their perfume. We didn't know why Mark wanted the flowers in the house and garden until we all returned. I thought it might be his way of mourning. I have never seen that before, and I have been to a lot of funerals over the years.

However, someone asked him what he was going to do with the flowers and he said he was going to take them to nursing homes around the Stockport area. I thought it was a nice gesture. He was quite good in that way. Normally, people leave flowers at the grave, but there was no grave because she had been cremated. We returned to our home in a daze.

My younger sister, Hyacinth, arrived the day after the funeral, from Jamaica. She had been delayed by the red tape about entering this country. She was distraught when I took her to the house and she saw all the flowers. She kept repeating, "Yvonne, Yvonne! Why did you do it?"

That was the same question we were all asking ourselves over and over again. She stood in the green room sobbing and reading the messages that were attached. Then she threw her arms around me and we cried together. She told me she had to make journey to be with us. It was not a pleasant first visit to England for her, but we tried to make her visit as pleasant as possible in the circumstances. Eventually, one by one they returned leaving us to grieve.

I remember looking out of our living room window. It was dark, even though it was midday and raining. I told myself I have to be strong. Those were the last words my sisters told me. But inside, my stomach was in knots. I told myself that I will get through this trauma by the help of God, as I have my husband, children, grandchildren, and friends.

But a child is irreplaceable. It was hard for us to comprehend what had happened, because Yvonne was in the prime of her life. She had so much to live for and she had so many plans for the future. We were not ashamed of her because of the way she took her life, but we were ashamed of the people who had driven her to her death. We wouldn't have been able to cope in the way we did if we hadn't believed in God.

We will remember her every day for what she meant to us, and for the void she has left in our lives. Even though I felt like I had a big hole in my stomach and it hurt so much. It is impossible for us to ascertain whether she made a rational decision to kill herself or whether it was just a passing phase of madness.

Wherever she is now, she is free from pain and whatever or whoever was tormenting her and drove her to her death. Yvonne, may the angels lead you into Paradise with your sunset smile. When it's a clear night I still go outside and look for the brightest star and think of you. You are the last thing I think of at night when I turn out the light and lie in my bed, and you are the first thing I think of when I wake each morning.

~ 13 ~

Yvonne's Inquest

19th July 1999

I woke early that summer morning. I lay still for a moment and recalled what I had to do that day, then I slowly slid out of bed, slipped my pink dressing gown over my still sleepy body and went downstairs.

As I pushed open the living room door, the door to the kitchen also flew open. I walked towards the kitchen and then suddenly I saw this huge black figure sitting next to the dining table, waiting for me. The figure hovered, and it had the look of an angel.

I suddenly went into a spell, speaking in a strange tongue. I flung my hands up and down as the black figure disappeared, but I kept speaking in this strange tongue. Eric was still in bed, but when he heard the commotion he rushed down to see what was wrong.

"Valerie... Valerie! What's the matter?"

But I was filled with this almighty power and just wriggled from his arms. He stumbled around me and tried to calm me down but nothing could stop me until this profound power subsided in its own time. When it did, I tried to explain what had happened to me.

I was going to Liverpool to attend the inquest with Yvonne's husband. My daughter Maureen told me not to go because she said it would kill me. But I told her that I wanted to go. I wanted to hear how my daughter had died. "If I don't go," I told her, "then I will never know because Mark won't come and tell me any details." So it was just the two of us, apart from the Coroner's people.

That evening, after the inquest, Mark dropped me off and then went home. I went into the living room where the rest of the family were gathered, and close the door. Suddenly, the door burst open. We all looked at each other, but nobody spoke a word. There was nothing in sight, so we carried on talking as if nothing had happened.

I will always remember what happened that morning of the inquest, and every time I open the door the memory of it comes flooding back. We told our vicar what was happening and he came to view our house then went round the rooms with Eric while I sat quietly in the living room. He said it had been the Holy Ghost who came round that morning to guide and protect me, because I had such a harrowing day to face.

But now I can still feel her around me. I sometimes get a profusion of perfume that comes and goes, and reminds me that maybe Matty is still around.

PART FIVE
IN SICKNESS...

~ 1 ~

What a terrible year 1999 was for us. We had lost our daughter and were trying hard to hold on. But it took all my strength and I knew I was losing my grip. I was crying uncontrollably all the time, night and day. I could find no peace in my heart. My GP told me that I was suffering from depression... I think I had worked that one out for myself.

Eric was at the end of his tether because he depended on me to look after him. He was as traumatised as I was about Yvonne, but I was getting worse with each day. In fact, I wasn't with it most of the time. I just wasn't functioning at all. Eric told me one morning that he was deeply worried about me, because I had kept him awake for several nights and the strain was beginning to affect him. I remember feeling that I was on the brink of something, but I wasn't sure what.

Eric, with our best friends Elvie and Pat, took me back to the doctor. I vaguely remember being there. I have no memory of what took place. After a few days I was told that I was in Stepping Hill Hospital psychiatric ward. I wasn't shocked to hear this, I was just relieved to be getting some help, because I felt so desperate. Pumped up with pills, I was as high as a kite and although I was still very ill, I felt better for being there. Beds on those wards were like gold dust and I felt very grateful to be there and receiving treatment.

They patched me up and sent me home, even though I was still suffering from anxiety and panic attacks. My mood was still at rock bottom. It was hard because I could barely take care of myself, but I still had Eric to look after. I was on some very powerful drugs to calm me down.

I remember cooking some Saturday soup with brisket on the bone and a lot of vegetables, but I felt bloody awful. I can only describe my mental state at that time as being in a torture chamber. I left the soup and walked out into the garden. It was early June, the weather was pleasant and the bees were buzzing around the flowers. I wanted to touch the flowers, but suddenly everything began spinning round and I had to go back indoors.

"Go and take another one of those tablets," Eric said.

I had been given *Diazepam* to calm me down, and *Zopiclone* to help me to sleep. I don't know how many tablets I took. I can say with complete honesty that when I went upstairs I had no intention of overdosing myself. But that's what I did.

From what I was told afterwards, Eric came upstairs to check on me. He found me on our bed, with pills scattered over the cover. He didn't call an ambulance, but phoned Maureen, our daughter. Luckily for me, she was not on duty that day and dashed straight to our house, a 20- minute drive away. She tried to resuscitate me while she waited for the ambulance. I was lucky. They managed to get my heart going again.

I remember finding myself in a bed with cot sides and a mask over my nose and mouth. Everything was strange. I didn't know where I was and I couldn't get my breath. I began to panic again. The doctor told me both my lungs had collapsed. I had developed pneumonia. Whatever I had didn't matter much. My main worry was drawing my next breath.

That night, I felt as if I was drifting off somewhere dazzlingly white. There was a powerful brightness and I made up my mind I was going there, because I was struggling so much to get my breath. It was so bad that I really did think each one was my last.

"This is it," I thought. "I'm going..."

Somehow, I managed to survive the night and it was amazing that I did. God was not ready for me yet.

That was the second time I had pneumonia. The first time was in 1986. That was bronchial pneumonia. I had been to my GP who diagnosed bronchitis but it got worse so Eric took me to Withington Hospital. I didn't even have enough breath to tell them my name, I was told that if I had come five minutes later, I would have died. I can remember lying there, drifting, and I could see my open grave waiting for me, with the pile of earth at the side.

I think it was a close call, but God saw that I had so many things I wanted to do. He was merciful and gave me strength, and I came back to health. But only for a time. The next big worry was a lump in my right breast, which was swollen. The lump was removed and the biopsy showed it was not cancer, but a cyst.

I was okay for a while and then I found one in the other breast and that had to be removed as well. Naturally, it was a very worrying time for all of us. I found myself having to go to hospital every three months for five years to have these cysts aspirated. My breasts were like pin cushions.

The good thing about it all was that I was left with a pair of covetous Double D breasts. They may not be like Jordan's, of whom I am a great fan, but they were more than enough for Eric, he loves them and calls them his 'silk balloons.'

"They are perfectly alright," he said. So if my husband gave his approval, what could anyone else say?

But I had suffered a relapse and had to be taken back to Hospital. I had a total nervous breakdown. The death of our beautiful daughter was proving too much for me to bear. Finding myself in the psychiatric ward again was very daunting, but it was the best place for me. Eric, with his Parkinson's Disease could not look after me. I needed to be in hospital.

When I began to recover and saw what some of my fellow-patients were like, I felt lonely and desolate. When I looked around at what I had come to, I realised that we were all ill, but that there were some terribly disturbed people on that ward. It was so noisy I thought my head would explode. Some of them were drug addicts or alcoholics and some were self-harming, slashing their arms with razor blades or whatever they could get their hands on. Frankly, I was scared. Some days I was absolutely terrified because they were so vile.

I shared a room with five other women. One of them had some sort of obsession with clothes. All she did was change into different outfits and then walk around the ward before standing near the day room door like a doorman for a while, and then change her clothes again. It was very sad.

My progress was slow and I still wasn't feeling at all well. What Sir Winston Churchill termed as his 'Black Dog,' or Spike Milligan's depression, was still dragging me into the wilderness. I felt alone, frightened and very confused. Some days I would sit in a chair, with a cloud of blackness overshadowing me. I could hardly believe that I had ended up in a place like this. My mind was in a dreadful state. I couldn't remember much, and I felt ashamed of what was happening to me.

Then my psychiatrist talked to me about ECT, electro-convulsive therapy. I didn't know any thing about it, but he explained that it might help me. When I asked Maureen about it, she said I should not have it because it was barbaric. I was confused and tried to read the leaflet. I did not understand what I was reading, so I simply put it down and thought about what the doctor had said to me. I felt lower than I had at any time in my life. I was the only one who knew how I felt and I didn't like it.

What had I to lose? I decided to have the treatment.

As the nurse led me down the endless corridor to the treatment room, I felt like a lamb going to the slaughter. I remember being given an injection in my left hand and that was all.

"Valerie? Valerie!"

The nurse was calling my name as I came round and then I was given a cup of tea and two biscuits. It was a strange feeling, but I decided that it was my only hope. Nothing else had worked and I wasn't going to be put off.

I ended up having twelve shots of ECT and I honestly believe it was that treatment that put me on the road to recovery. After a while I was able to come out for a day, and then I was allowed home for weekends, and finally I went home.

A nurse came to see me once a week to find out how I was doing, but it was really hard on me because I had to care for Eric, even though I was sick myself. Donna, a home help, had been doing the shopping for Eric when I was in hospital and she continued for a while after I came home.

Eventually, everyone stopped coming and we were left on our own to get on with it. I was still weak and exhausted, but I would do what was necessary and then lie down. I have always believed that where there is life there is hope, so I kept going. I fought a constant battle with the Black Dog for a long time.

After the breakdown, my weight ballooned due to the various medications I was taking. I lost my confidence as my clothes didn't fit me any more. Suddenly I had another big battle to fight and I didn't know if I would have the strength to defeat it. But one day I woke up and decided I was going to do something about it. No one could do it for me.

I had started to wake up in the night, out of breath. It was asthma, but I didn't know that then, until I had seen my doctor. He said it would be beneficial if I could lose some weight. When I got home I phoned Weight Watchers and arranged to go to their next meeting. I was shocked when they told me I was over 15 stones. I was 5ft 6ins tall and never had a weight problem before. I told myself that I had taken the first step by going to the meeting. I sat and listened to the achievements of some people and thought if they could do it, so could I.

I cleared the cupboards and the fridge and restocked it, basically with the same kind of food, but I was going to use them in a different way. I lost 6lbs in the first week. Fantastic! But the second week I lost only ½lb. I was so disappointed, but I soon learnt to understand how my body's metabolism worked. There was no rush and I took things slowly.

However, I was still taking the same medication so I was fighting a losing battle. I begin to go for walks and be very strict with myself and worked hard to reach my goal. Eventually, after nearly two years, I lost 3 stones. I must have walked hundreds of miles, apart from my work-out routine. I bought 3 stones of cheap flour and stacked it up in the garage. What a shock I had when I saw the pile there! It took a brave person to stand there and look at it, but I did and I was so glad that I had persevered to get my life back.

I was so different from the woman I had been... hospitalised for months and pumped up on drugs to the extent that I was literally stoned out of my mind day and night.

But now I was reborn. Eric loved the new me and couldn't keep his shaky hands off me and I loved it. When I was in hospital I never gave a thought to sex or passion, but now I was raring to go. I felt sexy again, yes… and ready for it!

When Eric was in hospital for 5 months in 1978, I was in my prime and I didn't get any nookie for a long, long time. So what did I do about it? I put some records on our Bluespot radiogram and danced. It took my mind off all the fantasy and passion that was building up inside me like a hurricane ready to shoot.

So now you know, girls. When you don't have a man in your life, just put the music on and bop around the room. You will soon reach a full orgasm. But it depends how easily you reach those heights; some people's bubbles burst quicker and easier than others. However, it worked for me and I hope it can work for you. While you are reading this, have a laugh… go on. If someone is sitting next to you they will wonder what you are laughing at and start laughing too. The whole world will laugh with you and everyone will feel so much better (whether they have the real thing or not). Try and be happy with what you have until you get what you want.

~ 2 ~

I always wondered why Eric was so accident-prone. I couldn't pinpoint what was going on; he was forever injuring himself. Over the years he has broken so many bones in his body. Things were getting worse as he got older, but after so much trauma in our lives already, I guessed that anything could happen.

It was in May 1995, after we returned from another trip that I noticed he had a problem. He tumbled in the garden, in the living room, in the kitchen. Nowhere was safe. The funny thing was he always made a joke about it.

"Oh, I can't hold my diesel oil anymore," he joked and laughed. He loved the garden and spent a lot of time in it. In one corner was his vegetable plot. We were always fighting battles with the slugs but the freshly picked produce tasted divine. We had lots of strawberries in the summer and they were tastier than the shop- bought ones.

Once summer was over, Eric more or less went into hibernation.

His body became stiff and rigid and I had noticed that his writing had become fine and spidery. He would avoid writing and ask me to do it for him. But I wondered why he kept falling down and I worried when I was at work. He would never tell me if he'd had a fall unless I noticed a bruise or cut and then he would admit that he had 'slipped over.' It hurt his pride to admit it. I suggested that he go to the doctor and get checked out, but he made excuses, saying that he was just getting old and making a joke of it. But I wasn't convinced.

The falls were getting more frequent. One day, I made him a cup of tea and noticed that when he picked up the cup his right hand was shaking. I knew it was going to be difficult to get him to go and see the doctor. I decided that I would say something was wrong with me and ask him to come along with me. He had no idea the appointment was for him...

I began to explain to the doctor what was going on with Eric and how long since he began to fall. Eric gave me a look that could have cut me down. The doctor asked him a lot of questions and did some tests on him. When he picked things up, his hand began to shake.

"Nurse Bartley," the doctor said, "what do you think is the matter with your husband?"

"I think it's Parkinson's disease," I answered.

"You are spot on."

Dr Hussein said he would refer him to the Neurologist at Stepping Hill Hospital as a matter of urgency. We walked out of the room, Eric holding my hand, his stick in the other. It was a bit of a shock, but I was relieved that what I had suspected was now confirmed. Eric was cross with me because I hadn't told him that the appointment was for him.

"What difference would that have made?" I asked. "You still wouldn't have gone to the doctor."

Poor Eric looked crestfallen.

"Listen, now we know what it is, we will fight it together,"

Squeezing my hand, he managed a smile. "Yes. We will."

At the hospital, they did all the tests and confirmed the diagnosis.

On the way home he was very quiet.

"Cheer up, it may never happen!" I said.

"It has happened already," he replied.

"Never mind," I said, but I could see that it was getting to him. I told him I had no intention of locking him away, we would continue enjoying life together.

We had started to on foreign holidays after the girls had married.

We thought that it was time to do some globetrotting. Suddenly, I was about to live my childhood dream, when I would spin the globe around and pick out all the places I would like to visit.

September 1988 we went to Spain, and met a nice couple. It turned out that we were on the same flight, and they were from our area. We became very friendly with Alan and Mary and exchanged addresses and kept in touch. One evening I was reading the *Manchester Evening News*. There, in front of my eyes was the headline I found hard to bear. Mary and her granddaughter had been walking along the pavement and a car ran into them, killing them both.

I wanted to phone Alan, but what would I say to him? I just sent him a sympathy card and then after a while I wrote him a letter. We kept in touch and he sent me his new address when he moved. He has a new partner now, but it just goes to show that none of us know what tomorrow will bring.

Anyway, what happened to Mary brought it home to us even more. I had injured my back at work with a patient, so I decided to give up work to be with Eric. We brushed up on our swimming. He could swim, but I was hopeless, I was just trying to keep him going, really. I also enrolled at college to try and catch up with the education I had missed all those years ago. I was very nervous but I was determined to move forward, even though it was a big step for me.

Slowly, I became hooked, and the following year I took my GCSE exam in English. I had never taken an exam before, but the support and encouragement from Jane and Barbara, my tutors, paid off. I got a C and I was delighted.

Eric was very pleased for me and encouraged me in everything I did, knowing how determined I was. Nevertheless, I was still having trouble with my spelling. Barbara told me she was going to give me a test to find out if I was dyslexic. It turned out that I was and it was a relief to know that there was a reason for my inability to spell correctly. I will always have this problem, but I will not let it stop me from being creative. I could have chosen a ghost writer to write my book, but I wanted to do it myself. A ghost writer cannot feel the pain, trauma and the feelings of hopelessness I have suffered. When I'm writing, I'm reliving every moment of what I have been through. I can feel the hardship, deprivation and despair. It has to come from my heart and no one else can tell it for me.

In a way, by writing down everything I have held so tightly inside me all my life, I feel a tremendous release. It is like being re-born.

I would like to encourage anyone else who has dyslexia to take life by the throat. You're not done yet, and you'll be amazed what you can achieve. But you have to be determined and reach for the stars. People with this condition can be very creative and artistic. Many famous people are dyslexic; they have used their creative abilities to overcome it.

I went on to take a Creative Writing course and learned the different styles of writing. It was something I really enjoyed, although I sometimes had to juggle my two roles as student and carer. I did Levels 1, 2 in Creative Writing and level 2 doing just poetry. I found this amazing because I was never into poetry before. In fact, I wrote my first poem at the beginning of my course. It goes like this:

Adult Reflection

If you have a dream
that you want to fulfil.
Take my advice
and do the real thing.
When I thought
that I couldn't
do anything,
I went to a class
to do the real thing.
On the first day
with my brain full of rust,
all that was said
didn't mean a thing.
Now I'm there
I begin to see
that Adult Education
can fulfil my dreams.
Rushing to discussions
to achieve my ambition;
writing with passion
that reflects my imagination.
Adult Education.
Now I'm here to seek,
build up my confidence,
lose all my fears.
Writing short stories
with words full of colour
push me on top
of the education barrow.

It just goes to show that if you want to do something badly enough, you will succeed if you keep trying. I just wanted to prove that I had a brain and, given the chance, I could have done better. But I'm delighted with what I have achieved and at the same time managing to be Eric's carer.

But still I was not satisfied because I was writing everything in longhand and could not type. So I bought a second-hand computer and enrolled for some lessons in computing. For some reason I was frightened of the computer. It was frustrating, but as you know by now, I don't give up that easily. I wanted to learn to use the computer so that I can type up my writing and get to grips with the technology. I didn't want to get left behind. There is still a lot for me to learn about computers and I hope to continue, but at the moment I know enough to do my writing and I'm very happy. But the busier I'm the more I seems to thrive.

All this time, Eric's condition was getting worse, but I kept taking him to different places all over the world, while he could still walk.

I was always looking out for a last-minute bargain, and the good thing was that we could usually go within a week or two – but it was sometimes possible to book and be gone in five days. It has become a standard joke with our friends, but we have been to some fantastic places. We have been cruising in places like the Panama Canal and Catalina Island.

We went to San Blas Island where the native Indians live very primitively in their huts, sleeping in hammocks. They hunt and fish for food. It is what I would call a desert island. Our ship dropped anchor and we were taken by tender boats to the islands. When we'd had enough of barbecuing, swimming and sunbathing, we were taken back to our ship, *The Sunbird*, to relax and do whatever we fancied.

Eric was still able to walk with the aid of his sticks but he was helped at the airport with a wheelchair. We just did gentle activities that would not wear him out too much. We have met some lovely people on our travels and that makes the holidays more enjoyable. I can honestly say that we were treated very well and with respect everywhere we went.

People can't resist Eric's sunshine smile. It is like a magnet. He is always smiling, even though he is stiff as a piece of board and shaking.

That always embarrassed him, but once people knew what the problem was, they said they admired him and he was a lucky man to have such a caring wife to look after him. But I was the driving force behind our exploration of the world.

After what we have been through, especially the time when we stared at death down the barrel of a gun, every second of the day is important to us. I was just keeping him on the go.

Once we flew to Barbados with my best friend Elvie, her husband Pat, her brother Huppert and his wife Norma, for a week's cruise and a week's stay. With some other tourists, we went down Harrison's Cave on a tram, where a 40-foot water fall was, wearing safety helmets. Of course, Eric kept us all amused.

"What if the tram breaks down? How the hell am I going to get out?"

We laughed. "Don't worry," we said. "We will carry you."

It was a fantastic day out. We had never been in a deep cave before, so it was a new experience for all of us. That evening, we planned to have dinner in one of the restaurants. There were two flights of stairs to climb. Eric was in need of a rest when we reached the top and sat down on a green plastic chair. The next thing we knew, he had fallen off the chair onto the floor. One of the chair legs had broken. It was not Eric's fault. He didn't know the chair was broken, but that was our romantic dinner up the Swannee, as he banged his right shoulder badly and Elvie and I had to get a taxi to take him to hospital. Thank God he didn't break anything, but he could have done.

Poor Eric, he was very shaken and upset and thought he had ruined the evening. But as I said, he is accident-prone and seems to be drawn to things that will hurt him. That is why his illness makes me feel so nervous and edgy all the time.

The first time Eric and I went on a cruise, we embarked at Southampton and sailed to Spain, Lisbon and Madeira. We spent five days crossing the Atlantic and then on to Barbados, St Lucia, Antigua and Dominica. It was cold crossing the Atlantic, but once we reached the tropics it was fine. We were delighted to watch the flying fishes leaping gracefully out of the Caribbean Sea and gliding back into the water. It was really spectacular; we had never seen that before. Most of the passengers were soaking up the sun as our ship glided through the Caribbean.

When we disembarked at Barbados, we walked out to the welcoming tune of *I'm Dreaming of a White Christmas* being played on the steel drums. That was it... Eric started to jam to the music and I had no choice but to join him. It was wonderful. Happiness shone out of his face like the sun. We walked around until it was time to join the ship and set sail in the spectacular sunset.

We became hooked on travelling and as soon as we had saved enough money we were off on another trip. They helped Eric to cope, and it's true that there is always someone worse off than yourself. We met an 89-year old blind man on our first cruise. He was in a wheelchair, but he got a neighbour to take him. He fought in both World Wars and lost his sight in action. He told us that he just wanted to smell the sea and hear the sound of it and feel the swell of the waves. It was a pleasure to listen to him. At least my husband could see, even if he had a bit of trouble sometimes finding his sea-legs.

We met a couple from London on the cruise, Philip and Vilda. They came originally from Grenada. We became friends and sunbathed together on the top deck, sipping rum punch. They had planned to visit a friend from London who had returned to Dominica. So when we disembarked, their friend came to pick us up and took us back to her house. We spent most of the day with her and had dinner there. Then she took us back to our ship, *The Emerald,* and we sailed off with the last rays of the sun into the ink-blue sea.

We were interested to know how the ship sailed, so we made an appointment to meet the Captain. He explained about port side (red) and starboard (green) and some other technical aspects concerning navigation. I asked quite a few questions because I was very intrigued. One question I asked was if he could show us where we were on the map. Using the compass, he showed us the exact spot and told us that in the old days, the Captain would come out onto the bridge with binoculars and look at the moon and stars. Now we have moved on and modern technology gives us an instant, accurate result. After the lecture, we were ready to soak up more sun and cocktails. We'd had another perfect day.

Life seemed blessed even though Eric was ravaged by this terrible disease. Well aware that life is what we make it, I didn't want to be saying, twenty years down the line, that I wished we had done this or that before he reached the stage when he was unable to travel.

Shortly after our return from the cruise I decided that I would like to visit Africa. One Sunday morning we were having a lie-in and switched on *Teletext*. They were offering a week's B&B in Serrekunda, Gambia. I thought it was reasonable so I booked it. Banjul, here we come!

It was a five-hour flight but it soon passed and we landed at Banjul airport. Eric and I were as excited as two kids to be in

West Africa, where some of our ancestors originated. Just to breathe the air and feel the African sunshine was magical. We were told that Kunta Kinte, the central character of *Roots* by Alex Haley, came from the nearby village of Juffure, which made the visit very special for us.

When Eric and I were walking along the beach the next day, people were coming up to us and saying, "Welcome, Brother; Welcome, Sister," as they shook our hands. The people were friendly. But, of course, some of them were too friendly, and we soon discovered why.

They followed us as we walked along the beach, telling us stories about their mothers, fathers and brothers and so on and what had happened to them and how hard their lives were. They were not openly begging, but it was obvious that they expected money from us. We soon discovered our own way of dealing with them.

We became friends with one of the security men at our hotel and he promised that on his day off he would take us out and show us the real Gambia, the places the tourists do not normally see. I was well up for it, but I wondered how Eric would cope as Broco warned us that we would have to change mini-buses many times.

Our first port of call was a look around the market. The women were dressed in brightly coloured kaftans with matching headscarves which were wrapped in some beautiful styles. Everyone called out to us to buy something.

As we walked around we came to the fish market. I was not prepared for what we were about to see. The women sat fanning the flies off the fish. There must have been millions of them. However, I never heard anything like the noise of the buzzing flies every time the brush, newspaper, and palm leaves rained down on them.

We quickly moved on through the crowds and waited for the mini-bus to our next stop. We passed through some small villages and flat, open plains. When we left the bus we walked down a dirt track which led to a small village with thatched huts. Eric and I walked slowly behind Broco as he called to the villagers in his native language. Then a woman walked towards us. She was tall, slim and barefoot, and traditionally dressed in African costume.

The yard was swept and the chickens were scratching and clucking. Two straggly dogs growled softly and then lay down again. Broco introduced her to us and we shook hands. She turned around and hurried into the hut, stooping at the small entrance. I was surprised to see her come out with two chairs for Eric and me to sit on. She and Broco sat on a nearby plank of wood. I felt very humble, as it brought my childhood back to me. These conditions were very similar, with the chickens and dogs in the yard.

There were some palm trees nearby and as we sat, I noticed white plastic bottles hanging from them. Intrigued, I asked Broco to explain. He told us that someone climbs up the trees and pierces through the bark, then the bottles are fixed into position and the milky juice is collected and made into palm wine. Of course, we were asked to taste it and I'm not going to tell you it tasted like champagne, but it was good nevertheless. I was sure that if I drank enough of it I would soon get plastered.

After we left and walked down the track, we came to the most amazing sight. Huge platters were laden with fish that were being dried in the sun. Then we went to the factory where the fish were smoked. We didn't stay there for many minutes because the wood smoke was stifling. The sea was a stone's throw away and I could see canoes bobbing on the waves, approaching the shore.

I love to be where the action is, to see something new and different. There was a group of women kneeling in the sand, babies on their backs, scraping fish. I asked if I could take a photograph and they agreed. That really made my day. There was a lot of stingray lying on the sand, their broad, flat shape unmistakable.

I love fish. "I would love to buy some fish to take back," I said to Broco, "but we have nowhere to cook them in the hotel."

"Buy the fish," Broco replied. "I will ask the Chef to cook it for you."

I was delighted, but as we headed back to the Kotu Strand Hotel under the hot afternoon sun, I was worried about the fish going off. But they were fine.

We invited Broco to have dinner with us that evening and I ordered a bottle of wine to celebrate our wonderful day out in 'the real Gambia.' It was very kind of him to take us. As we ate our meal, we watched a magnificent sunset descend the sea. Daylight crept away and dusk turned into black night.

Later, Eric and I sat on the terrace in the November breeze, watching the sea water spraying the sand as the tide came in. A puff of wind ruffle through my hair and the nearby palm trees, the rustling branches sending back snatches of distant dogs barking. My deep sigh was one of contentment.

We sat and watched a couple performing some traditional African dancing to the rhythm of drums. They were certainly jamming to the beat and twisting and bending their bodies as if they were rubber. We retired to bed after that because Eric was very tired. I was too, but I knew if he overdid it, he would be too tired to walk along the beach the next day.

We just relaxed in the sun under a thatch umbrella the following day, sensually rubbing suntan lotion into each other's bodies. I began to feel excited and Eric was horny, so we disappeared towards our room, passing the hibiscus plants kissing in the breeze. The water raining down from the shower did nothing to dampen our fire. Damp-dry and still entwined, we sneaked into bed and when we awoke it was black and the tree frogs were calling.

But all good things come to an end; we were due to leave the following afternoon. I was wishing we could have stayed another week. Broco was sad to see us go and we promised to write to him.

We checked in at the airport and were asked by officials to open our cases. When they had finished with us we sat on white plastic chairs to await the flight. The runway was red and dusty. It was the most primitive airport I had ever seen, but we took off safely and were soon homeward bound. I promised myself that I would return to Gambia.

Home again. I went to Longsight on the Friday. I felt happy, in fact on top of the world. I was wearing my kaftan and I had my head wrapped in the fancy way I was shown by a African lady where I bought the outfit. I bumped into someone I knew.

"Hello, Valerie," She said. "Oh what a way you look posh, that is lovely."

I thanked her and told her we had just come back from Africa yesterday. Well, the woman glared at me for a moment and then shocked me with these words.

"Africa? What is there to eat out there? All the time they show on TV how people were starving and dying there!"

I was so vexed that I felt I could hit her. The strange thing was that I didn't like this woman whom I will call BB. She was a trained nurse and supposed to be an educated woman. Africa is a vast continent.

It didn't mean that because we had been there we'd had to starve. However, I didn't give her the pleasure of explaining that we had been very well fed, thank you. I just told her I was in a hurry and left her standing there. I was so annoyed that she had just thrown cold water over my happy, sunny African glow.

When I told Eric, he said, "You should have stayed to talk to her... ask her where she goes for holidays? I tell you, someone needs to take her out there, on Safari and leave her with the lions."

His comment sounded so funny that I burst into fits of laughter.

It broke the tension and I regained my happy mood again. He was so right. We have always been a couple to enjoy what we can afford in life. In spite of the difficulties I shared with my husband, we still wanted to enjoy ourselves for as long as possible. It wasn't the end of him, but rather the beginning of a new phase in his life. Through our travels we have met some great people and become friends with many of them.

We have been members of the Parkinson's Disease Society for many years now and it has helped to be able to pick up the phone when he is struggling and speak to someone who understands what we are going through. They are well worth supporting and I have helped with fund-raising campaigns whenever possible, even if it is just selling raffle tickets. Every little helps.

~ 3 ~

Two out of five people with Parkinson's Disease develop Dementia. It is commonly cited as one of the most distressing complications of the condition, both for the sufferer and his or her carer.

There is a wide range of symptoms associated with PD such as hallucinations, anxiety, apathy and depression. These are the factors which often result in the person needing nursing home care.

Will the day ever come when better treatments are available to help improve the quality of life for people living with this disease? The symptoms and effects can be devastating to family life.

Eric suffers from an overwhelming sense of tiredness, a lack of energy, and a feeling of exhaustion. It can be any one of these, or maybe all three rolled into one. He is tired and lethargic throughout the day and falls asleep frequently. At night his sleep is impaired by involuntary movements and he sometimes falls out of bed. This is not the case every day, however. Some days he feels quite well and able. On other days he is exhausted. Many activities that he loved, such as gardening, requires conscious and sustained effort. He is therefore depressed, moody and feel of little value.

The increasing signs of my husband's bizarre behaviour coincided with his almost imperceptible slide into Parkinson's. That slide accelerated as his condition deteriorated, changing him from a charmingly unconventional individual to someone with a tenuous grip on life and a frightening disregard for his own safety.

The confident, energetic, fun-loving man I loved was unrecognisable. Trembling involuntarily, his face sometimes a vacant, stiff mask, he was dependent on a wheelchair, and someone to wash him and to turn him over in bed. Life as we knew it had ended. At first, I found it almost impossible to deal with and for emotional support, I called the Samaritans. I did not know where to turn to for help. Life was becoming a treadmill. Lack of sleep meant that I was tense and miserable, but how can I relax in the midst of such turmoil?

It is not uncaring to sit tranquilly somewhere apart while family life goes on without me for a time. This is what I'm doing as I write this, and in this short time to myself, I hope I can recharge my batteries and come back able to achieve twice as much. After all, my boiler and my car both need servicing. Without proper care and attention they will break down, so servicing myself is not selfish, but sensible. I'm seeking quality rather than quantity. I am putting my feet up and, as I am away from home, I do not have one ear cocked in case I am needed. I arranged this time for myself so that I can be completely off-duty. I can choose to take a long, luxurious bath, walk in the park, have my hair done, go to the cinema... we all have our own ideas of heaven and just knowing that my moment has come, temporarily lifted the weight from shoulders.

However, it is not always easy to relax. My surroundings may have been tranquil, but I found it hard to switch off. So, convincing myself that it wasn't a sign of weakness to ask for help, I asked my doctor's advice. I found that it was possible to relax, and then to be able to deal with the problems that caused the tension in the first place.

When I feel that the whole world is pressing on my shoulders, I write down my worries and then tackle them one by one. It's amazing how a list like that has helped me get my life in perspective.

I believe Eric had the symptoms for a few years before he visits the doctor.

Other alarming symptoms of the disease were hallucinations and delusions (visual misinterpretation associated with Parkinsonism) and visio-spatial orientation – difficulty in judging space around him and failing to accurately assess the distance between objects in relation to himself. This meant he would often bump into things as he walked past them, particularly in confined spaces.

As these problems began to worsen, Eric became more depressed and self-pitying. He had always been a cheerful, happy-go-lucky guy and I found myself having to be tough on him.

There were issues concerning Parkinson's and Sex. Living with PD means coming to terms with the way a loving relationships will change. *Relate* counsellors and sex therapists believe that finding a way to overcome and adapt to sexual inadequacy is key to ensuring your relationship and sex life remains fresh and fulfilling.

Part of coming to terms with degenerative illness is about recognising that the future will not be the one you perhaps dreamt of. Identifying how the relationship will be affected is part of the process of managing expectation. Some couples fear that when an illness is diagnosed, it means giving up their sex life for good, but this need not be the case.

As a person come to terms with having PD, he may begin to feel differently about himself and withdraw from his partner. Not wanting sex is natural at such a time. Identifying the reason and communicating with your partner is crucial so that he are she can understand the changes and the reasons for them and allow him space and time.

As partners become carers, this can affect the couple's relationship to the point where they no longer feel an equal part of it. Many couples enjoy finding new ways to be intimate together. If the side effects of Parkinson's mean that you cannot do all the things you used to in your lovemaking, adapting new routine and finding ways of being sensual together are really worth investing. Changing the time that you make love to accommodate energy levels can work for some and adopting different sexual positions can also mean discovering more about each other. Keep talking to each other throughout and give yourselves time to overcome any limitations.

Erectile dysfunction is a well-known physical side effect of Parkinson's. Most men will experience problems obtaining and maintaining an erection at some point in their lives. However, those with Parkinson's can access medical treatment from their GP free of charge. Eric was having this problem for a long time and it damaged his manly pride. Rather than admit that he was unable to maintain his erection, he used to blame me for the fact that I was getting no satisfaction and it caused many arguments and frustrations.

A less common condition is hypersexuality. This is due to the side effects of certain medication that is used to treat Parkinson and is equally disruptive to the normal way of life. This is when sexual impulses become more intense, often spontaneous and compulsive. The demands for sex can be excessive, again causing distress and disagreements.

It is important to realise that this condition is a direct result of medication, and not a personality disorder. GPs can help individual cases but Eric did not want to discuss it, either with his doctor or PD nurse, because he was so embarrassed by it.

Finding ways to be close to each other by incorporating cuddles, hugs, strokes and kisses will enable the couple to maintain an intimate connection. Even when your sex life becomes less active, maintaining a sensual relationship can be achieved by sharing massage, using aromatherapy oils to relax and open up the senses, bathing together, trying new foods and finding ways of laughing together. Keeping a sense of humour is so important. But it is not always that easy and there were many times when I began to wonder for how long I could cope.

It is worth contacting your GP and *Relate*, both of whom offer support and help with sex counselling and therapy.

What is Lewy Body?

I was told that Eric could have Lewy Body, which is dementia with Lewy Bodies (DLB). Lewy bodies, I understand, are microscopic protein deposits in the brain, associated with brain death. They are named after the man who discovered them. The significant difference between PD and DLB is the location of these protein deposits in the brain, In PD they are found mainly in the mid brain which is responsible for movement and audio-visual co-ordination. In DLB, however, they are found at the front of the brain which is involved in memory function.

DLB is the second most frequent cause of dementia in older people after Alzheimer's Disease. There are, however, vast numbers of people suffering from different forms of dementia. I am no doctor, but over the years, since my husband has been diagnosed with PD, I have learnt so many revealing facts about these degenerative illnesses. I really think that having this insight into causes and effects has helped us to cope with the challenges.

PD is caused by the death of neurotransmitters in the area of the brain called dopamine. Control and regulation of movement is gradually lost, and the core symptoms of slowness and stiffness emerge. Knowing these facts is helpful in enabling me to understand the illness better and I can honestly say that, in spite of all that we have endured, we have managed to keep smiling most of the time. But we have also had our dark days of misery when the tears have flowed in plenty.

~ 4 ~

As a carer I have certain rights and I want other people out there in similar circumstances to realise that help is available and they must claim their entitlements in order to help ease some of the pressures brought about by a partner's illness.

First and foremost it is my right to be free from inhuman and degrading treatment under Article 3. The right to be free from health risks that carers face could be an issue under this clause. If Public Authorities know of carers who are suffering mental health problems or physical illness as a result of caring, and do nothing to alleviate or prevent it, that could constitute a violation of their human rights.

Under Section 8, carers have rights to privacy and family life just like every citizen. A framework is offered to ensure that the rights of the elderly or disabled person are balanced against the rights of the carer, but in reality, this rarely happens. Social Services teams tell carers that they cannot have the services they require until their needs have been assessed. Then we are told that even if we have an assessment, we will not receive any more support.

These attitudes and failure to apply current legislation deter and prevent carers from meeting their basic but important needs, which include keeping up family relationships and social ties. We hear plenty of spin about care in the community, but a clear picture emerges of carers being let down because of cost, staff shortage or attitude. The lack of resources available to satisfy carers' legal rights could itself be considered a breach of the Human Rights Act.

Imelda Redmond, of Carers UK, states: 'Carers tell us time and time again that they feel their human rights are being infringed when they are not given a chance about caring. We are not talking about just a few people; there are six million carers throughout the UK. Every year, around two million people become carers. This gives an indication of the potential scale of the issue.'

Robert Meadowcroft, Director of Policy of Parkinson's Disease Society, said: 'We are pressing for greatly enhanced support for those who are providing care for people with Parkinson's.'

People like me should have access to carers' needs assessments, respite care and improved financial support. Both central and local government must respect the rights of those of us who provide vital support, and urgent action is clearly required.

It was my own dogged determination that finally got things moving in our case, but not everyone has the strength of character that seems to be needed to get anywhere these days. Those unable or unwilling to speak up for themselves will just be left by the wayside, forgotten, to make the best of it and it is a shameful state of affairs.

In our case, when Eric's condition began to deteriorate, our doctor phoned Social Services on his behalf. They promised to send someone to see him. Nobody came. Then I phoned and asked if someone could come and see my husband who was falling over all the time.

Nobody came. A year passed and still nobody came. One day, near the end of my tether, I drove Eric to an advice centre.

We sat and waited our turn then I pushed him to the desk. I explained to the lady what had been going on and asked her if she could phone Social Services for us. She took one look at Eric, shaking like a branch in the wind and immediately phoned them. She was very direct in her manner and spoke with authority and urgency. She told us that they would be sending someone to see us in a few days. This was when Mr Mark Pilbeam a Social Worker came into our lives and he has been a great support to us.

When I was a young girl in Jamaica, I used to see people shaking and I was told that they had bad nerves. I believed that was the case until I took up nursing and discovered the real cause. But there are other illnesses that cause people to shake, and one of them is clinical depression. Depressed people do not suffer solely from low moods and a negative outlook on life. They have difficulty concentrating, poor appetite, sleep problems and tiredness and a lack of sexual energy.

There is a greater awareness of PD now, but there is still a lot of work to be done. Many of the underlying issues of Parkinson's are not apparent. It is an insidious and fluctuating disease. How many of us really understand the overwhelming fatigue? How many times, in a restaurant, has Eric been considered to be drunk because he has knocked something over, and he staggers and slurs his words?

I have often wished that my husband might want to donate his brain to Parkinson's for research, in the hope that it may one day help other sufferers of this terrible illness. However, it has to remain unspoken. I cannot say it to him because, the way his mind constantly changes, he might think I want to kill him for his brain.

Eric often tells me that he feels worthless. This, with his feelings of hopelessness, guilt together with his painful slowness, sometimes makes him feel suicidal. He can't go for a walk or swim any more. I used to take him to the pool, just to let him exercise his body, but I had to watch him like a baby. One day I took my eye off him for a moment to talk to someone and the next thing we heard was a strangled grunting sound. He was disappearing down the deep end and swallowing water.

I had to get help to bring him out of the pool and I was so frightened by what happened, I never took him again. It was a shame because the water used to help loosen him up. I took him to the doctor and he arranged for the physiotherapist to see him. The physiotherapist came a few days later with some papers containing exercises and instructions on how to do them. She left the papers with me. That was not what I expected to happen. I expected her to work on him, not to leave it to me. He has never seen another physiotherapist since.

I think that after you reach a certain age, they more or less give up on you. But I'm a persistent person, so I always fight his corner. I have to be persistent, to get up each time that I've been knocked down, and to take another step forward. I have been through some tough times in my life, yet somehow I managed to come through whatever the problems were. Out of bad can come good, and maybe life can become a huge success. Well, I am my own rock... I am a fighter.

However, it is a sad fact of life and the nature of people to build you up and then shoot you down, like a bird. But I don't see my life as a tragedy. It is just my fate, my destiny. Some people get more trouble than others but I somehow got more than my own share.

~ 5 ~

This chapter breaks my heart, but it has to be written because it affected me and my husband very much, although most of it was directed at me.

Since I overdosed, Maureen had treated me with contempt. She had no respect for me anymore and the way she spoke to me was terrible. She would never have spoken to her friends in that way, nor treated them in such a degrading manner.

We had fallen out so many times. But still I tried to be there for her, as a mother. In January 2006 she went into hospital for major surgery and for thirteen days I drove from Stockport with Eric to see her every day. Her husband didn't visit because they were having problems.

I used Eric's wheelchair to push him. I was so tired, but I kept going, even after she left hospital. On the Sunday we went to visit her, Colin, her husband, was there. We didn't need to be lawyers to realize that something was going on. Then Maureen told us that she and Colin were splitting up. Eric and I both burst into tears, we were all in tears. They had been together since they were eighteen, and now they were forty-four.

Our grandchildren, Warren and Georgia, took it badly. I tried to reason with Maureen, but nothing worked. Since Yvonne died she had been finding it hard to cope and I suggested she had some counselling. But she said she didn't need it, and that I was the one who needed it. She had her friends and her work as a midwife but the breakdown of her marriage seemed to make everything worse. She seemed to throw everything at me.

It was becoming so bad that I felt I wanted to disown her. It's not as if I have been a bad mother. I have always helped her out over the years, but I came to the conclusion that enough was enough at the end of the day. I was the one who gave birth to her, gave her life. We did not bring her up to disrespect us or anyone else.

On 1st June 2007, I decided I would treat Maureen and her children, and my son, Andrew, to a holiday. On 2nd March, Maureen's birthday, Andrew had been involved in a terrible road accident in which he broke both arms and sustained other injuries. Having been knocked off his motorbike, he was very lucky to come out of it alive.

I thought it would be good for us all to chill out for a week, and have a rest, but Maureen managed to have a fight with us over something trivial the day before we were due to leave. Since then, our relationship had been very strained.

All I can say is that you can do and give too much, until it is simply taken for granted. And then to be treated as if you have never done anything is heartbreaking. I wanted us to be friends and have fun together as mother and daughter. I am not an unapproachable person, but Maureen had some issues and until she addressed them, I guessed there would be no change. I was determined to get on with my own life in whatever way I was able to, because life is too short.

So I try and have some fun, enjoy myself and above all, keep on writing, because I enjoy it very much. When I am in a good frame of mind and my writing is flowing, I can so easily lose myself in my creative world. Writing can take me somewhere beautiful, somewhere sad, and somewhere happy, where I can let my imagination run wild.

~ 6 ~

We continued to travel, even though I had to push Eric in his wheelchair. We visited countries not too far away from England. We had done most of the long-haul flights before he became too frail to withstand such long journeys.

In January 2006, Eric kept asking me to take him to Jamaica so that he could visit his older brother. I told him that maybe his brother had died. After all, they had not been keeping in touch, and I did not want him travelling all that way for nothing. However, he won and I booked our tickets. Then disaster struck.

Two days after booking the tickets, Eric had a fall and sliced his left ear in two as he crashed into a glass panel in the door.

Thank God I was there, or he would have bled to death. I had only just gone upstairs to do some writing on this book when I heard a loud bang. I ran down the stairs to find him with a piece of glass stuck in his head. I could feel panic rising inside me, but I remembered what I had to do.

When I dialled 999 they told me to apply pressure to the bleeding, and that's what I was doing with a clean kitchen towel.

He was lying on the floor, moaning, when the ambulance arrived.

The paramedics took over then, and told me to go and wash my hands. When we got to A&E the doctors tried to stop the bleeding, but they had to give up because he was losing so much blood. He had to undergo an operation to stitch his ear back in place.

I took a taxi home at 5.50 am. No one knew what had happened until I got home and rang the children before they left for work. That was how 2006 started for us. I was finding it so much harder to cope with Eric and his illness, but somehow I kept to my vows, 'for better, for worse; in sickness and in health,' even though I was at breaking point.

Nevertheless, it was the last straw that broke the camel's back.

My computer wasn't working properly, so I called someone to come and check it out for me. We had just finished supper when the doorbell rang. I left Eric sitting at the table and took the guy up to the computer in the back bedroom. The next thing was Eric shouting right behind me. He had taken the stairlift and followed us upstairs. He was in a jealous rage and very hostile, shouting that I had run upstairs to have sex with this guy. I was shocked at his outburst and very embarrassed. I felt that I could have strangled him with my bare hands.

I was in floods of tears and decided that I would not sleep in the house with him that night, so I put my coat on and took my keys. By this time it was 11 o'clock and he had been ranting since six. I went for a walk. No where special; just walking around different streets. My mind was in a terrible state and I just felt like ending it all because I could see no way out of the nightmare that I found myself in.

I sat on a wall at the end of our street for an hour or so. There was no traffic. Just two cats having a fight... or was it sex? Anyway, I remember thinking what hell it was in our house and how peaceful it was out in the street. I decided to move as I felt a bit scared. Anything could happen at that time of night when it was so quiet. I sat in one of our garden chairs and tried to think what I could do. I knew I couldn't sleep in the house with him because I wouldn't be responsible for my actions. I was likely to harm him if he continued his aggression.

I took a torch and went in the garage. I sat in there and threw the travel rug around me. It was after 2 am, but I couldn't go off to sleep because my thoughts were running away with me. However, I knew that something had to be done. I would not take that sort of behaviour from him. I had put up with enough crap and simply wasn't prepared to take any more, sickness or not.

I knew when it was 7 am as I heard traffic in the street again. But I must have fallen asleep. The next thing I knew, it was 9.30. The carer David must have come and got no answer when he came to help bath Eric. I rang my son, Andrew. He was starting his shift at 11am and promised to look in on his way to work. But when he came and saw the situation for himself, he rang Maria at work, and she rang our doctor.

The doctor came with a social worker and I was kept out of the way while they discussed what they were going to do with him. This was July 2007 and we were having some decent weather. We could have gone out and enjoyed the weather if things hadn't been so impossible.

Dr Crook came upstairs to me. She told me that they had given Andrew and Maria the names of two possible homes where Eric could go. They took him away and I just went to bed and cried. I knew that it was the beginning of the end of our lives together. I was so distraught. It was like a bereavement, I missed him so much, I wondered what was wrong with me. I had wanted to be out of his presence when he was behaving so badly, and yet I couldn't bear to be without him once he had left.

The worst part was having to explain to people what had happened, and how it had all started. It was so stressful. I went into depression and didn't actually visit him for a few weeks.

I knew I looked awful and I didn't want him to see me like that. When I did go to visit him I was horrified. Both his eyes were badly bruised and nearly closed. and he was still accusing me of 'having it off with that guy in the bedroom' so I walked out.

He was deteriorating and obviously wasn't being properly cared for. Mr Mark Pilbeam, the Social Worker, decided that he should be moved to a different nursing home. But after he was moved, he kept falling and injuring himself. The staff told me that he was very challenging. Well didn't I know that already?

I used to visit him most days. I felt that I must, even though I was exhausted. He would cry and beg me to take him home. He said he had not been bathed for days. The policy of the Home was a bath once weekly, but he had not had a bath for nine days. He was always a very clean person and this distressed him beyond words. I was disgusted, but that was nothing to what I felt when, one day I went to visit and they told me Eric was in his room. When I opened the door he was sitting at the wash basin in his birthday suit, trying to wash himself.

I was shocked at this sight. He looked so vulnerable. I put my hand in the water and it was cold. I ran it out and replaced it and began to wash his back. The water was filthy and I had to replace it again to wash his front. Again, it was the same and I repeated the procedure until I got down to his feet. I was appalled when I looked at his feet. They were being eaten away by some kind of fungal infection.

I creamed his body and dressed him and splashed him with some of his favourite fragrance. When I had him settled back in his wheelchair I pushed him to the office and described what I had just found to the lady in charge. She said she would arrange for the District Nurse to come and attend to his feet. Two visits later, no one had come and I was so disgusted that I went out and bought some spray for Athletes Foot. I assumed that was the cause of the infection, but I didn't know for sure.

That was the kind of treatment Eric received in the nursing home and I was paying a whacking amount of £535 a week to watch him deteriorate. It affected Eric more than anyone knew. He was so distraught that he deliberately smashed a drinking glass in the washbasin and then swallowed the pieces. He'd had enough of his illness and the way he was being neglected in the home, and decided he would be better off dead. The staff didn't phone me, but they phoned Andrew and Maria, telling them what had happened. Maria had to break the terrible news to me.

I made a dash to Stepping Hill Hospital and found him lying in bed with the cot sides up. He was grey and his eyes were closed. I thought he was on his way out. He had an X-ray and we could see the glass inside his stomach. The doctor decided not to operate as it was too risky, so they waited for nature to take its course. The glass damaged him internally but he pulled through.

He was in the bed numbered 2, and over the next two weeks, five people died in bed numbered 1 next to him. This made him even more depressed. I took the opportunity to explain to him that, even though he wanted to die, he would have to wait until his time came. All those patients in bed number 1 had come to the end of their time and died peacefully. But I have to say that it was quite morbid when I went to visit him and again found a different patient in the bed next to him.

Next, he had to be assessed by a psychiatrist. I was told that they wanted me to be present. So I had to sit there next to him, listening while they discussed what might have tipped him over the edge. I knew what had contributed to his distress. I was blown over by the intensity of the doctor's questioning. Eric was 83 years old at the time and I thought it was too much for him to cope with.

Two weeks before Christmas of 2006, Eric was found a bed on the psychiatric ward. It was a very distressing time for me and the family. Somehow I found the strength to bring him home with the help of my grandchildren for Christmas dinner. They came with me to the hospital and helped to get him into the car. When we got home, they were a Godsend, helping to settle him into the house. Between us we managed it, and it was wonderful to have him at home for Christmas.

Andrew and Maria came down early to help me bath Eric and then returned later for Christmas dinner, which I had been up late preparing on Christmas Eve. It was wonderful when all the family arrived, but Eric just sat in his chair, smiling, although he was clearly unwell. I will never forget this. I wanted him to sit at the table, with the family. But he wouldn't have it. He just wanted to stay in his chair in the living room. In the end, I sat in there with him and fed him with his Christmas dinner. Then I had mine on a tray on my lap. But it was no big deal. I was just happy to have him home. Andrew and Maria took him back to hospital on Boxing Day in the evening.

I continued to be there for him and visited almost every day. He kept asking to come home and when I explained that I couldn't cope on my own he became aggressive and abusive towards me, accusing me yet again of having another man. He thought that was the reason I didn't want him to come home. I found this very difficult to deal with. I knew I was not doing any such thing. I was giving him a hundred and ten percent and that was my reward. He knew what he was doing. He told all the hospital staff he met and anyone else who would listen.

I found it not only distressing but also embarrassing. Most of them knew it was not true, but it was soul-destroying, all the same.

There was one time when he had kicked off on the same old subject and I came out of the ward and drove my car into a concrete post in the car park. I knew I had parked in a very tight spot and had to take care, but in my anger I yanked the wheel round quickly and went straight into the post. Another time, he was sitting with some more patients and asked me to take him to his room. When we got there, he very calmly said, "Valerie, aren't we husband and wife?"

"Of course we are," I told him.

"Then why are you having it off with all these men?"

I couldn't bear him to start again. I was ready to kill him and I walked out before I completely lost it.

Andrew and Maria were walking towards his room as I stormed out. They led me back into Eric's room.

"What's up now, Mum?" demanded our son.

I told him, saying I could take no more of it.

Andrew spoke to his father. "I don't want to hear it, either. Come, Maria."

As they walked out, I let the brake off Eric's wheelchair and pushed him back to the day room. "They only just came," I told him, "and now they have gone. And I am going, too." I marched blindly down the corridor, passing Andrew and Maria talking to a staff member. When I reached my car I started crying and, hardly able to see through the tears, I drove off. I turned the corner and realized that I should not be driving in this state. I pulled up and when Andrew and Maria turned the corner, they saw me and stopped.

Andrew took me to their house and Maria drove my car. We sat down with cups of tea and had a long talk. When I pulled myself together again, I drove myself home. It was pitch black and the rain was throwing down. I felt devastated and cried and cried when I got home. I had never felt so alone and lost.

Since the early part of 2007, I have been saying that I would just like to take off to a desert island where I don't know anybody and nobody knows me. I have felt completely beaten. I know in my heart that I have given everything to Eric. I have told him so many times that there is only my life left to give and I can honestly say that there have been many times since then that I have felt like giving that up, too. But, you know, there is always some voice in my head that speaks to me and tells me to hold on, even though I am desperate and ready to give up.

Yes, I do know that it is Eric's illness that makes him behave the way he does. But when he is saying these things, he seems to be quite rational. He has all his faculties and knows exactly what he is saying.

Sometimes he forgets what day it is, or what he has just said even though he can remember what he did years ago. I feel a deep sadness when I see him like this. Parkinson's has taken everything from him. He is Eric Bartley, the man I married all those years ago... and yet he is nothing like him. I have lost him and that is what is so hard to bear. I knew that if I did not take care, I could end up on the same ward as him. That was where the demented geriatrics ended up and my instinct was to run like hell out of it.

One day, after a meeting with Eric's psychiatrist, I was very distressed and Mark, his social worker, suggested to me that I went away for a while.

"Why don't you go and visit your sister?" he said.

I said I would think about it, but it was strange that he had said that, because I had been toying with the idea for some time. But I kept thinking that it was wrong to leave Eric. What would the children think of me, leaving their father when he was so ill? How silly I was not to think of myself just for once. I would be of no use to him or anybody else if I broke down again. I did not want to end up in the same state I was in after Yvonne died, and yet I knew I was heading that way.

~ 7 ~

I booked a holiday to Egypt in January 2007, for two weeks. It seemed an obvious choice for an once-in-a-lifetime adventure. I had always wanted to visit Egypt, but Eric always said he didn't want to go there because there is too much trouble in that part of the world. I told him I would go on my own one day, and that day had come.

I was excited to be going to the land of the pharaohs. I was told that the temperature would be over 70°, but when we touched down at Taba Airport it was freezing. As we set off to our hotels, we started to descend quite sharply and there were a lot of hairpin bends, making me feel uneasy. The landscape was otherwise barren. Dusk seemed to fall quickly and before long the night was black. I just prayed that we reached our hotels safely.

With such a steep descent it was like going into a pit, but it must have been a very deep valley. At last, I could see some lights twinkling in the distance, assuring me that there was life somewhere in this place.

When I finally arrived at the Radisson Hotel, my home for two weeks, I was shocked to find they had airport-style security. Our bags and cases all had to be scanned. I did feel slightly uneasy, but little did I know that I would have to put up with that wherever I went. It was normal procedure in that part of the world.

I was delighted with my room, which was spacious and modern. It even had a fridge, which was good to see. This was the second time I had gone on holiday on my own since Eric had to give up travelling. I was trying to get used to my own company, which took some doing, but I was determined to be a true adventurer.

I awoke to the sound of birds twittering. I sprang out of bed and opened the door to the balcony. It was 7.45am. There was the Red Sea in the distance. The sun was shining but there was a cold wind blowing off the sea. After a shower I went for breakfast. I strutted into the dining room and hung my fleece over a chair at a table for two. I was vexed that I needed an overcoat to walk from my bedroom to the dining room, where I had to go through the security scan again.

After breakfast I went to the Welcome meeting. I looked at some trips to Cairo, Jerusalem and Petra. Nothing can compare with what I saw and learnt on those three-day trips, which included a visit to the pyramids. I don't think a visit to Egypt is complete without seeing the Pyramids and the Sphinx. The Egyptian Museum is a must.

My trip brought my geography lessons to life. I couldn't believe I was passing beneath the Suez Canal, something I was taught about all those years ago. The cruise down the River Nile while having dinner was unforgettable with all those belly dancers swinging their hips full of trinkets.

Wow! Cairo was a crazy city, inhabited by 18 million people and the worst traffic and pollution of any city on earth. The pyramids towering above made me feel wonderful, and yet insignificant. It was hard to avert my gaze from their magnetic appeal. It felt odd to be so near to something that is famous in the mist, even though it was almost midday. The enjoyment of my trip to Egypt was shaped by the knowledge and expertise of the guide – and believe me, a guide is essential. It would be no good at all without one.

I didn't go inside the pyramids because I felt it would be claustrophobic, so I sat on the steps, touched them, and breathed the atmosphere of antiquity. However, I soon realized that if I sat there much longer my peace would be interrupted by hawkers selling their trinkets. I got up and mingled with the sea of tourists, all mesmerised by these historic monuments.

I couldn't get over how barren the area was, but of course it was all desert. I stayed overnight and visited the Citadel the next day.

Wandering around the beautiful Mohammed Ali mosque was very calming and exactly what my spirits needed, even though my legs were dropping off.

We set off back to Taba at midday in hazy sunshine. I was secretly dreading all the border checkpoints where they came on the bus and checked us all out. We had an armed guard throughout our journey, sitting in the front seat of the bus.

The light faded, and a glorious sunset gave way to darkness until it was soon pitch black. I could not close my eyes and relax because I wanted to see what was going on. Not that I could do anything if something happened. Lots of people were zonked out, but not me, and I was dead tired. It was 11pm when we reached the hotel and I felt exhausted, but I was glad I had done it, in spite of a tummy upset. The next day I just chilled out and went for a walk along the beach.

On 16th January we visited Petra in Jordan. We travelled by bus, boat and then bus again, to get there. I was stunned to see the mountains and the roads covered in a blanket of snow. I just had my short fleece coat, and used a shrug as a scarf. It was freezing. Petra is the cradle of civilization. It has retained its Old Testament charm. I took a horse and cart when I heard how far I would have to walk down the valley. I sat in my seat bumping up and down as the horse galloped downhill full tilt on the cobblestones. I held on for dear life, frightened out of my wits.

The horse seemed to know every stone that his hooves thundered on. The shimmering rose-red sandstone towered high above as we descended through a long and winding gorge. There were some ancient monuments, hundreds with their magnificent facades hewn out of the rock face. Then we suddenly reached a small, flat area. I was surprised to see a film crew and loads of men on camels, hanging about waiting to do their scene.

I tried to block out the cold and soak up the magnificent views. There was a number of Bedouins selling souvenirs. Most of the group walked back up, but I took the cart because I knew I would find it very difficult. As it was so cold, I knew it would spark off my asthma, making it difficult for me to breathe. I felt like a slab of ice. However, I managed to fulfil another dream.

We trooped into a restaurant and I had a huge bowl of soup which I was told contained bits of bull's penis. I didn't really care, it was just what I needed to defrost me. On the boat trip back, which took two hours, we were all given a blanket. I wrapped myself from head to foot, leaving only my face uncovered. Someone gave me another blanket – I was literally like a frozen slab of meat. Some of them were laughing at me, but I didn't care. I had three choices – freeze to death, get pneumonia, or look like a mummy, which wasn't a bad thing as millions went to Cairo to see them.

On 20th January, I took the coach at 3 am with a group of people to go to Jerusalem. It was a very long drive through the desert to the Dead Sea at the lowest point on earth. I didn't go into the sea but stood and watched the brave few who went into the ice cold water. I saw them coming out with their hands full of salt balls that looked like crystal. I begged for one and was given two, which I will always treasure.

Next we drove to the Jordan Desert and drank in the panorama from the Mount of Olives. We visited the old city of Jerusalem, the holiest city of the Jewish religion, and traced the last journey of Jesus. I saw so many wonderful, awe inspiring places... the Garden of Gethsemane, the Church at Gethsemane, the tomb where they laid Jesus, Mary's tomb and the Wailing Wall. I made a wish for my family and friends and myself and pushed it between the cracks in the wall.

Just before we reached the airport for our flight back to Taba, a thunderstorm broke. The security at the airport was very intense and I was asked some ridiculous questions like... why did I come here... what did I do... where did I visit? I was taken aback but I answered very politely that I always wanted to visit this part of the world because of its fascinating history and I loved embracing different cultures. My passport was viciously stamped. In all, I have fourteen stamps on it from visiting those countries.

We took off at 8.25 pm in the thunderstorm. Minutes into the flight, the plane was hit by lightning. It took a few minutes before the pilot announced, "Ladies and Gentlemen, we have been hit by lightning and I am returning to the airport." Everyone seemed calm, but I said a prayer in my mind. My stomach was turning over, but I knew if it was God's will He would get us down safely. And He did. When we landed there was a round of applause. I was so relieved, but my heart was pounding for quite a while afterwards.

We were well looked after and given drinks and little cakes, and after two hours we boarded the plane again. I was nervous but with a few deep breaths, I calmed down a little. However, the drama of the way the plane was dropping out of the sky will stay in my mind for a long time. The rain may have stopped, but the turbulence was terrible. I felt sick and scared and was relieved when we finally landed at Taba airport. The pilot certainly earned his money on that trip.

It was 1.30 in the morning when I reached my hotel, tired after walking in the hills. But I am so glad now that I went and didn't leave it until I was too old. I wanted an adventure, and an adventure is what I had. If I am honest, I could have done with another week just to recover from those trips, but it had all been truly wonderful.

I was still plagued by a tummy bug and visited the doctor the morning before checking out of the hotel. I was worried about having to rush to the washroom on the flight.

The guide that took us round Jerusalem said, "When you get back home, tell your friends that it is safe to come to Jerusalem."

I smiled and said to myself, "What an adventurer enjoys, an ordinary traveller may not." I would leave them to make up their own minds.

I couldn't have any alcohol for the whole of my holiday and as the coach pulled away I raised my bottle of water gently in the air... a toast to Egypt and her eternal treasures.

~ 8 ~

I was thankful for Mr Pilbeam's suggestion that I visit my sister. What I needed was someone to give me some encouragement and that was exactly what he had done. I attended to the household bills and made sure that nothing was in arrears and two weeks later, on 21st October 2007, Andrew and Maria came at three in the morning to take me to Manchester Airport. I was on my way, but the trouble started before I even went near the aircraft!

My flight was 6.20 am to Gatwick and from there I was to take a Virgin flight at 9.20 am. When I reached the desk at 7.45 I was told it was closed. I didn't understand, because the flight wasn't leaving for another hour and a half. I was taken to the British Airways desk and they booked me on a midday flight. I couldn't believe it. I had to phone my sister who was fast asleep as it was 3 o'clock in the morning there.

The other problem was this flight was going to Kingston and I would have to get an Air Jamaica flight at 11.45 pm back to Montego Bay where my sister would meet me. I began to think that everything I touched was a problem. Nothing ever seemed to be easy for me.

The flight to Kingston lasted ten hours and I was very tired. I can never sleep on a plane. When I was sitting around at the airport for eight hours, I had time to think and reflect. There were moments when I asked myself what I had done and then I calmed down and amused myself by watching the passengers going to board their flights. For some reason, I felt I should punish myself for what had happened and I refused to buy myself a drink or anything to eat. I think I would have been sick anyway, as my stomach was churning so much. The air conditioning was on, but my body felt like a hot spring.

Eventually, my flight was called and I seemed to float towards the departure gate like a butterfly. In no time, the plane took off into the black night sky for the short flight to Montego Bay. By now I had taken off three times and my third landing was about to take place. I felt at times that my journey would never end, but of course it did. We touched down safely and I couldn't wait to collect my luggage and walk out into the warm night and the arms of Hyacinth and my niece, Shauna.

But there was another journey of an hour and a half to Ocho Rios. I was feeling disorientated but like a true adventurer, I still chatted to my family. The blanket of stars seemed to be following us as we drove along the coast road. I could smell the sea and hear the waves breaking onto the shore and a few knots in my body began to untangle. It was 2.30 am when I tumbled into bed. I didn't have to wait long for sleep to come.

In the morning Hyacinth and Shauna went off to work and I had a lie in. I was jet-lagged and very tired. I went out into the garden and checked out the fruit trees. The recent hurricanes had damaged most of the trees and blown the fruit away. I found myself squinting against the glare of the sun, but it felt so good. I applied a good dose of sun cream and walked around the yard in my shorts and a skimpy top, soaking up the warm sunshine. I was in Paradise again, and yet I still had to try and detach myself from Eric's voice repeating in my head that I had another man. I could hear him telling everyone who came his way. I knew it was going to take some time for the trauma to subside, if at all.

I walked around the garden most days for gentle exercise. When it rained I paced up and down the verandah, trying to clear my mind and drinking lots of water. My days were very quiet, apart from having the radio on. I had time and space to reflect... to turn myself inside out.

After a few days I tried to write, but not a lot came. I was still so drained. It was best to leave it for a while. Some days I felt lonely and I was nervous, remembering what had happened to Eric and me when we were held up by the gunmen. When I was not walking, I locked the grille to the verandah for protection.

Icis wasn't well before I came. I wanted to help her in any way I could but I knew that I had to get some rest and regenerate myself first, before I could feel strong enough to help her. Hyacinth was at breaking point, trying to hold down her job whilst driving out to see Icis and give her support. When I heard that she hadn't seen Icis for a while, I knew that as the eldest sister, I had to do something while I was in Jamaica.

Hyacinth and I had a long talk about the situation and she decided to let Icis come and stay while I was there.

"I must warn you, Valerie," she said, "you are the one that's going to be here on your own all day with her. You have come to recharge your own batteries, so it's a lot to take on, you."

But I'm a person who always likes to help someone when they are down. Even though we didn't get on when we were growing up together, I had to hold out an olive branch. When we went to pick her up from her home at Discovery Bay, I shouted her name a few times, demanding that she open the door. She had no idea that I was in Jamaica.

"What has happened?" she cried, goggling as we threw our arms around each other. "When did you come? It is so good to see you!"

I asked how she was, but it was clear that she wasn't well. In fact, she was very ill. She had lost her ability to cope and become anxious and depressed since her husband had gone to America.

I told her I was on my own as well, Eric was in hospital and that life wasn't easy, but I had to find a way to cope. I asked what would make her feel better and happy again. Her reply? For a family member to take her in and look after her. Immediately I saw scenes from our childhood flashing in front of me. She never could cope with anything on her own.

She said, "I know that one day someone is going to find me dead in this house."

I broke down in tears when she said that.

"Please don't say that," I begged. But she had a point. I told her we had come to take her with us to Ocho Rios. She had already been invited a few weeks ago and even though her case was packed, she was still undecided. Anyway, we bundled her and her case into the car. She sat in front with Hyacinth and I shared the back seat with Haille, who was just eight weeks old, Hyacinth's first grandchild. It was the hurricane season and the rain was hammering down as the wind raged, and thunder and lightning flashed and clattered in the skies. I felt a bit scared because the windscreen was misting up. Hyacinth had to let the window down to help clear it and of course the rain found its way into the car. But at least it was warm rain.

As the car turned into the yard, Icis said, "Thank you, Lord." I was saying the same thing in my mind. I edged out of the back seat with Haille in her car seat. Her hazel eyes were wide open and she was sucking contentedly on her dummy. As soon as we went indoors we had some refreshments and sat down to talk, talk, talk.

Icis agreed to go to the doctor on the Monday and we said we would take things from there. I was to be nurse to our sister for the next seven weeks...

On Sunday, we were up early to go to the beach as planned. Icis was all for it, but when we got there she refused to go into the water. It was 6.45am and the sea water was warm at that time. But Icis chickened out and wouldn't budge. I watched her pacing up and down on the sand and decided I would go to her, to see if I could persuade her to join us.

"Leave me alone!" she shouted. "Go away!"

I went back into the water with Hyacinth and Marcia, enjoying the freedom to swim and splash about in the relaxing water. When I looked back I saw she taking off her T-shirt. I held my breath, hoping she was coming to join us, but a few seconds later she put it back on. Poor Icis! We knew that half of her wanted to come with us, but the other half was scared stiff.

Icis stayed on dry land. She said there were morays in the water.

We kept telling her it was only clumps of seaweed, but she didn't believe us. Then she said she didn't want her clothes to get wet. Now, come on, who is going to worry about getting their clothes wet down on the beach, huh? We laughed at her, although we knew she was not herself. But that's Icis. All her life she has wanted to be the main attraction. It was no big deal and we didn't push it. There was no point in winding her up unnecessarily.

However, I was glad to be there for her when she needed someone. She was child-like at times, seeking attention. The tablets prescribed by her doctor made her very sleepy, but when she was awake she made up for it by eating everything in sight. It was almost as if she had just discovered food. We were happy to see her eating, though, because she needed some flesh on her bones.

We knew when she began to feel better, because she started telling us what to do. She seemed to forget she was a guest and not in her own house. She was very irritating when she started blistering her mouth off about what she wanted to eat. The meals had already been planned by Hyacinth and I told Icis I was only doing what the lady of the house had told me to cook for dinner.

But I had to let some things go, and change the subject and talk about our childhood. Some things she insisted she couldn't remember, but at other times she admitted that she had been mean to us and behaved very badly. She laughed, saying that she had to do something to get out of doing those jobs. She thought they would kill her.

"Yes," I told her, "and sometimes I wanted to kill you! Then, can you imagine the uproar?"

We laughed and it was a good way of easing the tension.

When Hyacinth returned from work she sounded her horn, and I rushed to the verandah to greet her, like an excited child.

She has a lovely smile. "How was your day?" she asked me.

"Oh, it was good. I mustn't complain."

"Please do if you have to," she said, giving me a broad wink.

She looked at Icis. "Hello, Sis. How are you today?"

Icis scratched her head. "Not too bad. I had some sleep and Valerie was busy in the kitchen when I woke up."

"Well," Hyacinth replied, "we are waiting for the day to come when you will be in there cooking up a storm."

"I am not peeling any green bananas to stain my hands," Icis retorted, laughing like a mischievous child.

"Somebody has to do it so that you can roll up your tongue, though!" Hyacinth was not amused and neither was I.

When dinner was served, Icis was first at the table. A part of me couldn't help feeling sorry for her. She had lost her marbles somewhere along the way. My thoughts were that life was too short and when I returned home I didn't know if

I would see her again. I might never have the pleasure of cooking dinner for her again. By the time we had finished eating, I had buried her words under the tiles on the kitchen floor.

I made sure that I had my time and space to do my exercises around the yard. Sometimes she watched me and at other times she sprawled out on her bed with the fan to cool her. I didn't mind because it gave me some peace. I didn't want to hear her religious lecture all the time. She was a Jehovah Witness.

I could see her improving each day which was wonderful. It made me feel good because I had put a lot of myself into seeing that result. I have always been a good listener and now I was on my way to being a counsellor. I'm one of life's givers, not a taker. But it is so rewarding when I can bring back a smile to someone's face.

Aunt Helen came to take Icis and me out. We planned to go to the hairdressers to get glammed up. Icis wanted to do something about her grey hair. It had passed salt and pepper a long time ago. Well, her hair came out sort of blonde and the colour really suited her skin tone. I just had a shampoo and blow-dry and Aunt Helen had highlights in hers.

It was amazing to see the transformation of Icis. She stood in front of the mirror, twisting her head and smiling. She seemed to be reborn, reminding me of a rose beginning to open as the sunlight catches the petals. We almost had to drag her away, as we were going to have lunch at Jack's Wood Grill. The sun was blisteringly hot and I was glad to have my shades at hand.

We joined the line and I ordered fried festivals, which are dumplings, with jerk chicken and sorrel juice to wash it down. It was all soul food and for me, a real treat. I didn't have that kind of food very often.

Aunt Helen was waiting for her food to be cooked so I went upstairs with Icis to find a table. We had Aunt Helen's drink on a tray. Icis, having a love affair with food at that time, started to gobble her food down as soon as she got to the table. Down went the jerk fish and the fries and then, in her rush, she gulped down Aunt Helen's juice.

I was embarrassed. I wanted to thump her because I was blazing. I had to bite my tongue and hold the ice-cold drink to my mouth. We just made a joke about it and didn't let it spoil our day.

There was no stopping Icis after that. She wanted to go and look round Jazz Girl. After wandering around for ages, she bought a white sleeveless dress with embroidery on the bodice, she was happy.

Aunt Helen dropped us home, and as soon as she had gone Icis was keen to start cooking supper. I was surprised, because she had been had been complaining that she couldn't do any cooking because of pain in her fingers.

She started preparing the vegetables. I could hardly believe she was the same person who had been lying around in bed for most of the time. She peeled yams and made dumplings. She was buzzing like a bee. All I could say was, "Thank you, God."

She, in return, said, "Thank you Jehovah."

When she had finished, she took off her apron and announced that she was going out for a walk. My eyes bulged and I held my breath as I watched her disappear down the road. Shauna saw her as well, and phoned Hyacinth to tell her how lovely it was to see aunty Icis out for a stroll.

It was almost dusk when Hyacinth arrived home from work and stars were beginning to light up the sky. There was quite an air of excitement. Suddenly two figures appeared at the gate. Marcia had walked Icis home. As she walked onto the verandah, Hyacinth sprang to her feet and gave Icis such a hug.

"You look so good sis, you must keep it up now."

As my sisters clung to each other for another moment, the light went off and we were plunged into blackness. Hyacinth quickly went into action, bringing back childhood memories. She fumbled her way inside and found Mamma's old shade lamp on the sideboard. She put it in the middle of the dining table while Icis struck a match.

"Let there be light," she said, and we all burst out laughing. I felt quite emotional as I watched the dim glow casting shadows, just like it was all those years ago.

Icis said she was going to the shop to buy a flashlight. She was in top form and there was no stopping her. Off she went, up the hill in the darkness with Gevante, Hyacinth's five-year-old step-grandson. I sat there quietly with Haille in my lap. I could not believe what I was seeing.

Hyacinth plucked the little girl from me. "Come," she said. "Let's go and see what our Icis is doing."

I laughed. "Listen," I said, "I haven't got eyes like an owl. I'm frightened of falling."

"You will be fine. Just hold on to me," she said. And I did. I held on for dear life.

When we reached the shop there was a line of people waiting to buy flashlights. We ended up buying two so that we could see better to walk home and I was mighty relieved by that.

We were all hungry now and looking forward to the dinner that Icis had cooked. We used the flashlights in the kitchen to see what we were doing and the dining table was soon groaning with food. Hyacinth graced the table and thanked the Lord for the wonderful recovery that Icis was making. We all tucked in and it was lovely. We told her so, and we meant it.

The power was off for four hours and for a while I stood outside in the yard. The sky was ablaze with stars. Hyacinth was pointing upwards and naming some of them. There was a time when I could have done the same but I could not identify one of them. I also saw the fireflies for the first time since I had been there. I said they had come out especially for me and we all laughed like a bunch of kids.

The next day it was announced that there was an all-island power failure. That had not happened for years. They laughed again when I said I was just about to have my shower when suddenly the waterfall turned to a few mean drips. But I was geared up for it. I felt quite at home in third world conditions and we did quite a lot of reminiscing that night. I went off to bed with my head full of wonderful memories.

My nephew, Brant, and his wife, Gillian (Haille's parents) left for their own home after the lights came on. I helped with Haille when Hyacinth picked her up from day care, so my time was being spent in a family environment. We planned to go to Bois Content. I wanted to go and paint our parents' tombs.

On the Saturday morning, Hyacinth and I got up early and off we went with our paint and brushes. Icis didn't come. On the journey, I took in the views and the old and new landscapes that sat side by side, changing moods with the seasons. It was a nostalgic journey and when we reached Old Walk Lane, I knew that I was really home. Nothing could ever change that.

Hyacinth sounded her horn and our brother, Clement, came rushing up the lane. There were plenty of hugs and kisses as the eldest and the youngest met up again. It meant a lot to us. Clement's wife was standing by, watching, and then she fell into my arms, laughing with the excitement. We walked down into the yard, our eyes moist with tears of joy.

I walked the few yards from the verandah to our parents' graves. Hyacinth and Clement joined me and looked on as I talked to Mamma and Poppa and then we went back to the verandah and sat down. As we talked, I was looking out at their tombs. Clement busied himself chopping green coconut for us to drink.

"Thank you," I said. "Is there any rum?"

"No."

I was joking. If I started drinking rum, I might not get the painting done. We talked for a while and then got cracking. I love to paint because it can be very relaxing, but it was the feeling of somehow touching my parents with every stroke of the brush that gave me the most joy. I knew they were entombed, but it was the feeling of being close to them again that mattered to me.

Clement and his friend helped us and, as the saying goes, many hands made light work. We had a break for lunch – boiled breadfruit, green bananas, salted mackerel and tomatoes – and then went back and finished the job. It was a flying visit but my mission was completed and I was happy. Hyacinth wanted to leave by 3 pm. She didn't want night to catch us snaking up the mountain road; she was afraid of the pot holes and the blinding headlights. And so was I.

Clement packed some food and sugar cane in the car boot. I was looking forward to getting my teeth into the sugar cane, but I will have to watch my crowns. My jaws are not so strong as they had been all those years ago, but what the hell? I would give it a go.

As we drove along we saw a woman sitting at the side of the road braiding hair. High on the bank side we could hear reggae music pounding away, and then there were the menacing street hustlers toting for business, calling out, "Nice lady, come buy something from me." As we crawled through Old Harbour in the traffic, it brought back memories of all those years ago.

Then we approached Bog Walk, which is breathtakingly beautiful with its idyllic mountains, lush green foliage and vivid tropical flowers bathed in almost mystical light. One lyrical Rastafarian described the road ahead as 'the stairway to heaven.'

"I don't know about that," I said, because, although I wasn't driving, I was braking like hell with my foot every time I saw some mad driver overtake three or four cars on those treacherous roads. They were narrow and winding and they must have been crazy to drive like that.

But we made it safely back to Ocho Rios by dusk and we thanked the Lord for bringing us home safely.

Icis was lying down reading her bible. "How did you get on?" she wanted to know.

I was tired and longing for a shower so I spoke to her briefly and left it to Hyacinth to tell her. If she had come with us, she would have known all about it, but of course she chickened out as usual. Where there was work involved, she would run a mile.

I was beginning to think about returning home and as the time drew nearer I was feeling butterflies in my stomach. I was worrying about what I would have to face with Eric. People might think I had spent three months in the Caribbean and would return home, reborn and fit as a frisky filly. But it was not like that at all. I had felt like a mother hen and I needed to step back and give myself some space.

Icis told me she wanted to stay on for another week after I had gone. I reminded her that was not the arrangement. We had planned to take her home two days before I left. We knew why she wasn't keen to return to her own home. She liked being waited on. Anyway, that was the last of my worries. I was busy packing and getting my hair braided.

On the Friday evening, Icis began to pack her things. Hyacinth had told her bluntly that she was taking her home in the morning. I sat there with my lips sealed, scrutinising the seething expression on Hyacinth's face. I knew that she really meant it.

Saturday morning came and Icis threw her case into the car. She was sweating profusely and muttering to herself. I heard her say, "What I need is people around me to help me, not to be on my own and become a recluse."

My heart was beginning to pound, but there was nothing I could do to make it any better for her. I was on my own, too, but I wasn't making a big deal of it. There was no point.

We stopped at the supermarket so that she could get some shopping. Even that seemed to be an effort for her, even though we helped her. There were still a lot of tropical storms around and it was bucketing down. I tried to make light of the situation. I said, "Icis, you are lucky. You can travel home by road, but I will have to go six miles up in the sky and just hope I come down safely."

When we arrived at her home she seemed to perk up a bit. I suppose she had to, really. We helped her to bring the shopping in and she discovered that the fridge was frozen solid.

"Pull the plug out, and open the door" I told her "it's warm. It will soon melt soon."

"I don't want my meat going off," she said, pulling a face.

When she went into the garden she found someone had been stealing her fruit. All the best were gone. She found a small sowersap and knocked it down with a stick and Hyacinth found one ripe mango. We went back inside as the rain began to hammer down again.

"Valerie, we will have to love Icis and leave her," Hyacinth said. "We have a lot to do, come on."

On the verandah we all hugged each other fondly. The sky was dark and the thunder roared. We dived into the car and I waved to Icis as Hyacinth drove out on to the gravel road, spraying the chippings into the culvert with the rainwater.

The journey was a little subdued but we managed to have a joke about the situation, and after all it is better to laugh than to cry. It was still throwing it down when we arrived home and we poured ourselves some juice and sank into the couch to relax, knowing that we had done our best for our sister Icis.

I had lost some weight and my pants were very loose. In fact, they were falling down. That didn't make sense to me because I had been eating well. My skin was as smooth as a baby's bottom and I had a nice tan... oh yes, we *do* go darker in the sun. When I reached home I would have my lighter bits and my very dark bits to show off.

Hyacinth had not specified what to cook for supper. It was Friday, when anything would do. She went and pick up grandchildren. She had had a mixed day, as a friend from America had phoned and told her that her daughter had died in a road accident. She was sad, and went to lie down for a while.

When she got up, she sprang a surprise on us. "Get dressed, girls!

We are all going for a meal down town."

We had a lovely Chinese meal. The atmosphere there was very enjoyable and I was tapping my knife and fork to the rhythm of Bob Marley's 'No Woman No Cry'.

Gevante exclaimed, "Auntie Valerie, mind you don't wake Haille with the noise!" He was only five years old, but already very protective of his baby sister.

I felt very happy to have three generations of the family gathered here for my farewell meal. Okay, I was into my sixties, but hey, I was alive, and dancing with life. I have had to be a strong woman to stand by my man, but that extra strength does not last for ever. I had no one to perform my wifely duties with anymore, and missed the touch of Eric's lips, holding him tight, and whispering lovers' talk with him. The house would be empty when I got back, with a pile of letters and junk mail waiting behind the door. I had geared myself up to anything that was thrown at me. I was still able to hold my head high, but I dared not think for how much longer I could do it.

We were enjoying ourselves so much that nobody noticed it was beginning to rain. Brant did not have a car, so he borrowed his mother's to take his family home first and then returned so that Hyacinth could take the rest of us home. We were the last to leave the restaurant – a good sign – and we joked about it as they closed the door after us.

When we got home, the three cats, Socks, Zoe and Havana were curled up on the verandah waiting for us. They were all so different in character. Socks was aptly named, with her four white paws. She was a good hunter but allowed Havana to snatch her kill. Lizards were not safe when she was around. As we sat talking, Socks jumped into my lap and we didn't see Havana go past, into the kitchen.

"Hyacinth," I said, suddenly noticing what looked like blood on the floor, "where has that come from? Is it blood?"

She looked to where I was pointing." Looks like it," she said, and got up, following the trail to the kitchen. Then I heard her shout.

"Havana, what's that you've got? Valerie, she has caught a rat!"

"What?" I was up on the couch in an instant and then froze to the spot.

"She has been flashing that about for some time, there is a lot more blood here," Hyacinth called. "I am going to get it here on the mat and pour some hot water on it, watch out!"

I made a grab for the door key, and opened the door and ran out to the gate. I was absolutely petrified. As I stood near the bank I saw Hyacinth pulling out the mat with this huge great rat on it.

"Valerie! Valerie! Where are you?" she called.

I was unable to answer, paralyzed with fear. I watched as she poured the water on it and two of the cats circled around it.

"Valerie? Where are you?"

"I'm out here by the gate."

"Well you can come in now. It's gone"

I peered across the darkness and in the light from the doorway, I saw Havana grab the rodent and run down the steps with it. I went back inside, taking care not to stand anywhere near the spot where it had been.

Hyacinth was as bright as brass after performing her ritual.

"They bring them in here many times, as if to say,' aren't we clever, look what we 'a got'."

"What?" I was horrified and my heart was still pounding. The room smelt of the rat's blood. It was a strong, overpowering smell.

"I'm used to sorting them out when they bring 'em in. I think they catch 'em in that bush at the back," Hyacinth cheerfully informed me.

I felt sick to my pit. I took some deep breaths and tiptoed to the bedroom with the feeling I wasn't going to sleep well that night. Just two more days before I flew home. I wanted to see Eric again... but what would I find?

"What a dramatic way to end my holiday," I said aloud.

"You were lucky they never brought one in before," Hyacinth replied.

My eyes bulged and my head swam when it was mentioned next morning. I spent all day scanning the place in case there was a repeat performance. Even now I shiver when I think of it.

Aunt Helen came and had Sunday dinner with us on her way back from church. She looked very glamorous as usual in a cream suit and matching hat. Nearly seventy, she always wore her heels, claiming that she couldn't walk in flat shoes. How I wished my sister Icis could take a leaf out of her book. Helen, a widow and a JP, kept herself occupied doing charity work and many other things. When she was leaving, we kissed each other on both cheeks and she drove off down the lane like a woman half her age, the wheels spinning up a cloud of dust in the evening sunshine.

I sat quietly on the verandah, replaying a few memories from the past three months before retiring to bed. Later, as I lay in bed, a green frog jumped in through the window. Another fright! I screamed and freaked out as it jumped towards the door. There were some things I was definitely not going to miss when I went home!

As dusk fell softly into darker night, the telephone rang.

Hyacinth rushed to get it.

"Guess what?" she asked, putting the phone down. "Courtney just told me he is coming from Kingston at 11am to take you to the airport."

"What? I thought you said you would take me?"

"Yes, but Valerie, if he wants to come, I can't stop him," she smiled, her shoulders jumping up to touch her ears.

"Well, the more the better," I replied.

"At least we will have air conditioning in his posh car. That will make such a nice change for you and me!" Hyacinth laughed like a child full of glee. Courtney was her ex-husband and they were the best of friends.

It was sad for me to leave my family who had been there for me when I needed a bolt hole. Courtney arrived on the dot of eleven.

"Are you ready, Miss Valerie?"

We hugged. "Yes, I am."

"Where is your case? In the bedroom?"

With a few long strides he was in and out in two seconds, all 6ft 4ins of him, with a cheerful grin on his face. I settled in the back seat and enjoyed being driven by my ex-brother-in-law, soaking up the views as we went along. When we reached Discovery Bay, I said, "I wonder what our Icis is doing now?"

"She might be still snoring," Hyacinth said.

We laughed. "Icis is Icis, bless her," I said.

"When you coming back again to Jamaica?" Courtney wanted to know.

"If you don't mind, I haven't gone yet..."

"Well, you will be back for the sunshine, if nothing else," he teased.

"Okay. Don't rub it in." But I was thinking of cold, wet Manchester and what lay ahead.

When we got to Montego Bay Airport we said our last goodbyes and then I walked away without looking back. My eyes were like two hot springs. The desk had just opened up and two people were ahead of me. Just as I was being checked in, the computer crashed. The assistant went to another screen and managed to finish my booking and I walked away, through immigration, not knowing or caring that all the computers were about to crash.

However, because all passengers had to be checked in manually, long delays ensued and our 5.20 flight finally took off at 9.30 pm. By then I was tired and not in the least looking forward to the nine hour flight to Gatwick. As I have said before, although I enjoy flying, I can never sleep. Those moments of turbulence can be very hairy sometimes.

I was seated next to a woman with a young baby and a three year old girl. It was a bit ear-piercing at times, especially when they both cried at the same time. But what could you do? We were all locked up in a tube miles above the earth with no control of our lives. You have to be tolerant of coughs and splutters and cheesy feet. It is true that my nose is very sensitive, but I am not a snobbish person and I will talk to anyone to break the ice. That is part of being adventurous – otherwise you may as well forget it. If you don't ever open your mouth, how will you find out anything?

We arrived at Gatwick at 8.45 am. I was cross-eyed. I need to take a connecting flight to Manchester and the place was heaving with people hurrying about in all directions. But my flight to Manchester was not until 11.45, so I had plenty of time. Of course, it did not go smoothly for me... there *had* to be a problem.

When I tried to check in with my hand luggage, which was basically some of my work for this book and a couple of other books, I was stopped because I also had a litre of Sangster's rum cream. I was quite entitled to bring it into the country, but anti-terrorist regulations in this country meant that I was not allowed to take any liquid onto the plane. It would have to go in with my main luggage.

I tried protesting. "I have just come off one flight with it, I haven't left the airport."

It didn't work.

"Put your papers in this carrier bag," she said, handing me one and then put the bottles in your hand luggage. Easily solved."

"But it will get broken on the carousel. The bags go flying all over the place."

"Go and buy some bubble wrap, then. That will protect it."

God, I was getting fed up with this. "Buy some where?"

She pointed. "There are some shops over there."

I shuffled off, cursing under my breath. My eyes felt full of gravel. Eventually I found a likely shop.

The man laughed in my face. "I have sold out."

"Damn it!" I stamped my foot, frustrated at what I considered to be unnecessary hassle. For a moment I freaked out. I was exhausted and my head was bloody pounding. Taking a deep breath, I asked him politely if he had any odd pieces of plastic wrapping.

"I'll look in the bin." He fished around and came up with some discarded bubble wrap and some paper.

"Bingo. That will do," I said. "I'm in business now."

He laughed and I grinned back at him. I wrapped the bottles and put them into the bag. My writing would travel with me in the carrier bag. With a spring in my step now, I went back to the desk and checked the bag in.

By now my stomach had started to complain and I made a dash to the washroom. No sooner had I come out than I had to rush back in again. I suddenly felt nauseous and nervous. What on earth was wrong with me? Then it dawned on me that I was nearly home and had no idea what I was going to face with Eric. I took some deep breaths to compose myself and occasionally glancing at my watch.

A lady came and sat beside me and I struck up a conversation with her. It turned out that she had come off the same flight from Jamaica, and was also travelling alone. She was waiting for a flight to Edinburgh. As I said, talking to people you meet is part of the adventure of travelling. She told me that she had been to her brother's funeral and I told her I was sorry for her loss.

She was an albino and didn't look as if she had even seen the sun, let alone been to a warm country. As we talked, it was as if we had known each other before. The time passed quickly and it was time for me to get to my boarding gate. We said goodbye fondly and I walked off into the crowd, knowing this was the last leg of my journey.

It was a small British Airways plane with just one cabin with green leather seats. My window seat was near the back. I was cold. Maybe it was because I felt so tired. As I looked round, I saw a young woman walking down the aisle towards me. She was dressed in a long tweed coat and Russian fur hat, and carried a designer handbag. She came and sat in the seat next to me. No sooner had she sat down she began coughing her guts up and blowing her nose like a trumpet. Boy, that was all I needed. I pick up bugs very easily.

I turned my face towards the window and pulled my scarf over my nose so that I wouldn't breathe in any of her germs. She was blowing her nose practically non-stop and I felt embarrassed on her behalf because everyone was looking at her. But trust me to be the one sitting next to her with such a stinking cold! I sat with my scarf over my nose and my face turned away for the whole journey. I didn't care much what she thought; she wasn't thinking about me. She didn't even apologise.

I was relieved when the plane touched down. As it taxied in, I was still holding my scarf for dear life. The woman had not said one word to me, but I didn't mind. That would have meant moving my scarf.

I collected my luggage including the bottle of rum, which was still intact, and walked out in the rain to the taxi rank. There was no one there to meet me because they were all at work. I was my own woman and trying to get used to it and be strong. This would be my life now. As the taxi joined the motorway I found myself wondering if my home was okay. I would soon find out.

~ 9 ~

When the taxi pulled up outside and I stepped onto the pavement, and I thanked the Lord. I opened the door to a pile of letters and junk mail.

The house welcomed me after being locked up for three months. I lit the fire and made a cup of Camomile tea before taking a long, lingering bath. Then I crawled into bed, but it was 2 pm. I lay there, waiting for sleep to come and eventually, it did.

When I woke up, I phoned Lillian, my next door neighbour, who had my spare keys. She was ninety-three years old, but she watched my house like a hawk. She was pleased to see me back and told me how she had missed me. I often went in and had a cup of tea or a glass of sherry and a natter with her. I told her I would see her tomorrow and then I phoned my son and daughter to get the latest news about their father.

They said he had missed me like crazy and thought I had gone off with another man. Maureen had warned him not to mention it when he saw me and I was glad she had pulled him up about it. That was the one thing that drove me mad, because he accused me of it every time I saw him.

I went to visit him Wednesday afternoon. When I arrived he was sitting in the dayroom with some other patients.

When he clapped his eyes on me he stretched out his hands and said, "Come, come." His face lit up like the full moon. I bent down and gave him a lingering kiss.

"I'm so glad to see you," he beamed.

"I'm glad to see you, too." I said.

All eyes seemed to be fixed on us.

"He missed you very much," one elderly man told me. "You will be alright now, Eric, she's back."

"I won't be long," I said. "I'm going to get your wheelchair so that we can sit in your room and talk."

I came back with it and Toby, one of the male nurses, helped me to get him into it. He was so excited that he began to shake.

"Calm down," I told him.

"How is Hyacinth and Icis? Maureen says that's where you've been."

"But I told you that's where I was going before I left. You didn't believe me, did you?" I was trying to stop myself from erupting into a ball of flames.

"I'm so glad you're back. I missed you so much."

"Well, I hope you are not going to start giving me ear grief again," I told him.

"No, I won't," he promised, holding on to my hand like a love- bird.

Because of his insecurity, I did sometimes feel sorry for him. I was giving my all to him, but he didn't see it that way.

The trolley arrived with the patients' supper. It was five o'clock and time for me to go. I pushed Eric back into the dayroom, and kissed him and I left. It was black outside and very cold. When I got home I breathed a sigh of relief that Eric was okay with me.

That night I began to sneeze. I could feel that I was coming down with a cold. I knew then that I had caught it from the trumpet blower who had sat beside me on the plane. I came down with the most horrendous chest infection and I never left the house again for three weeks. It took two lots of antibiotics and a bottle of revolting medicine to put me on the road to recovery.

But before all that, I went round to visit Lillian my neighbour in the afternoon. She told me that she felt jiggered, a phrase she often used when she didn't feel well.

She said, "Well, I told myself I'm not seventy, I'm not eighty... I'm ninety-three. I think I'll be going soon."

"You won't be going anywhere," I said. "You will be here for your one hundredth birthday."

She pulled a face. "We'll see."

I kissed her, as I always did, and left. But I was not geared up for the next bit. When Isabella, another neighbour, went in with some shopping on the Saturday, she found her dead in her chair. When I was told, I was devastated. She had been like a mother to me, and a really good friend. The thought crossed my mind that she had been waiting for me to return from Jamaica, to give me my keys.

Isabella rang Lillian's only sister and told her what had happened. The police and ambulance arrived and then her sister and her daughter. I was in shock, and went indoors. I looked outside just in time to see her body being taken away. Isabella and I went to her funeral and our names were mentioned in the Minister's eulogy, much to our surprise.

Whatever we did for Lillian, we did it from our hearts, with love, and I can only hope that if I live to her great age, I will have some kind neighbour to do the same for me.

February 14th, Valentine's Day, and I was having a lie-in when there was a knock at the door. I looked out of the bedroom window to see a man holding a huge bouquet of flowers. Grabbing my dressing gown, I rushed to the door, and he plonked the flowers in my hand. I was taken aback but when I read the card, I was blown away completely.

They were from Eric. He is a very romantic man and that is the kind of thing he used to do a few years ago before his illness. I couldn't help wondering who he had asked to get them for him. Maureen and Andrew said it wasn't either of them.

It took me two weeks to find out. I rang Eric's social worker. "Have you visited Eric lately?" I asked him.

"Yes."

"Oh, I was wondering who bought me those beautiful flowers on his behalf."

"Well, it was me," he replied, laughing. "I had to help the guy out. He is still very romantic and it goes to show that whatever your age and circumstances, it doesn't stop you from showing how you feel."

I have to admit that I was delighted, and so proud of him. I had never had flowers that lasted for four weeks. Every night I put them in the porch. Eric's love was ingrained in the flowers and in my heart.

At the moment, my writing is my love life. But I don't want to be a sexless old maid who never gets the chance to enjoy smouldering kisses in a crushing embrace... it would be such a waste. Perhaps I'm wishing for a lot. They do say what you don't have, you don't miss, but I don't know about that. I miss it a bloody lot!

I went to visit Eric shortly after he had sent me the flowers. It was a bitterly cold afternoon and the raw north wind cut like a bacon- slicer. He was sitting in his chair, dozing. I touched him gently and he opened his eyes.

"Hello, Romeo," I greeted him.

"Have I got a new name now?" he said.

"Yes, you certainly have."

I planted a soft kiss on his lips before pushing him to his room.

"Thanks for the flowers. They are beautiful."

"I know how you love your flowers, and I have to show you that I still love you... more than ever."

"I know." The tears were welling up in my eyes, but I bent my head and brought my face close to his lips, caressing his shoulders and chest. After several moments in a savage clinch, the chair almost tipped over, causing bodies and lips to part. Eric was furiously jerking with uncontrollable passion and a heavy longing gathered in my chest. So I kissed him again and we were like a fire smouldering beneath the surface. We blazed as he pulled me into a furious embrace and the chair tipped precariously again.

I pulled away. "This is going to cause an accident," I said, and sat in the armchair as we laughed like teenagers. That is one thing he hasn't lost – his passion. His hormones are still raging and he always says, "If I die now, what a way to go." People might think that when you reach a certain age, your feelings for love are blown away with the wind. In our case, they are as strong as ever. It's just a pity that we find ourselves in a terrible situation over which we have no control.

On our wedding anniversary, 31st March 2008, we had been married for forty-six years. Had Eric been more active, we would have gone away to some faraway place for a romantic holiday. I dreaded saying anything about the date, but in the end I did. He told me he had remembered but found it too painful to mention. We had to console ourselves with our memories of the wonderful times we had all those years ago. I did feel a little sad when I came home.

On the Sunday afternoon, the phone rang.

"Is that you, Valerie?"

"Yes?"

"Eric wants to speak to you."

After a short delay, I heard Eric's voice. "Hello, Valerie. It's our wedding anniversary tomorrow. Can you bring my black suit and a bottle of champagne?"

"Why? Where are you thinking of going?"

"Nowhere, but I want it."

"Okay," I agreed. "I will see you tomorrow."

I put the phone down and stood still for a few moments, staring at the wall. Then I went in the cupboard under the stairs, took out a bottle of Brut and put it in the fridge. I decided I would get some roast chicken from Spice, a West Indian take-away, down the road, that would tickle our taste buds.

I took two champagne flutes and some white serviettes. When I arrived, he was sitting beside his friend.

"Eric," someone called out. "She is here!"

He was beaming as I kissed him. "Happy Anniversary," I said.

"And to you as well."

We soon disappeared into his room. We had to be on our own for this moment. When my old man works out his fantasies in his head, anything can happen. I brought my face close to his and we had a steamy kiss. I don't relish quick, cheap sex. I like it sensual, smouldering... and even dangerous. But there was no chance of that, so we made the most of the scorching situation we found ourselves in.

"You little fireball," I said, laughing my head off, "that's a good place we've been." I shook my head, still laughing. "You're wicked. Shall I open the champagne now?"

"Wait a bit..." he said.

"I have brought you some roast chicken."

"Oh, I'll have a piece of that," he said with glee.

We took a portion each and tucked into it.

"Shall I pop the cork now, Eric?"

"Yes, if you are going to have some."

"I can only have a few sips because I am driving."

"Well don't bother opening it, then. Take it back home and I will have a can from the bedside cupboard."

I did open the bottle. Then I poured the Champagne into the two flutes. "Cheers!" and I took a few sips. He drank hard and long from his.

"Cheers!" he replied, with a wink. He hadn't mentioned his black suit, which I hadn't taken and hoped he wouldn't remember.

Faced with life on my own, I knew that I had a husband who loved me endlessly. We shared one last kiss before I walked out into the chilly evening air with the opened bottle of champagne I would finish on my own.

© Valerie Bartley 2009

POSTSCRIPT

Most grandchildren don't see their grandparents as anything other than their grandparents. Put on this earth for that purpose alone. That illusion was shattered when I first read the draft of this book. Turning the pages, I soon learnt that my Grandma was Valerie Hancel, Valerie Bartley; a daughter, sister, wife and mother, before she was a Grandma. Truly getting to know this magnificent woman has been one of my life's greatest honours.

The book is, in many ways, an important historical text. Grandma and Grandad were part of the 'Windrush Generation' that worked so hard to make better lives for themselves and their children in Britain. Grandma had to bear great burdens to forge that life for her family. Speaking about her life with Uncle Andrew, he told me that when he was young, he always wondered when his mum slept, as she often worked multiple jobs to put food on the table while caring for Grandad. And yet through all that struggle and perseverance, she always maintained a love for living. As soon as I'm able to, I look forward to visiting Bois Content and seeing Jamaica through her eyes and meeting my extended family.

Since finishing her book, Grandma's life has continued to have its ups and downs. Grandad (Eric Abijah Bartley) passed away on the 8th November 2019 at the age of ninety-six. Until the very end he was full of love for his wife, family and friends. His funeral was a testament to his life. Grandma was a picture of beauty and dignity. The church was packed with people who adored Grandad, and he is buried with his daughter, my Mum, Yvonne Matilda Bartley. Grandma is sad that Grandad never got to see this book published, but I'm sure he'd be so proud of her perseverance in finishing the book and publishing it.

Grandma has recently opened a new chapter in her life by moving to Romiley to be closer to Grandad, Mum and the rest of her family. All her grandchildren remain emotionally, if not physically close, thanks in no small part to a deep bond fostered around Grandma and Grandad's dinner table over Saturday soup as children. The family is rapidly growing with seven great grandchildren and counting. This book will be a lasting legacy of her life, passed from generation to generation of Bartleys, Parsonages, Watersons and Greenwoods, so we can all truly get to know this extraordinary woman.

Miles Andrew Greenwood, February 2021

CPSIA information can be obtained
at www.ICGtesting.com
Printed in the USA
LVHW090039280521
688706LV00001B/5